American Civil Wars

CIVIL WAR AMERICA

Peter S. Carmichael, Caroline E. Janney, and Aaron Sheehan-Dean, *editors*

This landmark series interprets broadly the history and culture of the Civil War era through the long nineteenth century and beyond. Drawing on diverse approaches and methods, the series publishes historical works that explore all aspects of the war, biographies of leading commanders, and tactical and campaign studies, along with select editions of primary sources. Together, these books shed new light on an era that remains central to our understanding of American and world history.

EDITED BY DON H. DOYLE

American Civil Wars

The United States, Latin America, Europe, and the Crisis of the 1860s

The University of North Carolina Press *Chapel Hill*

The University of North Carolina Press has been a member of the
Green Press Initiative since 2003.

Library of Congress Cataloging-in-Publication Data
Names: Doyle, Don Harrison, 1946– editor.
Title: American civil wars : the United States, Latin America, Europe, and the crisis
   of the 1860s / edited by Don H. Doyle.
Other titles: Civil War America (Series)
Description: Chapel Hill : University of North Carolina Press, [2017] | Series: Civil
   War America | Includes bibliographical references and index.
Identifiers: LCCN 2016019379| ISBN 9781469631080 (cloth : alk. paper) |
   ISBN 9781469631097 (pbk : alk. paper) | ISBN 9781469631103 (ebook)
Subjects: LCSH: Civil war—America—History—19th century. | Slave insurrections—
   America—19th century. | America—History—1810– | America—Politics and government—
   19th century. | United States—History—Civil War, 1861–1865. | United States—
   Foreign relations—19th century. | Latin America—Foreign relations—19th century. |
   Europe—Foreign relations—America. | America—Foreign relations—Europe.
Classification: LCC E18.83 .A45 2017 | DDC 973.7—dc23 LC record available at
   https://lccn.loc.gov/2016019379

To the memory of our colleague

Christopher Schmidt-Nowara

1966–2015

Contents

Figure

Acknowledgments

This project was supported with a generous grant from the Collaborative Research Grants division of the National Endowment for the Humanities. Their funds allowed me to bring in more than a dozen scholars from all parts of the United States, Europe, Mexico, and South America for three days of paper presentations, discussion, and collegial exchange that transcended the often forbidding frontiers of academic specialization. I am very grateful to Lydia Medici, program officer at the NEH, for her very helpful assistance in preparing the grant proposal.

The University of South Carolina provided an ideal setting for our conference, unparalleled administrative support, and, after our conference dispersed, an extraordinary academic setting that allowed me time to work with authors in transforming their conference papers into parts of a common intellectual enterprise. My special thanks to Lumi Bakos, Travis Weatherford, Jim Twitty, and Abby Callahan for administering the grant and making everything go smoothly.

Special thanks to Matt D. Childs and Tom Lekan, who as directors of the university's History Center contributed essential funds and organized a seminar with Erika Pani and Stève Sainlaude that previewed the conference for faculty and students.

Funds from the NEH also permitted me to hire as special assistant to the project Chaz Yingling, a young historian and PhD student at USC. Chaz performed wonderful service on so many levels, but his lasting achievement for this project is a website that will continue to inform scholars on this subject in the future: American Civil Wars: A Bibliography: https://sites.google.com/site/americancivilwarsbibliography/. Readers are encouraged to send suggestions for additional citations to: civil.wars.americas@gmail.com.

On behalf of all the authors, I thank Mark Simpson-Vos for his interest in this project and his expert shepherding of the book manuscript through the process of review, revision, and editing. Mark and the entire UNC Press team have been a delight to work with.

Thanks also to the anonymous reviewers selected by UNC Press whose knowledge of the field and perceptive critiques of earlier drafts made this a better book.

The authors of this book joined in this work with an unusual spirit of collaboration that is all too rare in the discipline of history, divided as it is into isolated spheres of geographic interest. One vital sign of the reigning spirit was that every single author turned in the initial conference paper on time. Every author came to the University of South Carolina prepared to join in mutually beneficial conversation. In the conference and over food and drink during our three days together new friendships were forged and new ideas hatched.

The last evening of the conference my wife, Marjorie Spruill, and I invited everyone to our house for the Matías Romero Banquet. We named it in honor of the indefatigable Mexican ambassador who staged widely publicized banquets at Delmonico's in New York to promote the very idea that inspired our conference: that the civil wars raging in Mexico and the United States were one and the same, each rooted in rebellions against the popular will. Filling the night was music of the nations involved the crisis of the 1860s, from "La Marseillaise" and "Battle Hymn of the Republic," to "Adios Mama Carlotta." It was a night to remember. Everyone returned home energized by the allied ambition of our project. The same spirit of collective enterprise carried us through several rounds of revision, and I remain amazed and gratified by the élan of my colleagues on this project.

A little more than a year later, all of us were deeply saddened to learn that one of our colleagues, Christopher Schmidt-Nowara, died tragically in Paris last summer. None embraced the collaborative nature of our project with more gusto than Chris. He was the best of us. After the conference, and through various rounds of review and revision, Chris and I carried on a lively exchange. He took time to give my introductory essay a careful reading and made several astute, helpful suggestions on how I might improve it. I was going to meet him in Paris when I heard of his sudden death. The only consolation is that Chris's brilliant essay (which Matt D. Childs and Anne Eller graciously helped me edit) is included in this volume, and that its publication gives us the opportunity to honor him by dedicating this book to his memory.

Introduction

The Atlantic World and the Crisis of the 1860s

Don H. Doyle

For more than a century and a half, historians have told the story of America's Civil War within a familiar nation-bound narrative. Most accounts center on the growing tensions between North and South over slavery, the clash of arms, the generals and political leaders on each side, the civilians at the home front, and the ordeal of Reconstruction. It is a quintessential American story about the nation's defining crisis.

This book takes readers away from the battlefields and political debates in the United States to view the conflict as part of a larger global crisis that seized the Atlantic world in the 1860s. Our book joins the international turn among historians endeavoring to understand the modern past as something more than the sum of national histories. In addition to expanding the frame that normally surrounds the U.S. Civil War, our goal has been to situate the war and Reconstruction within a transnational complex of upheavals that included multiple civil wars, European invasions, separatist rebellions, independence and unification struggles, slave uprisings, and slave emancipations.

The various points of turbulence we examine were all connected to a vast web whose radial cords attached to Washington and Richmond but also fastened at Mexico City, Havana, Santo Domingo, Rio de Janeiro, and other nodes of power in the American hemisphere. Other radials spanned the Atlantic to connect at London, Paris, Madrid, Rome, and myriad points between and beyond these major centers of state power. Tremors at any point in this web reverberated to distant connections in the network, constantly creating new dangers, and opportunities, for different actors in this dramatic decade.

The schematic diagram in figure 1 illustrates the scope and nature of this vast complex of wars, invasions, and emancipations that spanned the Atlantic world. However, it cannot fully convey the violent currents of influence and reaction that ran through this network of nations and empires, nor the dynamic unfolding of events during this tempestuous decade. In addition to identifying the multiple civil and international military conflicts taking

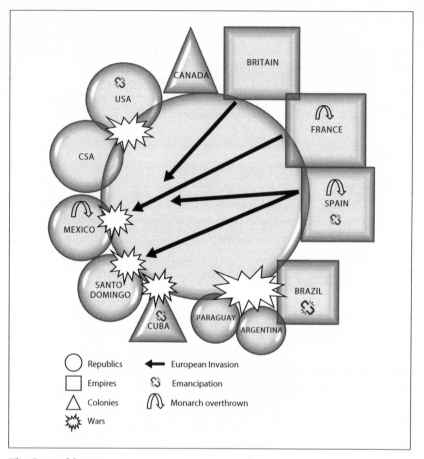

The Crisis of the 1860s.

place in this decade, it also indicates the several emancipation measures that took place, including outright emancipation in the United States and the gradual emancipation through the free-womb laws passed by Spain in 1870 and Brazil in 1871. Though all these events connected in some way to the developments in the United States, we invite attention to the entangled web of history that connected all of these sites of contestation to one another. Each of the essays that follow will examine this larger complex through the author's expert knowledge of one or more distinct sites of conflict within the web.

Our notion of a multi-faceted, interconnected set of crises derives from an understanding that all these violent upheavals were not just coincidental with, but also connected to, the U.S. Civil War. The U.S. imbroglio was not always the first cause in this dynamic scheme (Mexico's Reform War preceded it), but it often *enabled* ensuing events. The European incursions in Latin America that took place in the early 1860s, for example, would have been far riskier had the United States not been ensnared in a protracted civil war. Likewise, had slavery been preserved within an independent Confederacy, the future of slavery would have been fortified in the Spanish Caribbean and Brazil.

The crosscurrents of causation and influence did not always flow outward from the United States. They ran in various directions across the web of entangled histories. Thus, France's ambitions in Mexico, Spain's commitment to hold onto Cuba, and Britain's anxiety over defending Canada opened to the insurgent Confederacy the possibility of allying with European powers. The threat of such alliances, in turn, imposed limitations on what the United States could do in the face of the bold European incursions in the Western Hemisphere carried out in flagrant violation of the Monroe Doctrine. The U.S. Civil War erupted out of its own domestic political and social tensions. From the beginning, however, this conflict became enmeshed in multifarious international conflicts, imperial rivalries, and distant civil wars such that we cannot understand any one part of this crisis in isolation from the larger web of conflict and imperial ambition that pervaded the Atlantic world in the 1860s.

APART FROM THE COINCIDENCE and connections among the several intra-state and international clashes that constituted the crisis of the 1860s, there were also common political and social questions enveloping all these conflicts. Foremost among these was the future of slavery, a question of momentous importance not only to the U.S. conflict but also to the entire region extending from the Caribbean and Gulf of Mexico to Brazil. Many think of slavery in the 1860s as a barbaric relic of the past, doomed to eventual extinction within a modern capitalist world that required a free, mobile system of labor. However, the future of slavery was far from certain when the U.S. secession crisis erupted. Driving the U.S. South's bid for independence was its determination to protect slavery from a federal government that had fallen into the hands of the antislavery Republican Party. Southern secessionists had more in mind than simply protecting slavery where it existed; they saw independence as an essential prerequisite to fulfilling their dream of a tropical empire that would encompass the Caribbean and the territory surrounding the Gulf of Mexico. During its war against the United

States, expediency required that Confederate diplomats deny any such imperial ambitions lest they alienate potential allies, particularly Spain and France. Whether or not an independent Confederacy would have allied with—or conquered—new territories in Latin America, the world would have faced a powerful bastion of slave-based plantation economies spanning North America, the Caribbean, and Brazil, never mind the possibilities for expanding slavery into Central America and Mexico. As it happened, the defeat of the slaveholders' rebellion in the United States set the stage for the demise of slavery in Spain's Caribbean colonies, Cuba and Puerto Rico, and in Brazil. The long history of slavery in the Americas faced the beginning of the end as Spain, and then Brazil, placed slavery on a slow road to eventual extinction with the passage of free-womb laws, which granted freedom to the children of slave mothers. Subsequent laws passed by Spain in 1886 and Brazil in 1888 abolished slavery once and for all.

AT STAKE ALSO in the crisis of the 1860s was the future of the republican experiment, which had endured in the American hemisphere but had been all but extinguished in Europe. Just as some are inclined to see slavery as an atavistic holdover from the precapitalist past, there is a common tendency to see democratic forms of government as the inevitable wave of the future for the modern world. Looking back from 1861, the Age of Revolution that began in Europe with the French Revolution was largely a litany of failed revolutionary struggles and a testimony to the remarkable resilience of the Old Regime of church and crown. At the end of the Revolution of 1848, though some European monarchies had conceded civil liberties to their subjects and accepted constitutional limits on their powers, there were no self-governing republics of any size in Europe outside of Switzerland. Europe remained a bastion of monarchies and empires in opposition to republicanism, and even more to democratic ideas of universal suffrage.

The Latin American wars of independence (1810–25) brought onto the world stage a host of new republics, which reinforced the perception of modern republicanism as an American phenomenon. Mexico experimented briefly with a monarchy under Emperor Augustín de Iturbide (1821–23) before embarking on the republican experiment. All the other former colonies of Spain eventually followed the same republican path. Only Brazil, having served as the seat of the Portuguese empire during the Napoleonic invasion of Iberia, maintained a permanent monarchy after independence. The young Spanish American republics, rife with *pronunciamientos*, civil wars, *caudillos*, and revolutionary upheavals, were proof to conservative critics that the Latin "temperament" was ill suited to anything but the authoritarian rule of monarchs and priests. That the Empire of Brazil remained a notable exception to the tumult afflicting Latin America was not lost on critics of the republican experiment.

For all their troubles with self-government, Latin Americans displayed a tenacious devotion to republican ideals. Unlike Europe, which had largely repudiated the republican experiment in favor of monarchy, the Latin American republics did not revert to monarchy, except, as readers of this volume will learn, in Santo Domingo and Mexico where European powers interceded. During the 1860s, the entire American hemisphere as a whole became a contested site for the experiment in popular sovereignty.

European cynics believed that popular government, in whatever form, was inherently fragile, tenuous, and, sooner or later, destined to descend into anarchy and revolution, or into some form of despotism, especially under the strain of war, which they thought republics were ill equipped to conduct. Most conservatives, even many liberals, in Europe and the Americas, therefore, regarded "extreme democracy," with universal manhood suffrage and raucous party rivalries, more as a threat than a safeguard to individual liberty. Constitutional monarchy on the British model, with a strong parliament and freedom of speech and assembly, was thought to be the best guarantor of liberty and progress.

The vaunted Great Republic, as admirers frequently called the United States, had long been an exemplary model of popular sovereignty's success. By 1861, however, the secession crisis seemed to prove the rule that all such experiments were doomed to eventual self-destruction. Some monarchists, witnessing the failure of the U.S. example, predicted that all the republics of the Americas would gravitate back toward monarchy, or seek European imperial protection.

If the idea that the United States, or any of the Latin American republics, might abandon democracy and subject themselves to monarchy and imperial rule seems wildly implausible today, that is due to our present-minded conceit that progress in the modern world has inexorably followed a democratic trajectory. However, in the 1860s, the republican experiment seemed a proven failure in Europe and was about to enter a strenuous trial in its

American nursery. During the 1860s, the future was uncertain, and all things were possible.

France's Napoleon III was eager to assist the return to monarchy by transforming Mexico into a model of imperial order and Catholic moral authority. During the forty years since winning independence from Spain, Mexico witnessed no less than fifty changes in government. Liberals introduced radical reforms in the 1850s that curtailed the power and wealth of the church and extended civil rights to all citizens. When Liberals won control of the government in 1857, the Conservatives, backed by wealthy landowners and the Catholic clergy, plunged the country into a prolonged civil war known as the Reform War, which ended in early 1861 with the Liberals still in control of the government.

Having failed to defeat Liberal opponents at the ballot box, and then on the battlefield, Mexico's Conservatives turned to European monarchs to rescue them from the specter of republican rule. For decades Napoleon III had been considering Mexico and its strategic role in his global scheme to restore France to the imperial glory it had known under his uncle, Napoleon I, now on a global scale. The control and stabilization of Mexico were essential to his plan for an inter-ocean canal across Central America, the key to imperial mastery of the Pacific and Atlantic.

Mexico's salvation, according to Napoleon III's Grand Design, would also be the first step in the regeneration of the "Latin race" throughout the Americas. The Empire of Mexico, in time, would serve as a model and protector for all the troubled Spanish American republics and might even form an alliance with South America's monarchical anchor, the Empire of Brazil. With help from the insurgent Confederacy, Napoleon III's Latin American empire would impede the insidious influence of Anglo-Saxon republicanism emanating from the United States.

THE INTRUSIONS BY EUROPEAN powers in Latin America point to a third common thread, in addition to slavery and republicanism, running through many facets of the crisis of the 1860s: the issue of national sovereignty and territorial unity. Each nation-state involved in this story was seeking to secede, unite, expand, ally with foreign powers, or impose itself on other nations by conquest or diplomatic intervention. The national idea, which supposed that nations ought to contain coherent populations and that governments should represent the popular will, was still taking form in the mid-nineteenth century. The idea that a "people" have the natural right to govern themselves, a hallmark of liberal nationalist ideology, was seized by the insurgent slaveholders in the U.S. South. Unionists were left to assert the right of the existing nation to defend itself against rebellious minorities, an imperial stance that confounded European liberals. It was only the beginning of enormous legal and moral confusion surrounding such basic questions as the justification for international recognition, the legitimacy of insurgent states, the right of foreign powers to intervene in domestic disputes, and a host of other vexing questions that surfaced with compelling urgency in the 1860s.

The historic contest between principles of dynastic sovereignty and inherited privilege against those of popular sovereignty and human equality were suddenly playing out in real-life choices that politicians, diplomats, and ordinary citizens had to confront. If the Confederacy's claim to national sovereignty should be determined by nothing other than the capacity of an insurgent rebellion to defend itself militarily, were there not moral or legal grounds on which the family of nations might legitimately deny recognition? By the same token, should the people of Mexico or Santo Domingo decide they no longer wanted to govern themselves and invite a European prince to rule over them, was national subjugation also justifiable and legitimate? It was telling that even the most blatant usurpations of power were veiled in plebiscites, often specious but supposed to determine the popular will. Southern secessionists took great pains to deny their revolutionary intent, and several states took the time to hold popular elections to nominate delegates or, more rarely, to vote on secession itself. Maximilian insisted that the French carry out a plebiscite before he assumed the throne of Mexico. A similar bow to the fiction of popular consent took place in Santo Domingo to legitimize its return to the Spanish Empire.

The secessionist rebellion in the United States suddenly threw open new opportunities for France, Spain, and Britain to create, expand, or secure their imperial domain in the American hemisphere. Britain, worried that the United States would find some pretext to take over Canada, began recalculating its North American imperial policy. In 1863 it began fashioning a new a self-governing polity that was inaugurated four years later as the Dominion of Canada. In contrast, following a violent clash with discontented blacks at Morant Bay, Jamaica, the British imposed more direct control of Jamaica's colonial affairs.

Having proclaimed the annexation of Santo Domingo in 1861, Spain went on to provoke war with Peru and Chile, which many saw as part of a larger plan to take back its lost American empire. France took the prize for imperial ambition in the Americas. At its boldest expression, France's vision included proxy control of a vast Mexican Empire that would expand southward to incorporate the proposed canal through Nicaragua and northward to reclaim the territory ceded to the United States in 1848, including Mexico's former province Texas. Since Louisiana had severed its ties to the United States, the idea was floated that France might also assert its right to recover the vast territory Napoleon I had sold to the United States in 1803.

FAR MORE THAN just territory and geopolitical advantage were at stake in the global contest among rival European empires; the future of slavery and survival of democracy also hung in the balance during the crisis of the 1860s. Had the European powers actually intervened in the U.S. Civil War, or had the Union otherwise failed to defeat the rebellion, it would have meant a new lease on life for slavery, and not only in the American South. A Confederate victory would have rekindled the long-held Southern dream of a tropical slave empire in the Caribbean and Gulf of Mexico, either in alliance with the slave regimes of the Spanish Caribbean and Brazil, or possibly the conquest of the former. We must also consider that, had the South won independence, Maximilian's Mexican Empire, instead of being a nearly forgotten ill-starred adventure, would have played out very differently with an independent Confederacy acting as a buffer state protecting Mexico from U.S. interference. As it was, General Ulysses S. Grant sent Union troops to the Texas border in the summer of 1865 to intimidate French forces and fortify Benito Juárez's republican army with clandestine supplies of arms and ammunition. Had the French experiment succeeded in Mexico, it is also likely that the American hemisphere would have presented irresistible temptations for further European imperialist adventures.

Instead, soon after the Union victory in 1865, there was a major withdrawal of European empires from the Western Hemisphere. To some extent, this was part of a redeployment of imperial resources. The U.S. Civil War helped accelerate European expansion into warm cotton-producing regions of the world because it disrupted exports from the world's largest supplier of cotton. The 1860s witnessed the dawn of a new age of imperialism in Asia, the Middle East, and Africa coinciding with the withdrawal of Europe from the Western Hemisphere.

Compelling the European retreat was the emergence of the United States as a powerful military force, capable of mobilizing a massive citizen army, building a powerful navy, replete with ironclad ships, and sustaining unprecedented losses over several years. The Monroe Doctrine, which European powers scoffed at during the war, now became a viable deterrent to European plans for further colonization in the Americas. Britain's creation of a self-governing confederation in Canada coincided with the decision of Russia to cede to the United States all of its territorial claims to Alaska and the Pacific Northwest in 1867.

Spain, too, facing fierce guerilla resistance from republicans in Santo Domingo and mounting opposition from the Liberal opposition in Madrid, withdrew its troops in the summer of 1865. During the U.S. war, Spain had also taken aggressive action against Peru and Chile for supposed offenses to the Spanish flag, which led Peruvian and Chilean republicans to prepare for war and seek help abroad, including from the United States. Fearing another disastrous war in Latin America and revolutionary opposition at home, Spain's imperialists eventually swallowed their pride. With the United States serving as a mediator, Spain settled its differences with Peru and Chile and withdrew from South America.

In the fall of 1868 Spain suddenly faced dual revolutions, at home and in Cuba. Cuban republicans proclaimed independence and invited slaves to join them with vague promises of freedom for those who fought for Cuba's freedom. All during the U.S. war, American diplomats reported Cuban slaves chanting *Avanza Lincoln, avanza, tu eres nuestra esperanza,* (Onward Lincoln, onward, you are our hope), as though they knew their fate somehow hinged on the outcome of the war to their north. Now a rebellion for independence within Cuba seemed to realize that hope. Cuba's republican insurgency dragged on a decade without achieving freedom for Cuba, but it struck severe blows for freedom among Cuba's slaves. In 1870 Spain answered the Cuban republican promise of freedom to slaves with its own. The Moret Law emancipated all children henceforth born to slave mothers, and it promised freedom to slaves who took up arms for the Spanish crown against the republican insurrection. Brazil followed suit the next year with its own law for gradual emancipation. These free-womb laws would have continued slavery well into the twentieth century had it not been for Spain's enactment of full emancipation in 1886, followed by Brazil in 1888. A hugely profitable system of labor that had been integral to the economy, law, and society of American nations for centuries ended at last.

Meanwhile, Napoleon III abandoned his Grand Design to regenerate the Latin race in the American hemisphere. Facing both growing opposition from reinvigorated French liberals and the rise of a united German nation across the Rhine, in early 1866 he announced the French "civilizing mission" in Mexico was at an end. Mexico's republican forces, aided by arms and

volunteers from the United States, won stunning victories against Maximilian's diminished forces. The United States took an official response of neutrality, refusing to recognize or meet with Maximilian's government. In
June 1867, the beleaguered emperor of Mexico, having been captured, tried,
and sentenced to death, faced a Mexican firing squad. The shots fired that
day resounded across the Atlantic, a somber reproach to further European
ambitions in the Americas.

THE REVERBERATIONS FROM the Americas after 1865 shook the thrones of
Europe as well. The Union's victory gave republicans and other liberal reformers in Europe a thrill of vindication and hope that the republican experiment
might yet be revived in Europe. Political leaders, whatever distrust they felt
toward democracy's excesses, ignored the restive public mood at their peril.

British Radicals favoring expansion of voting rights mobilized immense
public demonstrations across Britain beginning in 1866. Facing massive civil
disobedience during "riots" in London's Hyde Park, Parliament enacted the
Reform Act of 1867, which vastly expanded voting rights among the middle
and working classes.

Spain, one of the more conservative countries in Western Europe, also
faced revolutionary upheaval in 1868. The Glorious Revolution toppled Queen
Isabel II from her throne and opened up a brief, troubled period of representative government.

In France the opposition to Napoleon III's Second Empire had been
galvanized by the Mexican fiasco and by Napoleon's flirtation with the Confederacy during the American Civil War. But the opposition came to a boil
when Napoleon provoked war with Prussia in 1870. After being ignomini-
ously captured by Prussian forces at the Battle of Sedan, Napoleon fled to
exile in England. France, the birthplace of modern European republicanism, cautiously proclaimed its Third Republic.

The 1860s began with a powerful separatist rebellion to preserve and expand a system of slavery in North America. This coincided with an equally
daring effort to defeat liberal reforms by the imposition of European monarchy in Mexico. It ended with the destruction of slavery, the retreat of European imperialism from the Western Hemisphere, and the resurgence of
liberal hope in the Americas and Europe. Those hopes can easily be over-
shadowed by what followed the 1860s: the failings of Reconstruction in the
United States, the return of despotism to Latin America, the rise of European and U.S. imperialism, the ascendance of scientific racism, and all the
horrors these forces would visit upon the twentieth century. But all that lay

ahead. For a moment, it seemed that the Age of Revolution, thought to have died in Europe in 1849, had shifted to the Americas to rescue the republican experiment from self-destruction and strike a lethal blow to slavery.

TO COMPREHEND THE MULTIFACETED crisis of the 1860s in all its complexity has required a form of collaboration all too rare among historians, who typically spend their careers mastering one geographic area within a coherent historical period. No one person could perform all the archival research and learn all the scholarship required for a full understanding of each part of the puzzle assembled here. Our volume demonstrates the value of teamwork among specialists who both pooled their knowledge and engaged one another's work as part of a common endeavor. Our project began with a conference held at the University of South Carolina in March 2014, which involved three days of discussion and criticism, leavened with welcome doses of convivial intellectual camaraderie. Each author brought a specialized knowledge of one piece of the puzzle, and each came away with an understanding of how their piece fit into the larger picture of this turbulent and crucial decade.

The result is more than a collection of specialized essays; this is a multi-authored book that addresses a sprawling geography within a coherent period. All the essays support a common endeavor and examine facets of a common project. The volume begins with four essays on aspects of the U.S. Civil War with particular attention to Union and Confederate foreign policy strategies. Three essays on the major European powers tell us how Britain, France, and Spain responded to the U.S. imbroglio, and how it shaped their imperial strategies. Finally, five essays examine aspects of Latin America's role in the crisis of the 1860s with particular attention to Santo Domingo, Mexico, Cuba, Brazil, and Spanish America.

We aimed our essays at students and teachers looking for a fuller understanding of the events in this tumultuous decade and wanting to understand the entangled histories of all the countries involved. We are aware that our essays cannot do full justice to the subject. Each essay includes a list of suggested readings for those readers wishing to pursue further research on the subject. Also, Charlton Yingling, who served as a graduate assistant on this project, has constructed a more comprehensive resource for researchers: American Civil Wars: A Bibliography, online at: https://sites.google.com /site/americancivilwarsbibliography/.

JAY SEXTON'S OPENING ESSAY on "The Civil War and U.S. World Power" focuses on the role of the Civil War in the realization of U.S. national and global power in the nineteenth century. Though the Civil War gave evidence of the immense military and economic power of the United States, he shows, the projection of that power on the world stage also required foreign collaboration.

Howard Jones's "Wrapping the World in Fire: The Interventionist Crisis in the Civil War" takes up Union foreign policy and the diplomatic contest between the Union and the Confederacy that unfolded in Britain and France. While the Union insisted that the conflict was a domestic quarrel and warned outside nations against interference, the Confederacy set out to court foreign recognition, if not intervention, which many understood to be the key to winning independence. Both Britain and France weighed the advantages of intervention against the threat of war with the United States, and their calculations played a decisive role in the outcome of the conflict.

The next essay deals with the less familiar realm of Confederate imperial ambitions and their effect on foreign relations during the U.S. Civil War. Patrick J. Kelly, "The Cat's Paw: Confederate Ambitions in Latin America," examines tensions between the South's aspirations for hemispheric dominance and its need to curry favor with European imperial powers and Latin American neighbors. In the maelstrom of civil war, Confederates found it expedient to deny their imperialistic ambitions in Latin America, and necessary to condone those of Spain and France as the South sought foreign allies in their struggle for independence.

The next three essays deal with the major European empires involved in the crisis of the 1860s: Britain, France, and Spain. Richard Huzzey's essay on "Manifest Dominion: The British Empire and the Crises of the Americas in the 1860s" reveals Britain anxiously recalculating the risks and opportunities presented by the crisis in the United States. Its interests in the Western Hemisphere, ranging from the Mosquito Coast and Jamaica to Manitoba, were but part of a rapidly expanding empire with increasingly important assets in India, China, the Middle East, and Africa, to say nothing of its primary concerns with the European balance of power.

Stève Sainlaude takes up "France's Grand Design and the Confederacy," which he explains was the pet project of Napoleon III to create in Mexico a counterbalance against the growing power of Anglo-Saxon Protestants in the United States. The American Civil War opened an ideal opportunity for France to carry out this long-considered project, and Confederate independence appeared to be essential to its success. As Sainlaude's deep research in French diplomatic correspondence reveals, Napoleon III's more sober-minded foreign ministers felt that France had more to fear from an independent South than a unified United States. Again, the South's long-standing enthusiasm for expanding slavery southward into a tropical empire cast a dark shadow over their diplomatic success with potential foreign allies.

Spain is strangely neglected in most accounts of the international context of the American Civil War, but as Christopher Schmidt-Nowara shows in his essay, "From Aggression to Crisis: The Spanish Empire in the 1860s," it played a major role in the crisis of the 1860s. Spain leapt to take advantage of the secession crisis, and sought to strengthen slavery and sovereignty in its Antillean colonies, Cuba, and Puerto Rico. Its aggressive foreign policy in the Americas backfired, however, and by the end of the decade, Spain confronted grave challenges to both slavery and sovereignty, like those that the United States faced earlier.

The remaining essays all deal with Latin America and the crisis of the 1860s. One of Spain's most perilous foreign adventures was the takeover of the Dominican Republic in March 1861. Anne Eller's essay, "Dominican Civil War, Slavery, and Spanish Annexation, 1844–1865," takes us to what will be less familiar territory for most readers. Dominican guerilla fighters and their Haitian allies, many of them former slaves, forced Spain to leave in defeat. Their valiant struggle also inspired Cubans and Puerto Ricans to take up their own quest for independence from Spain.

The French intervention in Mexico is far more familiar than the Dominican war, but it is too often reduced to a pat story of French intervention and Mexican victimhood. As Erika Pani demonstrates in "Juárez vs. Maximiliano: Mexico's Experiment with Monarchy," the idea of restoring Mexico to monarchy had been nurtured by Mexican Conservatives for decades. Their dreams of monarchical stability revived with the advent of liberal reforms during the 1850s. Conservative designs for the restoration of order and progress in Mexico became possible to realize once the U.S. Civil War suddenly opened the way for Napoleon III and his abiding interest in Mexico as the site for his Grand Design to regenerate the Latin race in the American hemisphere.

In her essay "Arms and Republican Politics in Spanish America: The Critical 1860s," Hilda Sabato views the role of violence and armed forces in the political life of the Spanish American republics, which, since the war for independence, had favored the figure of the citizen in arms to safeguard freedom. Republicans understood the use of armed force as a legitimate means of thwarting despotism and defending popular sovereignty. As they evolved, most Latin American republics chose to combine the tradition of citizen militias with that of standing armies, and this favored the fragmentation of military power and the widespread eruption of armed conflict. This violence peaked during the 1860s when wars and revolutions swept across most of Spanish America.

The last two essays deal with the end of slavery in its remaining American strongholds, Cuba and Brazil. Matt D. Childs's essay, "Cuba, the Atlantic Crisis of the 1860s, and the Road to Abolition," shows how two key external events set the stage for abolition in Cuba. The Lyons-Seward Treaty of 1862 between the United States and Britain banned participation by U.S. citizens in the Atlantic slave trade. An antislavery movement in Madrid pressured Spain to end its involvement in the trans-Atlantic slave trade as well, which meant an end to the replenishment of Cuba's slave population. Then, in 1868, the revolutionary independence movement that began the Ten Years' War promised freedom to slaves who joined the cause. In 1870, Spain countered with its own emancipation plan by promising freedom to all slaves who fought for Spain and to all children born to slave mothers.

With Cuban slavery on the path to extinction, the Empire of Brazil stood as the last nation sanctioning slavery. Rafael Marquese's essay, "The Civil War in the United States and the Crisis of Slavery in Brazil," shows that Brazil's political leaders were keenly aware of the implications of the Union's emancipation policy, and its ultimate victory, for their own country. Brazilians also followed closely the post-emancipation conditions of the South and debated what lessons it held for Brazil. In 1871, alone in a world that had repudiated slavery, Brazil passed its own free-womb law, which spelled the eventual end of slavery in Brazil, and all the Americas.

The crisis of the 1860s was one of the critical turning points in modern world history. It opened with what threatened to become a major reversal in the progress of the international antislavery movement and a mortal blow to the beleaguered republican experiment. By 1871, however, the eventual extinction of slavery in the Americas was assured, and a powerful resurgence of revolution and reform in Europe and the Americas promised a vigorous future for popular government. Democratic ideals of equality, liberty, and self-government would face grave new challenges ahead, but these typically arose from illiberal movements within democratic societies rather than from monarchists. The major consequence of the crisis that seized the Atlantic world during the 1860s meant that whatever new challenges these ideals faced in the future, at least for the American hemisphere it seemed clear that there was no going back to slavery and no return to monarchy.

CHAPTER ONE

The Civil War and U.S. World Power

Jay Sexton

Why study the U.S. Civil War? I annually pose this question to the British undergraduates enrolled in the Civil War special subject that I convene.[1] Surprisingly few say they signed up to learn about the birth of the modern U.S. nation, or the abolition of slavery, or even the great battles and generals. Instead, the most common response is that they want to learn how a vulnerable union of states became a great world power, one that rapidly caught up with and then surpassed the empire of their homeland upon which the sun never set.

In linking the Civil War to the rise of U.S. power on the world stage, these students propose a connection between the national and international history of the United States that has been the subject of surprisingly few scholarly inquiries. New Left diplomatic historians considered the Civil War in relation to the rise of late nineteenth-century imperialism, but the war itself remained secondary to the structural economic forces these scholars identified as shaping U.S. foreign relations across time.[2] The more recent global turn in the study of the Civil War has likewise touched on this issue, but the primary objective has been to identify connections and similarities between the U.S. crisis and other cases of contested national consolidation in the mid-nineteenth-century world.

Situating the Civil War in the narrative of the rising world power of the United States requires the fusion of traditional national history to this volume's agenda of examining the entangled histories of the United States, Latin America, and Europe. The consolidation of the United States in the 1860s constituted the culmination of a protracted, postcolonial period of insecurity. The Civil War was, therefore, instrumental to the realization and configuration of U.S. national power, defined here as the social, political, and economic relationships that made possible the destruction of Southern separatism and the projection of national interests in the West and beyond. Rather than calibrating national power in material terms (i.e., the number of ironclad ships, bars of gold in bank vaults, etc.), it is better understood in respect to the fluid relations between the various stakeholders that negotiated its nature and purpose. Focusing in this manner on the formation of U.S. power brings to light a perhaps unexpected twist: though the Civil War unlocked the immense power of the United States, the actors, institutions, and political processes that harnessed it were not always capable of moving in concert thereafter to project this newfound national power. Whether or not U.S. power was projected outside of the nation's borders depended not only on dynamics internal to the United States but, crucially, on the involvement of foreign collaborators as well.

IT HAS BECOME an axiom of recent historiography that the early U.S. republic constituted an empire, one that rapidly acquired new territories and subjugated native peoples.[3] The most recent overview of early U.S. foreign relations opens with a list of reasons as to why the Union should be considered an empire.[4] There can be little question as to the verdict of historians: the expansionism of the early republic—the annexation of the Floridas, Indian removal, the war against Mexico, the actions of filibusters in Central America and the Caribbean—should be understood as imperialist. The formation of the early U.S. empire, as with other empires across time, was not solely coercive. U.S. power also manifested itself as an ideological force that found appeal in foreign lands. It was because of the traction of the ideas of republican government and economic liberalism that the conservative elites of Europe viewed the distant United States as a "dangerous nation" with the potential to disrupt the established political and economic order of the Old World.[5]

Though it is appropriate to view the early U.S. republic as an emerging empire, one drawback of this emerging consensus view is that it can lead to anachronistically projecting U.S. power back in time. The Union was a regional power, of that there is no question. But its greatest strength—the newness of its institutions and ideas—was also its greatest weakness. The young United States remained vulnerable to imploding from within—as would happen in 1860–61. But the North-South slavery divide was only one of many internal divisions that endangered the early republic. The thirteen original states might have formed several regional confederacies. So too could have new states in the West, such as Texas and California, maintained their distance from the United States with the support of an Old World power, as would Canada. And the Union might have fallen victim to ideological and political divisions, such as those unleashed by the French Revolution, that did not exactly overlap with geographic regions.

Looming over all of these potential sources of fragmentation was the shadow of European, particularly British, power. If uncovering the imperial dimensions of the early republic is one trend in the recent historiography, another has been to examine an antithetical, though inextricably related, phenomenon: the so-called postcoloniality of the United States.[6] Here, the comparisons lay not with the great empires of world history, but with the similarly vulnerable states that emerged in Spanish America at roughly the same time. European, particularly British, power remained an unavoidable reality in the postcolonial Western Hemisphere, and the early United States was no exception. Nearly half the U.S. national debt in 1853 was held in Europe, chiefly in Britain; English novels took up most of the space on American bookshelves, even as U.S. authors and lexicographers labored to develop a national literature and dictionary of their own; the might of the Royal Navy might be turned against American commercial interests, as it had in the run-up to the War of 1812. Henry Clay feared in 1820 that the United States was in danger of remaining a "sort of independent colonies of England—politically free, commercially slaves."[7] As late as 1883, when Henry Cabot Lodge wrote of "colonialism in the United States," he referred not to U.S. expansion or policy toward Native Americans, but to the persistence of British cultural hegemony at home.[8]

When early U.S. statesmen conceived of what we now call "national security," they looked both inward (to their domestic divisions) and outward (to their weakness relative to the Old World). Their greatest fear was that these internal and external vulnerabilities would merge, transforming their independent union into fractious colonial dependencies, virtual western pawns of the European balance of power. This thinking can be seen even at the apogee of early U.S. nationalism. The lesson contemporaries took from the War of 1812 not only concerned the rising U.S. nationalism of the era, but also how conflict with Britain nearly had undermined the Union when a group of New England Federalists flirted with negotiating a separate peace deal with Britain. Even at the height of the so-called "era of good feelings," an arch-nationalist like Clay feared "that within five years from this time [1820], the Union would be divided into three distinct confederacies."[9]

An important development in U.S. foreign policy concerned the geographic expansion of its perceived security requirements. By the 1820s, U.S. policymakers asserted that the "peace and safety" of their Union was linked to the course of the Spanish American revolutions.[10] There were strong ideological and commercial reasons for the United States to support the independence of the emerging Spanish American states. But it was geopolitics that most shaped the foreign policy of the Monroe administration and the formulation of what became known as the "Monroe Doctrine." When the cabinet debated how to respond to the feared recolonization of Spanish America by the reactionary powers of the Holy Alliance, as well as whether to formally align with Britain in the matter, what most animated their discussions was the potential that a single act of intervention in the New World would trigger an all-out imperial scramble. Though Secretary of State John Quincy Adams doubted the capability of the Holy Allies to re-conquer Spain's former colonies, he worried that an attempt to do so would end up with Britain occupying Cuba and France in control of Mexico. "Then what would be our situation . . . ?" he asked in his diary.[11] Secretary of War John C. Calhoun predicted that in such a situation "violent parties would arise in this country, one for and one against them, and we should have to fight upon our own shores for our own institutions."[12]

The formulation of the Monroe Doctrine illuminates the way in which U.S. policymakers connected events far from their own borders to the security of their Union. But if there was agreement on the desirability of an independent and republican Spanish America, there was much debate as to the policies to promote this end. Indeed, Monroe's 1823 message, which proclaimed a prohibition on future European intervention and colonization in the New World but stopped short of committing the United States to any specific measures to uphold it, should be viewed as a compromise between assertive and passive policy options, as well as a middle ground between formally aligning with the British and formally rejecting its offer of joint action.

Historians typically present the Monroe Doctrine as the clarion call of U.S. empire, "a breathtaking assertion of hemispheric dominance," as it recently has been called.[13] U.S. policymakers later in the century certainly would interpret it as such, but it should be emphasized that the statesmen of 1823 deliberately stopped short of calling for any proactive policies to project U.S. power. The brilliance of Monroe's 1823 message lay in how it propagated a popular nationalist vision without committing the United States to policies that disrupted internal unity. In other words, the 1823 message was written with the intention of maintaining internal unity in a perceived moment of crisis, not harnessing or projecting national power in Latin America. It was a short-term success in this regard; as Clay put it, responding to the threat of European intervention in the New World will "create no divisions of opinion among us. . . . We shall, in regard to it, be 'all federalists—all republicans.'"[14]

But over time, more proactive readings of the message emerged. The very popularity of the Monroe Doctrine made it an attractive symbol for those seeking to consolidate support for their foreign policy goals. In a curious twist, what initially had been a source of nationalism became a highly politicized symbol that exacerbated domestic divisions when invoked on behalf of partisan or sectional objectives. When James Polk invoked what he called "Monroe's doctrine" in support of his aggressive expansionism in 1845, when Calhoun promoted a proslavery reading of what he called "Monroe's declaration" three years later, when Stephen Douglas christened the "Monroe Doctrine" in an 1853 speech that embraced Caribbean expansion, when William Seward linked it to his vision of an antislavery and commercially expansionist Pacific power, the nationalist dogma of 1823 became a lightning rod for domestic controversy. As Polk's war of conquest against Mexico demonstrated, the United States could achieve its most ambitious goals, but doing so ultimately undermined the Union itself.

The politicization of the Monroe Doctrine reflected a broader symbiosis between deepening sectional divisions and perceived foreign threats. An ominous development in the sectional crisis occurred when both sides of the debate over slavery came to see one another in the light of the British threat. Proslavery Southerners viewed the antislavery forces in the Northern states as pawns of the powerful British abolitionists. Meanwhile, the new Northern Republican Party interpreted slaveholding Southerners as aristocratic elite, an un-republican "slave power." The international context further led Northerners to see themselves as the guardians of 1776. An independent Confederacy might be sucked into the orbit of the British Empire, not least because of the powerful bonds of the transatlantic cotton trade. The long-feared introduction of European balance-of-power politics in the North American continent would be the inevitable result. "Our country, after having expelled all European powers from the continent," Seward lamented, "would relapse into an aggravated form of its colonial experience, and, like Italy, Turkey, India, and China, become the theatre of transatlantic intervention and rapacity."[15]

The revival of European intervention in the Western Hemisphere in the 1860s, most notably the French-led European intervention in Mexico (discussed in essays in this volume by Stève Sainlaude and Erika Pani) and Spain's attempted recolonization of Santo Domingo (examined by Anne Eller), once again, as in the 1820s, gave common cause to advocates of republican government in the New World. Indeed, it was during the 1860s that the "Monroe Doctrine" became entrenched as a symbol of U.S. nationalism and, thanks to appropriations by Latin American liberals, opposition to recrudescent monarchy. Many observers in the United States viewed European intervention in Latin America as interlinked with Southern secession. "The French invasion of Mexico," Union general Phillip Sheridan asserted, "was so closely related to the Rebellion as to be essentially part of it."[16] "The final success of the whole programme," Ohio Republican Joshua Leavitt asserted, "hinges upon the result of the first step, the breaking up of the American Union."[17] Northern Republicans thus linked the cause of the Union to the cause of republican government throughout the New World, imagining in the process an ideological kinship with the forces of liberalism. The conflicts of the 1860s, in this formulation, derived from the ongoing revolutionary struggles against monarchical oppression that had first begun in 1776 in North America and had carried on in the Latin American revolutions of the early nineteenth century and into the more recent European revolutions of 1848.[18]

The triumph of the Union in 1865 thus was understood by contemporaries in the North as the culmination of the American Revolution. Taking the cue from Lincoln's "new birth of freedom," historians have come to see the destruction of slavery as a fulfillment of the principles of 1776. But the Northern victory also was a climax of the Revolution in the hardheaded terms of geopolitics: the verdict on the battlefield provided resolution to a protracted, postcolonial era in which internal divisions threatened to undermine the Union's independence. The consolidation and permanence of the Union was the obvious prerequisite for the rising world power of the United States. The Northern victory foreclosed the long-feared nexus of foreign intervention and internal separatism. The viability of the U.S. nation was never again to be seriously called into question. Significantly, the powers of the Old World—unlike in Mexico and Santo Domingo—allowed the warring parties in the United States to settle their differences without foreign intervention. The failure of Confederate diplomacy must be seen as one of the significant explanations for the Union victory and, as a consequence, the emergence of the United States as a world power.[19]

The geopolitical developments that ensured the security and hemispheric ascendance of the United States should not be mistaken for a severing of transatlantic connections. The United States continued to be "entangled" with the Old World post-1865—indeed, many entanglements deepened as a result of technological advances in communications and transport. But these post-1865 entanglements presented less of a threat to the newly powerful nation than they had in the years of the early republic. Where transatlantic connections might be said to have been strongest—in finance and trade—there was a diminution of the coercive hallmarks of European interventionism or imperialism. To be sure, Americans after 1865 railed against foreign investment and British free-trade imperialism, just as they had in earlier times. But the alarmism of contemporaries should not obscure the newfound security of the post-1865 Union, nor the benefits it reaped from its international economic connections. Far from infringing upon U.S. sovereignty, the steep increase in foreign investment from 1865–73 helped to make possible a boom in railroad construction, as well as the refinancing of the massive Civil War debt at a lower rate of interest.[20]

The failure of the European recolonization attempts of the 1860s further enhanced the geopolitical position of the United States. Indeed, the decade that began with high hopes of "grand designs" in the New World ended with France cutting and running from Mexico, Spain withdrawing from Santo Domingo (though not from Cuba, where a major anticolonial rebellion began in 1868), Russia selling Alaska to the United States, and Britain reformulating its position in North America, where it acknowledged the confederation and "home rule" of Canada. The emergence of U.S. national power during the 1860s was not the central cause of these developments, which owed much more to the agency of those on the ground who resisted European rule and the contours of great power politics. Nonetheless, the retrenchment of the old imperial powers in the Western Hemisphere enhanced U.S. security and, further, left the newly reunified republic as the clear, great power of the hemisphere. This shift can be seen in U.S. invocations of the Monroe Doctrine: in the early republic, the doctrine often referred to the security requirements of the fragile Union; after the Civil War it became a manifestation of U.S. power in the Western Hemisphere. The ascendant position of the United States also can be seen, paradoxically, in the rapid demobilization of its military after 1865—the great million men army of the Civil War quickly withered to a small force mostly on the western frontier; meanwhile, the state-of-the-art ironclad navy that British naval planners had feared in 1865 soon became obsolete. The post–Civil War geopolitical context did not require a large standing army for, despite the occasional diplomatic imbroglio with Britain, there were no fundamental external threats to U.S. security—though the continued resistance of Native Americans did necessitate military campaigns in the decades after 1865. In sum, the geopolitical chessboard looked very different—and far more advantageous to the United States—in 1870 than it had only ten years earlier.

THE OUTCOME OF THE Civil War demonstrated the viability of republican self-government to observers around the world. "Whether this Union, with

all its beneficent promise for the future, should stand or fall," Seward declared after the war, "was a question of vital consequence to the human race."[21]
The war also made clear that for this form of government to survive its trial
by fire, it required the realization of unprecedented national power. If we
think of national power as something that requires development and man-
agement, rather than something that simply exists to be deployed by political
elites, the significance of the Civil War to the emerging world power of the
United States comes into focus. The war did much to determine the institutions, structures, and policies that would condition the frenetic development and exploitation of the new nation's vast territories and resources, as
well as oversee its engagements abroad.

The first issue to consider here concerns the Union war effort itself. How
did the North acquire the awesome power required to destroy secession?
The national power necessary to consolidate the Union was not created out
of thin air. The early republic possessed power—just witness its rapid territorial expansion, social integration, infrastructure development, and economic
dynamism. But the power of the early republic was decentralized and often
unintegrated, if not centrifugal: settlers in the West who disdained central
authority; seaboard commercial elites who more fully integrated into transatlantic economic networks than internal, national ones; and, of course, rising sectional interests that threatened the Union itself. Foreign, particularly
British, power also underlay that of the Union—one thinks here of the importance of British investment to U.S. infrastructure development or how
the Royal Navy upheld the Monroe Doctrine during the threatened European interventions of the 1820s. This is not to say that there was no precedent for structuring and projecting power on a national level in the early
republic. The recent work of Max Edling has made clear that the central
state could use its revenue-raising capabilities to mobilize military power in
moments of need.[22]

What was different in the 1860s was the amount of power that was needed
to crush Southern separatism. The great challenge confronting the Union in
1861 was how to harness on a national level the power of its institutions,
economy, and civil society in a moment of crisis. The British students who
study the Civil War often come to the first class with the misperception that
Lincoln established a centralized, "war-time socialist" state (something
along the lines of Britain during the Great War) to crush an allegedly decentralized Confederacy. To be sure, the U.S. state, as recent historiography has
made clear, assumed new powers and increased its administrative capacity
during the crisis of the 1860s.[23] Nonetheless, the Union war effort should

not be seen as the product of some new central command structure for it deeply drew from traditions of decentralized government and volunteerism, which were products of the antistatist political culture of the early republic. The secret to the success of the Union war effort was not simply the growth of the federal government, but its synergy with a nationalizing and patriotic civil society—voluntary associations like the U.S. Sanitary Commission, grassroots political networks and Union Leagues, newspapers, evangelical churches, and so on.[24] Lincoln's political genius lay not simply in how he managed a cabinet of rivals, but in his capacity to mobilize the pulpit on behalf of his aims, coax support out of skeptical editors, appeal directly to the people through his addresses and public letters, and, not to be forgotten, harness the power of state governments.[25]

In terms of political economy, as well, the key development in the war years was not simply the increased role played by central authority, but rather the relationships forged between Republican politicians and a newly powerful class of Wall Street capitalists. The genius of the financial legislation of the Thirty-Seventh Congress was how it fused the interests of capital and nation by incentivizing investment in the war effort and federating the major private banks of the North. The funding of the Union war effort— two-thirds of which came from borrowing—perhaps best illustrates the bonds forged between government, finance, and civil society. With the London money market skeptical of the Union's credit worthiness, the federal government turned inward, empowering a new class of financiers, such as Jay Cooke, to market bond issues to the wider public. Enthusiastic buyers, many of whom had never before entered the securities market, invested their savings in small denominational bonds to the profit of bankers like Cooke, who worked on commission, and to the benefit of the larger Union cause. The bonds of finance and the shared interests of profit thus fused together government, capital, and citizen in the Union war effort.[26]

The power that enabled the Union victory, in sum, was the result of complex relations and negotiations between the state, finance, and the varied institutions of civil society—all the way down to the individual soldiers who gave their lives on the battlefield. The realization of the Union's power required effective political leadership, the support of financial markets, and the active and coordinated support of millions of ordinary people on the home front and the battle front. The "people's contest" to which Lincoln referred on July 4, 1861, was not only a battle against Southern separatists, but also an internal challenge. Could the Northern states mobilize this power in a sustained manner on behalf of the nationalist objective of forcibly restoring the Union? Though there were moments when the outcome to this question was in serious doubt, the affirmative answer came some four years later. And it was the result not simply of increased centralization, but more so the synergy between the state, the market, and the public, all of which became more fully integrated at a national level.

Here we arrive at a second set of questions: was this form of national power sustainable and transferable? Could the awesome national power that was harnessed to crush secession be mobilized on behalf of other objectives? Answering such questions requires consideration of both the new nation's "domestic" and foreign policy histories.

There can be no question that the national power realized during the Civil War accelerated the United States' greatest imperialist project of the nineteenth century, the conquest and colonization of the West. No longer paralyzed by the question of slavery in the territories, the Republican-dominated federal government supported private individuals and corporations who sought fortunes from the exploitation of the nation's vast western territories. The nexus between individual citizens, the central state, and an emergent Wall Street that had been instrumental to the Union's victory in the Civil War turned its attention to the West, even in the midst of the great conflict. Legislation such as the Homestead Act and the Pacific Railroad Act (both of 1862), as well as the use of military force to subdue the resistance of the Great Plains Indians, extended federal support to the migrants and capitalists who settled and exploited the nation's vast western territories. When Seward journeyed west across the new transcontinental railroad in 1870, he was struck by how the destruction of the "slave power" had unleashed a "sudden and prodigious increase of national energy in the prosecution of internal improvements." It would not be long before Omaha would become a new commercial center and San Francisco "the Constantinople of American empire."[27]

When one turns to the post-war South, however, the picture looks rather different. Apart from a brief phase of "Radical Reconstruction," the Republican Party proved only partially able, and ultimately unwilling, to project national power into the vanquished Confederacy. The voluminous literature on Reconstruction has examined the restoration of Southern "home rule" in detail.[28] The point to make here concerns how the nature of the national power realized during the Civil War proved self-limiting during Reconstruction. The federal government was better suited to the task faced in the West (facilitating voluntary settlement, infrastructure development, and environmental exploitation) than to the challenges in the post-war South (imposing new forms of government and racial equality upon an intransigent white population in the context of diminishing political support in the North). The mobilization and projection of national power, in other words, required the active consent and participation of a wide cross-section of stakeholders—something that was lacking in the case of Reconstruction.[29]

A FINAL QUESTION to consider: how did the form of national power that emerged during the Civil War shape the United States' engagement with foreign peoples and powers? The historians who have most cogently situated the Civil War within the broader trajectory of U.S. foreign relations, those of the New Left, powerfully advanced the argument that the economic transformations of the war years—the growth of manufacturing and industry; the emergence of Wall Street; the political ascendency of Northern financial interests over Southern slaveholding ones—propelled the new nation onto the path of overseas expansion and imperialism. In advancing this argument, these historians provided a necessary rejoinder to the idea that the U.S. imperialist outburst of 1898 was some kind of "great aberration."[30] Instead, it became, in the words of Walter LaFeber, the "natural culmination" of processes set in motion in 1860.[31] This interpretation deservedly remains ascendant to this day.

One of the problems with this view, however, is that it overstates continuity and understates the crablike trajectory of the era's foreign policy.[32] Indeed, when one looks at U.S. diplomacy in the years after the Civil War, the pattern more closely resembles that of Reconstruction in the South than it does the conquest and colonization of the West. In the years immediately after 1865, proponents of an assertive foreign policy, such as Seward, Nathaniel P. Banks, and Ulysses S. Grant, drafted blueprints for the projection of U.S. power abroad, particularly in the Caribbean and Central America. Fuelled by a newfound confidence in the power of the nation, these plans included the annexation of Caribbean islands, support for the Cuban revolution that began in 1868, assertive policies aimed at gaining the upper hand in the battle for control of an anticipated isthmian canal, and federal subsidies for steamship and telegraph lines. Yet, similar to the fate of Radical Reconstruction, by the mid-1870s little had come of these plans, with the very notable exceptions of the annexation of Alaska and Midway.

Here emerged a dynamic that characterized the remainder of the nineteenth century (and quite possibly beyond): assertive foreign policies would be formulated, but only partially achieved (if at all) in the face of domestic and foreign opposition, often to be abandoned, only to then resurface after a fallow period. There is no shortage of examples of this pattern. Annexationists had long dreamt of acquiring Cuba; then they were prepared to settle for some kind of intervention in the Cuban Ten Years' War (1868–78); but then they had to accept a "wait-and-see" policy, before plotting again to take the island when rebellion resumed after 1895. There was a similar sequence in Santo Domingo; Grant invoked the Monroe Doctrine in support of his bid for annexation in 1870, only to have the Senate torpedo the plan. U.S. commercial interests, eventually consolidated under the banner of the Santo Domingo Improvement Company, emerged as a powerful presence on the island two decades later. When a debt crisis raised the specter of European intervention in Santo Domingo in 1904, Theodore Roosevelt invoked the Monroe Doctrine, this time to justify intervention rather than annexation. A parallel pattern can be seen in U.S. shipping and communications policy. In 1865, the Republican-led Congress showered subsidies upon the Pacific Mail Steamship Company, the nation's largest international shipping conglomerate that established a monopoly on the New York to San Francisco (via Panama railroad) route, as well as opened the world's first transpacific steamline service (San Francisco to Yokohama and Hong Kong) in 1867. But a corruption scandal led a hostile Congress to revoke the subsidy in the mid-1870s, leaving the company to the predation of the Transcontinental (Railroad) Association. U.S. shipping would not recover until the following century.

Answering why the projection of U.S. power abroad after the Civil War proceeded in fits and starts is one of the great riddles of nineteenth-century U.S. history. One way historians have sought to explain this is by uncovering the factors that inhibited full-blown overseas imperialism. Another (and complementary) way of confronting this problem is to approach the formulation and execution of foreign policy not as a set of discrete choices made by policymakers, but rather as a derivate of the politics of national power that emerged in the Civil War. Foreign policy, in this formulation, was a function of the interplay of the institutions and brokers of power in the United States. Had the Union constructed a more centralized, powerful state apparatus during its Civil War, one could imagine a scenario in which the postwar United States would have pursued a more coherent and assertive foreign policy. But this was not the case.

The projection of U.S. power abroad in the late nineteenth century was governed by a political process similar to that which emerged during the Civil War. Historians should be careful not to attribute too much power and influence to the statesmen who drafted blueprints of empire from their

perches in Washington. To be sure, the central state played a key role in setting the foreign policy agenda, but the extent to which national power was
amassed and projected depended upon the state's ability to harness the energy of non-state actors—or, alternatively, the ability of non-state actors,
both from within and outside of the United States, to co-opt the state in
projects of their own design. As was the case during the war, realizing national power required the active participation of a wide range of stakeholders.
For national power to be effectively projected in an era still marked by anti-
statism and a relatively weak foreign policy apparatus, cooperation between
the state (diplomats, consuls, the navy) and the non-state (missionaries,
exporters, investors, foreign lobbies and collaborators), mediated through national institutions (the Republican Party, new interest group associations),
was required. This meant, in effect, aligning on behalf of an objective political support from an administration and, in all likelihood, from Congress,
alongside those private actors and foreign collaborators who most often were
most often the agents of U.S. power on the ground.

The size and shape of such a political coalition depended upon circum-
stance and, crucially, the strength of the opposition, which forged similar
coalitions of its own. The annexation of Midway (1867) was achieved simply through coordinated action between Pacific Mail and the U.S. Navy.[33] It
did not take a formidable political lobby to acquire a few miles of uninhab-
ited rocks on the Pacific on which to store coal. Objectives that were more
controversial (most often as a result of the presence of non-white populations in coveted territories—compare the annexation of Midway to the failed
attempts to annex the Danish West Indies and Santo Domingo in the same
period) required a stronger and more sustained coalition. The late nineteenth
century is full of examples in which overseas ventures were undermined, or
even thwarted by, the failure of its proponents to forge a suitably strong political coalition. Political elites at times raced ahead of public and business
opinion (the Grant administration's Dominican scheme would be a good
example of this); more often business and missionary interests complained
that their activities were undermined by a lack of diplomatic and naval support from the central government. The relative weakness of the era's political elites did not help the proponents of active, expansionist policies—after
all, there were no Gilded Age equals to Lincoln when it came to giving purpose to the nation's global mission (though to what end Lincoln would have
promoted a postwar foreign policy is open to debate).

Given this context, it is not surprising that controversial plans for the annexation of overseas territories with "undesirable" populations did not

come to fruition. But the politics of power projection did not preclude the United States from asserting itself outside of its borders. It just lent itself to certain kinds of policies in certain kinds of places. The case of Mexico is the best example of the how the form of national U.S. power developed during the 1860s could be projected—or, perhaps more accurately, could become "entangled"—in a sustained manner outside of its borders. This U.S. imperialism took an anticolonial form, both in opposing European intervention and in promoting Mexican nationalism—though, of course, a particular kind of nationalism conducive to U.S. interests. U.S. policy toward Mexico actually began its shift from outright military conquest of the 1840s to the informal projection of power in the late 1850s. The French intervention in the 1860s heightened U.S. interest, not least because of how the pro-Juarez lobby within the United States, led by the charismatic Mexican envoy Matías Romero, invoked the Monroe Doctrine and the principle of republican self-government on behalf of their cause. The French intervention led U.S. policymakers to see the projection of U.S. power in Mexico as reactive and anti-imperial in nature, an important development in terms of limiting opposition in Congress. Though there were calls for a counter-intervention during the 1860s, the United States preferred to leave the toppling of Maximilian to Mexican Liberals.

Once this was achieved in 1867, Mexico began to become an economic satellite of the United States, "one magnificent but undeveloped mine—our India in commercial importance," as one U.S. booster put it. Another Yankee, former Union General William Rosecrans, envisaged that the introduction of U.S. capital and commerce would promote the "peaceful development of Mexico under her own autonomy," thus rolling back European influence, avoiding U.S. occupation, and fostering a profitable and stable relationship. The neocolonial relationship that emerged in the final decades of the nineteenth century owed much to risk-taking U.S. investors and financiers who poured money into Mexican railroads and mining projects. But it also was the result of the diplomatic support they received from their home government, and, more so, the hospitable policies of Mexican dictator Porfirio Díaz and the now finance minister Romero, whose pursuit of foreign investment and national development led them to draft laws and regulations favorable to Wall Street capitalists—this despite growing concerns of U.S. intentions among Mexican Liberals. By the end of the century, U.S. investment in Mexico totaled $503 million, making it by far the most important overseas capital market. This figure would skyrocket in the first decade of the twentieth century.[34]

In the case of Mexico, U.S. power was mobilized and projected because of the relative political strength of its proponents (a constellation of U.S. diplomats, business interests, and Mexican political elites) and the relatively uncontroversial nature (in Washington, that is) of the diplomacy that was pursued (informal rather than formal imperialism). This kind of power projection—informal imperialism spearheaded by non-state actors, but supported by the central state and foreign elites, and presented under the banner of an imagined tradition of unalloyed anti-imperialism symbolized by the Monroe Doctrine—could be seen as a de facto compromise between interests and ideals, costs and benefits. Indeed, old Civil War–era liberals who later became anti-imperialists, such as Carl Schurz, pointed to U.S. policy toward Mexico as an enlightened and cost-effective alternative to the full-blown colonialism promoted by the imperialists of 1898.[35] But when viewed through the prism of the politics of U.S. power, it might also be seen as the product of the institutions and relationships that harnessed the new nation's rapidly growing power. This is by no means to suggest that U.S. power promoted the sustainable development of Mexico, as was imagined by its proponents at the time. Paradoxically, as the United States embraced limited central authority at home, its presence in Mexico served to promote the consolidation of power under the Díaz regime, thus helping to sow the seeds of the socioeconomic inequality, rural discontent, and political repression that would trigger a revolution in the early twentieth century.

The central role played by Mexican Liberals and, in later days, the Díaz regime, also should be emphasized. Rather than view U.S. power as simply something that was projected outward from Washington and received in Mexico, it is more fruitful to approach the expansion of U.S. interests and power as a function of the complex relationships between the U.S. state, private capitalists and other non-state actors, and Mexican "collaborating elites," who, despite concerns of the growing *coloso del norte*, saw advantage in, or resigned themselves to the inevitability of, some form of collaborative partnership.[36] An interpretation of U.S. foreign relations such as this will restore the crucial role played by non-state players and foreign elites, thus more fully bringing "entangled history" into the historiography of U.S. foreign relations.

THE STUDENTS I TEACH have remarked that it is peculiar that historians have not more fully situated the Civil War into the broader narrative of the emergence of the United States as a world power. After all, when in class we discuss African Americans, women, nationalism, politics, warfare, religion, and finance we eventually end up considering how the Civil War constituted a watershed. Why scholars of foreign relations rarely have attempted to make an equivalent case is likely a result of the fact that the Civil War does not cleanly fit into the narrative of the rising world power of the United States.

Of course, as this essay has argued, it is difficult to imagine the United States becoming a great world power without the Union victory. By consolidating national control over a powerful internal separatist movement and by demonstrating its capacity to mobile immense national power, the conflict was beyond any doubt the prerequisite to the emergence of the United States as a world power, not least because it facilitated the colonization and economic exploitation of the West, the source of so much of the United States' wealth and power in the twentieth century.[37] But the institutions and political relationships forged during the war did not consistently lead to the accumulation and projection of national power, at least in the short term. Indeed, greater awareness of the politics of power consolidation that emerged during the war might shed fresh light on that old question "why did it take until 1898 for the U.S. to partake in the global trend of full-blown overseas colonialism?"

The limits of the projection of the national power of the United States were most evident in the decades immediately following 1865. If we take a truly *longue durée* perspective, the Civil War looks more like a classic watershed moment. It appears as such not only for how it catalyzed the nationalization of power, but also because of the processes through which power was nationalized. For all of the developments in the power of the U.S. central state and the military-industrial complex in the twentieth century, the foundation of its national power remained the synergy between government, finance, and a persistently antistatist civil society. It has become commonplace to argue that the Cold War was won not because of preponderant military power or a sounder grand strategy, but because the U.S. political system proved superior in harnessing and deploying its economic, political, and ideological power over the long haul, as well as appealing to potential collaborators outside of the nation's borders. It too was a "people's contest." If only dimly, the structures and processes born in the United States' great nineteenth-century war can be seen in its greatest challenge of the twentieth.

Suggested Readings

Bensel, Richard. *Yankee Leviathan: The Origins of Central State Authority in America, 1859–1877*. Cambridge: Cambridge University Press, 1991.

Carwardine, Richard. *Lincoln: A Life of Purpose and Power*. New York: Alfred A. Knopf, 2006.

Cox Richardson, Heather. *West from Appomattox: The Reconstruction of America after the Civil War*. New Haven, CT: Yale University Press, 2007.

Crook, D. P. *The North, the South and the Powers, 1861–1865*. London: John Wiley and Sons, 1974.

Edling, Max M. *A Hercules in the Cradle: War, Money, and the American State, 1783–1867*. Chicago: University of Chicago Press, 2014.

Go, Julian. *Patterns of Empire: The British and American Empires, 1688 to Present*. Cambridge: Cambridge University Press, 2011.

Hendrickson, David. *Union, Nation or Empire: The American Debate over International Relations, 1789–1941*. Lawrence: University Press of Kansas, 2009.

LaFeber, Walter. *The New Empire: An Interpretation of American Expansion, 1860–1898*. Ithaca, NY: Cornell University Press, 1963.

Schoonover, Thomas. *Dollars over Dominion: The Triumph of Liberalism in Mexican-United States Relations, 1861–1867*. Baton Rouge: Louisiana State University Press, 1978.

Sexton, Jay. *The Monroe Doctrine: Empire and Nation in Nineteenth-Century America*. New York: Hill and Wang, 2011.

Smith, Adam I. P. *No Party Now: Politics in the Civil War North*. New York: Oxford University Press, 2006.

Weeks, William Earl. *The New Cambridge History of American Foreign Relations, Volume 1: Dimensions of the Early American Empire, 1754–1865*. Cambridge: Cambridge University Press, 2013.

Notes

1. "Slavery and the Crisis of the Union, 1854–1865" is one of the longest running special subjects in the Oxford history syllabus. The roots of this course can be traced back to Allan Nevins' time as the visiting Harmsworth Professor in the 1940s.

2. The key works here include Walter LaFeber, *The New Empire: An Interpretation of American Expansion, 1860–1898* (Ithaca, NY: Cornell University Press, 1963); Ernest Paolino, *The Foundations of the American Empire: William Henry Seward and U.S. Foreign Policy* (Ithaca, NY: Cornell University Press, 1973); Thomas Schoonover, *Dollars over Dominion: The Triumph of Liberalism in Mexican-United States Relations, 1861–1867* (Baton Rouge: Louisiana State University Press, 1978).

3. For illustrative works, see Charles S. Maier, *Among Empires: American Ascendancy and its Predecessors* (Cambridge, MA: Harvard University Press, 2006); Julian Go, *Patterns of Empire: The British and American Empires, 1688 to Present* (Cambridge: Cambridge University Press, 2011).

4. William Earl Weeks, *The New Cambridge History of American Foreign Relations, Volume 1: Dimensions of the Early American Empire, 1754–1865* (Cambridge: Cambridge University Press, 2013), xvii–xxv.

5. Robert Kagan, *Dangerous Nation: America and the World, 1600–1898* (London: Knopf Doubleday Publishing Group, 2006).

6. For a recent examination of this literature, see Jay Sexton, "The United States in the British Empire," in *The Oxford History of the British Empire, Companion Series: British North America in the Seventeenth and Eighteenth Centuries*, ed. Stephen Foster (Oxford: Oxford University Press, 2013), 318–48.

7. Quoted in Kinley Brauer, "The United States and British Imperial Expansion, 1815–1860," *Diplomatic History* 12 (Winter 1988): 19–37.

8. Henry Cabot Lodge, "Colonialism in the United States," *Atlantic Monthly* (May 1883): 612–27.

9. Quoted in David Hendrickson, *Union, Nation or Empire: The American Debate over International Relations, 1789–1941* (Lawrence: University Press of Kansas, 2009), 118–23.

10. James Monroe, Annual Message to Congress, December 2, 1823.

11. JQA diary, November 26, 1823, in Charles Francis Adams, ed., *Memoirs of John Quincy Adams* (Philadelphia: JB Lippincott), 6:207.

12. Ibid., 206.

13. Weeks, *Dimensions of the Early American Empire*, 1:117.

14. Clay, "Toast," March 29, 1823, in James Hopkins, ed., *Papers of Henry Clay* (Lexington: University Press of Kentucky, 1858–1992), 3:405.

15. Quoted in Hendrickson, *Union, Nation, or Empire*, 225.

16. Quoted in D. P. Crook, *The North, the South and the Powers, 1861–1865* (London: John Wiley and Sons, 1974), 262.

17. Joshua Leavitt, *The Monroe Doctrine* (New York: Sinclair Tousey, 1863).

18. My understanding of this point has been shaped by Don H. Doyle, *The Cause of All Nations: An International History of the American Civil War* (New York: Basic Books, 2015).

19. For the importance of Civil War diplomacy, see Howard Jones, *Blue and Gray Diplomacy: A History of Union and Confederate Foreign Relations* (Chapel Hill: University of North Carolina Press, 2009).

20. Jay Sexton, *Debtor Diplomacy: Finance and American Foreign Relations in the Civil War Era, 1837–1873* (Oxford: Oxford University Press, 2005), ch. 4.

21. Frederick W. Seward, *Seward at Washington as Senator and Secretary of State* (New York: Derby and Miller, 1891), 3:495–96.

22. Max M. Edling, *A Hercules in the Cradle: War, Money, and the American State, 1783–1867* (Chicago: University of Chicago Press, 2014).

23. In addition to Edling, *Hercules in the Cradle*, see also Brian Balogh, *A Government Out of Sight: The Mystery of National Authority in Nineteenth-Century America* (New York: Cambridge University Press, 2009).

24. Adam I. P. Smith, *No Party Now: Politics in the Civil War North* (New York: Oxford University Press, 2006); J. Matthew Gallman, *The North Fights the Civil War: The Home Front* (Chicago: Dee, 1994), 109–15.

25. Richard Carwardine, *Lincoln: A Life of Purpose and Power* (New York: Knopf, 2006).

26. Melinda Lawson, *Patriot Fires: Forging a New American Nationalism in the Civil War North* (Lawrence: University Press of Kansas, 2002), 40–64.

27. William H. Seward, "Speech on His Travels," Seward Papers (microfilm, reel 187); William H. Seward and Olive Risley Seward, *William H. Seward's Travels around the World* (New York: Appleton, 1873), 25. For the broader context of the West after the Civil War, see Cox Richardson, *West from Appomattox: The Reconstruction of America after the Civil War* (New Haven, CT: Yale University Press, 2007).

28. The starting point remains Eric Foner, *Reconstruction: America's Unfinished Revolution, 1863–1877* (New York: Harper & Row, 1988).

29. This view of the retreat of Reconstruction is indebted to Richard Bensel, *Yankee Leviathan: The Origins of Central State Authority in America, 1859–1877* (Cambridge: Cambridge University Press, 1991).

30. This was the view of Samuel Flagg Bemis, *A Diplomatic History of the United States* (New York: Henry Holt and Co., 1936).

31. LaFeber, *The New Empire*, xxxi.

32. For a critique of the New Left interpretation, see David Pletcher, "Rhetoric and Results: A Pragmatic View of American Economic Expansion, 1865–1898," *Diplomatic History* 5 (Spring 1981): 93–105.

33. See the description of the annexation provided in Senate Executive Document No. 79, 40th Cong., 2nd sess.

34. For the United States and Mexico in this period, see Schoonover, *Dollars Over Dominion*; David Pletcher, *The Diplomacy of Trade and Investment: American Economic Expansion in the Hemisphere, 1865–1900* (Columbia: University of Missouri Press, 1998), 77–113; John Mason Hart, *Empire and Revolution: The Americans in Mexico since the Civil War* (Berkeley: University of California Press, 2006). "Our India" from Pletcher, *Diplomacy of Trade and Investment*, 77; "peaceful development" from Rosencrans to Seward, September 29, 1869, Seward Papers (microfilm, reel 107).

35. Robert Beisner, *Twelve against Empire: The Anti-Imperialists, 1898–1900*, 2nd ed. (Chicago: University of Chicago Press, 1985), 31.

36. For the classic articulation of "collaborating elites" as being key to nineteenth-century imperialism, see Ronald Robinson, "Non-European Foundations of European Imperialism: Sketch for a Theory of Collaboration," in *Studies in the Theories of Imperialism*, ed. Roger Owen and Bob Sutcliffe (London: Longman, 1972), 117–42.

37. Bruce Cummings, *Dominion from Sea to Sea: Pacific Ascendancy and American Power* (New Haven, CT: Yale University Press, 2009).

CHAPTER TWO

Wrapping the World in Fire
The Interventionist Crisis in the Civil War

Howard Jones

The British and French were among others in Europe and elsewhere closely watching the events in America that in April 1861 culminated in the Civil War. Many observers seemed curious or captivated; others calculated the strategic and economic benefits to their own countries resulting from a republic now vulnerable to outside intervention. What might they gain from a divided and perhaps disabled nation? Still others wondered what civilized peoples should do to preserve a republic endangered by a rebellion that might threaten the rapidly growing Atlantic economy and hence their own livelihoods. Some contemporaries suggested mediation; others urged arbitration; still others considered a forceful intervention in the name of peace but always grounded in self-interest. Britain and France pondered an intervention that could have permanently divided the United States and prevented it from becoming a world power.

PRESIDENT ABRAHAM LINCOLN insisted that the conflict was a domestic matter in which his chief responsibility was to preserve the Union, but he soon realized that events in North America would also play out on the international stage and perhaps draw in other nations. The Confederacy's emphasis on winning diplomatic recognition and the United States' determination to prevent this from happening, even to the point of declaring war on any nation (or nations) that recognized the South, would put the Civil War on the path to becoming a global concern.

The greatest foreign relations issue during the Civil War was the Confederacy's attempt to win nationhood status and thereby negotiate foreign military and economic alliances that could decide the outcome of the fighting. According to the traditional story, President Lincoln blocked British and French intervention on behalf of the Confederacy by using the Union's victory at Antietam as the impetus for announcing the Emancipation Proclamation and converting the war into a moral crusade against slavery. The interventionist story is far more complicated than tying it to any single set of events.

Neither Confederate president Jefferson Davis nor Lincoln had experience in foreign affairs, but both leaders felt certain that diplomatic recognition of the Confederacy would assure its independence. Davis was confident that Britain and France would acknowledge Southern independence for two reasons: the righteousness of the Confederacy's cause—self-determination—and the leverage of "King Cotton Diplomacy," which entailed holding back on its richest product to force outside help. He failed to realize, however, that self-interest almost always trumps ideals in foreign matters and that the South's bountiful cotton crops in the past two years had provided a surplus in Europe that would last into late 1862 and ease foreign pressure for intervention. Lincoln meanwhile sought to convince London and Paris not to meddle in American affairs. He quietly supported the actions of his fiery secretary of state, William Seward, who had earlier instructed the Union minister in London, Charles Francis Adams, to warn the British against recognizing the Confederacy. Now, in a declaration to British news correspondent William H. Russell on July 4, 1861, Seward sent a stronger warning to British leaders that if their government recognized the Confederacy, he would "wrap the world in fire."[1]

The first eighteen months of the Civil War were crucial, not only because of what happened on the battlefields in America but also because of what transpired in the courts of Europe. To discourage outside interference, Lincoln in April 1861 announced his intention to blockade Southern ports. His reference to a blockade, however, introduced the language of war to the American contest and opened the door to Britain, France, and other nations to follow international law and declare neutrality. Such action made it clear that the outside world believed it had a stake in what happened in the United States.

The British proclamation of neutrality on May 13, 1861, followed by similar proclamations from the French and six other nations, defined the Union and the Confederacy as belligerents entitled to deal with private foreign businesses—an act that put the European powers only one step away from extending full recognition of Confederate sovereignty. The British also implemented their Foreign Enlistment Act of 1819, which barred subjects from any activity capable of drawing the crown into the American war. But the Lincoln administration quickly realized that the belligerent Confederacy could float loans, buy arms, and contract the building of a navy.[2]

This was a "war so horrible," moaned Lord John Russell, who as British foreign secretary thought it a senseless conflict, both in its origins and, more important, in the mindless destruction it imposed on the antagonists as well as the outside nations dependent on Atlantic commerce. Southern independence was a fait accompli, he and many contemporaries concluded, both in Britain and on the continent; surely the United States could not subdue so many people and occupy such a vast territory. Ironically, however, Russell agreed with the South that secession was the solution and *not* the problem. To the Confederacy, secession would safeguard slavery. To Russell, secession would kill slavery. The South's departure from the Union, he asserted, would create two American nations and resolve the slavery issue peacefully: "One Republic to be constituted on the principle of freedom and personal liberty—the other on the principle of slavery and the mutual surrender of fugitives." A breakup of the republic, he told his minister in Washington, Richard Lyons, would promote the death of slavery by surrounding the new nation with free territory that might make it easier for slaves to escape. "For this reason I wish for separation."[3]

Lincoln's call for preserving the Union rang hollow in England and throughout Europe. Most observers had expected him to proclaim war against slavery, but he could not do so without driving the Border States and Union loyalists in the South into the Confederacy while alienating northerners unwilling to fight for black freedom. The Union's apparent lack of moral purpose confirmed Europe's perception of a pointless war. The illustrious democracy had imploded into anarchy, leaving the republican experiment in ruins and confirming the skepticism of British prime minister Lord Palmerston and others who had long opposed political and social reform as madness. As for Russell, England in the Victorian Era was the leading civilized country in the world and bore a moral responsibility to end the war.[4]

Russell, however, had more in mind: Intervention might serve the crown's interests, even though leaving the impression that it had taken the South's side in the war. By the fall of 1862, he had become convinced that the vicious fighting could compel a forceful intervention for economic as well as humanitarian reasons. Not only would a prolonged war devastate the economies of both North and South, but it would inflict collateral damage on the British and other foreign peoples heavily dependent on American trade. Russell found justification for intervention in a broad interpretation of international law that authorized neutral nations to step into a war that threatened their livelihood. The renowned Swiss theorist on international law, Emmerich de Vattel, had argued more than a century earlier that outside intervention was acceptable in a war inflicting "disaster and ruin" on the belligerents while seriously damaging the neutral nations.[5]

Emperor Napoleon III of France had a far less complicated view of what the war offered him and his country: a chance to satisfy the demands of self-interest. Could he use the war as a means for further weakening the United States while helping stabilize Mexico with a monarchical government that stopped the spread of democracy? But drawn as he was to the American conflict, he refused to take any interventionist action without England's lead. France and England had recently defeated Russia in the Crimean War, but their concert rested on shaky grounds, and he did not want to alienate his chief rival in Europe and thereby upset his expansionist plans on the continent. Napoleon agreed with the British that the Union could not subjugate the Confederacy. But he wanted the war to continue until the South gained independence and he could extend diplomatic recognition. With the United States divided, he had an opportunity to roll back its recent territorial gains in the Mexican War by first fulfilling the dream of his illustrious uncle, Napoleon I, who had sought to restore the French Empire in North America that the British had wrested away in the humiliating Treaty of Paris ending the French and Indian War in 1763.[6]

The younger Napoleon had a well-deserved reputation as a notorious adventurer—a loose cannon, Palmerston and others sneered—who regularly tempted danger by concocting risky schemes aimed at promoting French imperial interests. Napoleon III often acted without consulting or listening to his advisers. Both the British and his own colleagues feared that he would unilaterally intervene in the American war when he found it in his best interests.[7]

Napoleon's dreams rested on his "Grand Design for the Americas," a fanciful project that hinged on taking advantage of the American war to intervene (in cooperation with England and Spain) in Mexico on the pretext of collecting debts but in reality to replace the new republican government with a monarchy headed by Austrian Archduke Ferdinand Maximilian Joseph. Erika Pani, however, demonstrates in her essay that even though Mexican Conservatives supported a monarchy, they would not have unanimously chosen Maximilian. But the French emperor forged ahead, knowing that the ensuing tripartite intervention in Mexico in October 1861 would set a precedent for Europe's intervention in the American Civil War.[8]

The success of Napoleon's empire-building program was problematic because it heavily depended on French recognition of the Confederacy. Stève Sainlaude shows that the emperor lacked the support of two successive foreign ministers who served him in this tumultuous period. The Confederacy, they insisted, had territorial designs of its own and posed a greater threat to Mexico than the United States.

Napoleon's ambitious effort sent shock waves throughout the Union and would have stunned the Confederacy had it not offered a bridge to nationhood. In return for recognition, the Confederacy would assume the role of a friendly nation standing between a mortally wounded United States and a resuscitated Mexico under French control. Such a far-reaching project necessitated cutting off a greatly weakened American republic from Mexico by taking back Texas and the vast lands making up the Mexican Cession of 1848. But inherent in this scheme was a French economic and territorial threat not only to the Union but also to the Confederacy. French intervention in the Civil War would come at a heavy cost to Americans on *both* sides of the North-South line and hence prove as threatening to their republic as did their family conflict. Confederate leaders were not naive, however, and saw a saving grace in the matter: A greater French presence in North America might be worth the risk if an independent Confederacy emerged strong enough to hold Napoleon's empire at bay while, as Patrick J. Kelly establishes in his essay for this volume, reviving Southern dreams of expansion— and never giving up Texas.

BY LATE 1861, the outside world's prognosis that the Union could not win the war seemed justified when in July Confederate forces routed its troops at Bull Run. The outcome of the battle confirmed to Europeans as well as Americans on both sides of the issue that the Confederacy was in the war to win against Union forces who were not prepared to fight.

The Confederacy's good fortunes continued when less than four months after Bull Run, the United States and England appeared headed for war over the *Trent* affair. Such a conflict, Lincoln feared, could ally England with the Confederacy and guarantee Southern independence.

This first international crisis of the Civil War had its origins in early November 1861, when Captain Charles Wilkes of the USS *San Jacinto* stopped the British mail ship *Trent* in the Caribbean and removed two Southern emissaries—James Mason and John Slidell—who had run the Union blockade and were en route to England and France. Rather than take the *Trent* to an admiralty court as a prize, Wilkes seized the two Southerners as the "embodiment of dispatches"—hence contraband—and set off a fiery reaction throughout England over questions of honor and international law. To Union supporters, however, the free-spirited naval officer had heroically restored their government's credibility after the debacle at Bull Run while slapping the British for bestowing belligerent rights to the Confederacy.[9]

Perhaps Lincoln would have been on solid legal ground had he refused to settle on the basis of the threat to national security posed by Mason and Slidell's mission—to seek a European recognition aimed at destroying the United States; but he considered it far more important to maintain peace with England and, therefore, admitted that Wilkes had acted illegally. Even after the agreement, Adams remained shaken by the war scare and warned that British imperial interests were still a threat at sea and in the Western Hemisphere. England, he wrote a friend, would continue to "sit as a cold spectator, ready to make the best of our calamity the moment there is a sufficient excuse to interfere."[10]

Thus was the republic in peril from the outside as well as within. The vendetta-like fighting could rip the nation apart, allowing foreign intervention to finalize that division. If these events played out in Old World fashion, the French, as Sainlaude's essay will make clear, would be in position to pursue their expansionist objectives in North and South America, and the British, as Richard Huzzey notes in his essay, would extend their strategic and economic interest in Latin America. Americans soon faced one of the greatest truths of a civil war: A family struggle deeply weakens the entire nation, making it vulnerable to a foreign involvement that, in this case, could inflict great damage on *both* the Confederacy and the United States.

Americans on neither side could have known at the time, but European intervention appeared certain at two distinct stages of the war. In the fall of 1862, Palmerston seriously considered a mediation pointing to recognition of the Confederacy; and from the close of that year to the end of the war in April 1865, Napoleon pushed for an armistice that tied recognition to his objectives in Mexico. Had either project succeeded, the Confederacy would doubtless have emerged as a separate nation, leaving it and a severely impaired United States in the midst of a heightened British presence in Canada and Latin America, along with a French empire wanting to expand into much of today's U.S. midsection, American Southwest, and Central and South America.

The British seriously considered recognizing the Confederacy in late 1862 because of a unique confluence of events both on and off the battlefield. The prime minister had Russell's support for a mediation based on separation as the best means for ending the war. News had arrived in London of General Robert E. Lee's victory at Second Bull Run in late August and had surely convinced the United States to reconsider the wisdom of continuing the war. "The Federals," Palmerston remarked to Russell, "got a very complete smashing, and it seems not altogether unlikely that still greater disasters await them, and that even Washington or Baltimore may fall into the hands of the Confederates. If this should happen, would it not be time for us to consider whether . . . England and France might not address the contending parties and recommend an arrangement upon the basis of separation?" If either or both belligerents rejected mediation, the two European governments should "acknowledge the independence of the South as an established fact." Russell approved the approach. If mediation failed, "we ought ourselves to recognize the Southern States as an independent State." They agreed to call a cabinet meeting in October to discuss the proposal.[11]

Intervention, it appeared to Palmerston and Russell, would win widespread support in England. Already sickened by the bloodshed at Shiloh in April 1862, both the *Times* and the *Morning Post* appealed to the Palmerston ministry to recognize the Confederacy. The *Morning Herald* issued a humanitarian plea for peace: "Let us do something, as we are Christian men." Whether "arbitration, intervention, diplomatic action, recognition of the South, remonstrance with the North, friendly interference or forcible pressure of some sort. . . . Let us do something to stop this carnage."[12]

But just as Palmerston prepared to suggest mediation to his cabinet in late October, he learned that Lee had launched a raid into Maryland. Confident that the Confederacy would amass an unbroken string of victories, the prime minister delayed his proposal until that expected news provided the United States with greater reason to accept the offer. Russell again concurred, recommending that they invite the French to join the interventionist effort and, in accordance with the queen's recommendation, add more weight to the proposal by broadening the list of participants to include Austria, Prussia, and Russia.[13]

In the meantime, in Washington, another series of events had unfolded in July, just before the battle of Second Bull Run, which soon wound its way into British deliberations.

By the summer of 1862, Lincoln had become so concerned about the lack of progress in the war that he moved toward an antislavery position. But he had to show Americans opposed to abolition that emancipation was a weapon to win the war and *not* an objective of the war in its own right. Thus, Lincoln did not support abolition for moral reasons. The assurance of freedom might encourage the slaves to abandon the plantations and join the advancing Union Army.[14]

Lincoln informed Seward and Secretary of the Navy Gideon Welles of his interest in using emancipation to "strike at the heart of the rebellion." The decision was "a military necessity, absolutely essential to the preservation of the Union." In taking this position, he acted as commander-in-chief and averted any charge of violating the Constitution. To destroy the Confederacy, Lincoln asserted, the United States must destroy slavery.[15]

In late July, Lincoln met with his cabinet and read his planned proclamation of emancipation. The move was a "necessary military measure," he emphasized before declaring that, according to its provisions, all slaves in states still in rebellion by January 1, 1863, would be free. Seward warned that the British would denounce the move as a desperate attempt by the Lincoln administration to incite a slave rebellion and feel compelled to intervene. The United States must first win a major battle. Otherwise, premature emancipation would appear to be "the last measure of an exhausted government, a cry for help . . . our last *shriek*, on the retreat."[16]

Lincoln agreed to wait for a Union victory—which did not come until September 17, 1862, in Maryland. At Antietam Creek near Sharpsburg, General George B. McClellan's Union troops desperately grappled with Lee's Confederate forces as the two huge armies together suffered more than 23,000 casualties in the bloodiest single day of fighting in the war. Lee retreated into Virginia, leaving the Union Army standing alone on the field and claiming victory.[17]

In accordance with Seward's recommendation, Lincoln followed Antietam with a noon cabinet meeting on September 22, where he announced his intention to issue the preliminary Emancipation Proclamation.[18]

London immediately reacted to the president's proclamation with an anger energized by the visceral remarks made by its chargé in Washington, William Stuart, who had temporarily replaced Lyons. Far less temperate and reserved than his mentor, Stuart justified Seward's deepest fears by sending the home ministry a blistering critique of Lincoln's purpose that made its way into the newspapers on both sides of the English Channel. The president, Stuart bitterly warned, sought to instigate slave revolts throughout the South that would not only destroy the Confederacy but set off a racial firestorm that could consume the continent.[19]

Stuart's invectives had touched a national nerve. The *Times* of London ridiculed Lincoln for thinking himself "a sort of moral American Pope." That same city's *Spectator* supported the United States but found the proclamation exasperating. "The principle is not that a human being cannot justly own another, but that he cannot own him unless he is loyal to the

United States." To win the war, the *Times* indignantly declared, Lincoln would encourage slaves to "murder the families of their masters" while they were away on the battlefield. Would "the reign of the last President" come to an end "amid horrible massacres of white women and children, to be followed by the extermination of the black race in the South?" *Blackwood's Edinburgh Magazine* denounced the proclamation as "monstrous, reckless, devilish." To defeat the Confederacy, the United States "would league itself with Beelzebub, and seek to make a hell of half a continent." Lincoln had played his last card, according to a London *Punch* cartoon—the Ace of Spades.[20]

The rage in Britain quickly spread across the channel into France, where both conservative and liberal newspapers joined in a venomous attack on the Emancipation Proclamation. The conservative press predicted slave revolts and a "fratricidal war" that would engulf America in "blood and ruins." According to one paper, Lincoln "wishes to abolish slavery where he is not able to achieve it and to save it where he would be able to abolish it." Had Lincoln abolished slavery as an act of justice when the war began, claimed another paper, "All spirits, or philosophers or Christians would have immediately rallied to the cause of the North, which would have been that of humanity." A conservative paper insisted that the war had stalemated and that "an intervention by a third party was necessary to break the equilibrium."[21]

Thus did the Emancipation Proclamation add momentum to foreign intervention by leading both England and France to accuse the president of making a pact with the devil to win the war. The British and the French feared a racial conflict that would spread beyond U.S. borders and ruin cotton and wheat production for decades. The only way to end the fighting was through their joint intervention.

FORTUNATELY FOR THE United States, the British only initially underestimated the power of the Emancipation Proclamation in ending slavery. As Lincoln insisted, and as several leading members of Parliament concurred, the proclamation would promote Union victory in the war and necessarily lead to the death of slavery. John Bright, Richard Cobden, and the Duke of Argyll were among those who took this position. Henry Adams, private secretary to his father in the London legation, enthusiastically wrote his brother back in the United States, "The Emancipation Proclamation has done more for us here than all our former victories, and all our diplomacy." By early October 1862, Lincoln's proclamation had become increasingly popular in England. The British press soon joined workers in condemning slavery as a violation of freedom and praising the president for advancing the rights of mankind by destroying the very foundation of the Old South.[22]

Palmerston's cabinet, however, was deeply divided over the American question, but the British public did not know this and considered recognition imminent when, on October 7, 1862, Chancellor of the Exchequer William Gladstone praised the Confederacy in a fiery speech at Newcastle. His staunch support for intervention on humanitarian and economic grounds had allied him with Russell. Amid thunderous cheers, Gladstone proclaimed: "We may have our own opinions about slavery, we may be for or against the South; but there is no doubt that Jefferson Davis and other leaders of the South have made an army; they are making, it appears, a navy; and they have made what is more than either—they have made a nation." Then came his resounding conclusion: "We may anticipate with certainty the success of the Southern States as far as regards their separation from the North."[23]

Gladstone, however, had spoken without official sanction and aroused so much criticism of the government for seemingly returning to its imperial ways that Palmerston distanced his ministry from him. The chancellor denied supporting the Confederacy and maintained that he was and always had been neutral. His intention, he insisted, had been to show that Confederate independence was clear and that other nations must accept that reality and band together to end the war. But the move had backfired. The *Times*, *Saturday Review*, and *Illustrated London News* declared their opposition to intervention and wanted the battlefield to resolve the issue. And in Liverpool, as Gladstone came to realize, he had left Southern sympathizers with the erroneous impression that they had government backing in establishing an organization promoting the Confederacy.[24]

Soon after Gladstone's speech, Russell called for a cabinet meeting in late October, only to cancel it when he faced formidable resistance to intervention led by his highly respected colleague and scholar, Secretary for War George Cornewall Lewis. Military force cannot preserve the Union, Lewis declared to a friend; "You cannot conquer a seceding State." England must remain neutral and wait for the Confederacy to establish its claim to independence. Any suggestion of a cease-fire would encounter "heated and violent partisans" on both sides, not a "conclave of philosophers" calmly discussing the strengths and weaknesses of such action. Any form of intervention implied the South's existence as an entity. An armistice could work only when both antagonists want an end to the war. There was no compromise between Union preservation and Confederate independence. Union resentment for

British intervention of any kind could cause war, leaving Canada vulnerable to attack as winter approached.[25]

Lewis emphasized that the war itself must define peace terms. A mediation or an arbitration required a peace plan that would resolve a number of issues, including slavery, boundaries, and whether the Border States should be slave or free. "The sword has not yet traced the conditions of a treaty recognizing the independence of the South." Perhaps, Lewis declared in quoting Hamlet, "Better to endure the ills we have / Than fly to others which we know not of."[26]

Russell set aside his interest in an armistice. If sincere in advocating a humanitarian intervention in a war that had spun out of control, he felt an obligation to step in as a leader of a civilized nation. Russell saw higher issues involved, not pure self-interest; and yet, he knew that an end to the war would benefit the Atlantic economy by expanding Latin American markets and reopening the flow of American goods to Europe—which, of course, included England. That consideration surely in mind, he now emphasized that it was the "duty" of the "Great Powers of Europe" to intervene in an alliance comprised of England, France, Russia, Austria, and Prussia.[27]

Palmerston meanwhile supported a wait-and-see position about the war. He was convinced that only a lethal stalemate would drive the two sides to the peace table and finally force the Union to accept Southern independence. The "Pugilists must fight a few more Rounds before the Bystanders can decide that the State Should be divided between them."[28]

Russell preferred immediate action, insisting that intervention would help bring an end to this war before it worsened. He knew Russia's involvement was critical but thought the emperor "would not like to say that he preferred war and desolation."[29]

Russell saw another opportunity in late October 1862 when Napoleon called for a tripartite intervention made up of France, England, and Russia. The emperor, Russell learned, had proposed a mediation based on a six-month armistice along with a six-month suspension of the Union blockade. But unknown to Russell, Napoleon had earlier assured the Confederate minister in Paris, John Slidell, of two other ingredients in his plan: If the Union rejected the proposal, he confided to Slidell, this would provide "good reason for recognition and perhaps for more active intervention." Napoleon's thinly veiled reference to the use of force excited Slidell so much that he had difficulty responding calmly that such a step "would be judicious and acceptable." Not knowing, of course, that the British government was likewise moving toward a mediation based on Southern separation, Slidell warned Napoleon that Palmerston would doubtless reject any thought of recognition. Nor could Slidell have known that Russell had justified the use of force if the war threatened neutrals.[30]

When Russell received the proposal, he immediately called for a cabinet meeting on November 11. Although unaware of Napoleon's readiness to use force, the British foreign secretary had had enough experience with him over Mexico to know he would do anything to achieve his imperial objectives. What other corrective remained once the Union expectedly turned down the proposal?

Given the United States' unbending opposition to *any* form of outside intervention, Napoleon's proposal virtually assured a wider war. Yet Russell so desperately sought an end to the fighting that he refused to dismiss any chance for peace. As he remarked to Sir George Grey from the Home Office, the European powers owed it to civilization to make every effort to stop the war. "If a friend were to cut his throat, you would hardly like to confess, he told me he was going to do it, but I said nothing as I thought he would not take my advice."[31]

The British government could not have known for certain, but the Russians never seriously considered becoming involved in Napoleon's proposal. Not only were they leery of both the British and the French, but Tsar Alexander had just freed the serfs in March 1861 and rejected any alignment with the Confederacy. Furthermore, slavery was not an issue to the government in St. Petersburg, and the war had not jeopardized the Russian economy. Indeed, the Russian minister to the United States, Édouard de Stoeckl, had accepted Lincoln's contention that the Emancipation Proclamation was integral to the war effort. The Russian foreign minister, Prince Alexander Gorchakov, was like many of his countrymen who remained grateful to the United States for making its good offices available to his government in an effort to end the Crimean War against France and England. He informed Stoeckl that the government would do nothing to endanger this friendship.[32]

But Gladstone's indiscrete remarks had set off a national debate over intervention that forced the British government to make a decision.

Lewis immediately warned his cabinet colleagues that Napoleon's proposal meant war. In early November, he circulated a 15,000-word memorandum among them opposing intervention and insisting that the Confederacy had not earned its claim to recognition. Most noteworthy, his argument focused on the possibility of war with the Union rather than the issues of slavery or emancipation. He had written his memorandum in collaboration with his stepson-in-law, William Vernon Harcourt, who held the first Whewell Chair in International Law at Cambridge University. Under the pseudonym of "Historicus," Harcourt had earlier published a number of letters in the *Times* of London arguing that the Southern rebellion was treason until it succeeded. "And thus the only real test of independence is final success." Like Lewis, Harcourt warned that recognition could cause war.[33]

Palmerston met with his cabinet for two days in November, vigorously discussing Lewis's memo in relation to the French proposal and the potential for war with the United States. Lewis admitted that Russell was correct in asserting that the American conflict threatened neutral nations. But perhaps fearing diminished support for his earlier recommendation to let the war decide the outcome, he warned that intervention at this point could lead to war with the Union. Recognition was "the acknowledgment of a fact." But the problem comes in determining when that moment of separation has arrived. "It is easy to distinguish between day and night; but it is impossible to fix the precise moment when day ends and night begins." Recognition cannot take place if there was any "reasonable chance of an accommodation." International law did not permit recognition while a "*bona fide* struggle with the legitimate sovereign was pending."[34]

The war had not yet rendered a verdict, Lewis insisted. Else the Lincoln administration would not have used the Emancipation Proclamation "to impoverish and distress the Southern planters, possibly even to provoke a slave insurrection." Nor would the seceding Southern states and their British supporters "be so eager to secure their recognition by European Governments." Premature recognition would make England an ally of the rebellious South and cause war with the Union. "If the Great European Powers are not contented to wait until the American conflagration has burned itself out, they must not expect to extinguish the flames with Rose-water."[35]

Lewis warned that a resort to force raised questions about the wisdom of intervention. A five-power alliance appeared formidable, but it would face great logistical problems in transporting soldiers across the Atlantic. Could its wooden vessels prevail over the Union's ironclads? Could its forces defeat the Union's armies? If successful in ending the war, a "Conference of Plenipotentiaries of the Five Great Powers" would gather in Washington to negotiate a settlement. "What would an eminent diplomatist from Vienna, or Berlin, or St. Petersburg, know of the Chicago platform or the Crittenden compromise?" Boundaries? Partition of the western territories? The status of slavery in the South and in the territories? Navigation of the Mississippi River?

"These and other thorny questions would have to be settled by a Conference of five foreigners, acting under the daily fire of the American press."[36]

Following the settlement would come the spoils. A collection of five powers might raise the military and moral effectiveness of the intervention, but it would also increase the likelihood of disagreements afterward. Such a "well-intentioned intervention might end in inflaming and perpetuating the discord." A five-power mediation was "an imposing force," but it was "a dangerous body to set in motion." In all the bickering over compensation, "England might stand alone."[37]

Lewis had presented a timeless argument against intervention. One nation's involvement in another nation's affairs assured problems that could lead to war. That Americans had gone to war with each other testified to the irreconcilable differences they had grappled with for decades. What compromise could there be between Union preservation and Confederate independence? Recognizing the South as a nation *before* it had achieved independence, Lewis warned, would ally the crown with a people in rebellion against their duly authorized government. The interventionist powers had no viable peace terms to offer, and premature recognition guaranteed war with the United States. Let the American war itself decide the verdict. England must remain neutral.[38]

After a day of discussing the issues raised in Lewis's memorandum, the cabinet overwhelmingly voted down Napoleon's peace plan in favor of a more cautious approach to American affairs that nonetheless left open the possibility of intervention. Palmerston expressed no opposition to the decision.[39]

Shortly afterward, the Russian government publicly turned down Napoleon's proposal.[40]

THE LINCOLN ADMINISTRATION was not privy to these discussions in London and appeared to be in desperate straits by the end of 1862. The Union Army's disaster at Fredericksburg; the ongoing cabinet crisis in which dissidents sought to remove Seward; the continuing struggle over intervention— "If there is a worse place than Hell," the president moaned, "I am in it."[41]

But his problems worsened: Almost in tandem with this critical moment, France emerged as a direct challenge to the United States . . . and to the Confederacy. Like the British, the French had converted to the belief that Lincoln's pronouncement on slavery had resolved that great issue by putting it on the road to extinction; but unlike the British, who recoiled from any involvement with slave-owning peoples, Napoleon decided this was the time to recognize the Confederacy as a pivotal step in fulfilling his imperialist goals: Lincoln's proclamation had quieted the antislavery groups in France who had rigidly opposed any action encouraging to the Confederacy.

According to Sainlaude, the French emperor's primary interest in the Civil War was to reduce U.S. power, but this was only one part of his vast range of imperialist objectives outside Europe that included Africa, the Middle East, and the Far East. Senegal in Africa, the construction of the Suez Canal in Egypt, his intervention in Syria, his initial forays into Cochin-china and Cambodia—all were integral to establishing France as the chief player in the Americas, Europe, and worldwide.

The crown jewel of Napoleon's Grand Design for the Americas was Mexico. The U.S. victory over Mexico in the 1840s had proved especially troublesome because of the vast territories in the southwest secured by the United States in the peace treaty. No longer was Mexico a barrier against American expansion into the rest of the continent as well as into Latin America. Furthermore, the civil war that erupted in Mexico in the late 1850s had resulted in a republican victory by 1861. His plan would right this wrong.

The Civil War was crucial to Napoleon's Grand Design and to his global objectives. He intended to place Maximilian on the Mexican throne, extend recognition to the Confederacy, and construct a four-party North American balance of power modeled after the German confederation: the North, the South, the West, and Mexico, each with equal power. To establish a Pacific-to-Atlantic commercial connection, he wanted a canal cut through Central America that would link the two oceans and make France dominant in the new Asian and South American fields of imperial expansion. Mexico's commitment to the Catholic Church would allow him to develop a closeness with Catholics in that country (and in Italy as well) and thereby help him institute his policies throughout the hemisphere (and in Europe). Napoleon's new Confederate ally would distract the Lincoln administration during the war and provide a buffer between the United States and Mexico. The new Mexican regime would attract investors as it underwent an industrial and agricultural transformation financially underwritten by the silver mines of northern Mexico and worked by its people along with American and European immigrants. The plan would thus dissolve much of the 1861 United States, allowing a French-controlled Mexico to shape the postwar American West by incorporating Texas and the former colony of Louisiana into a new empire that stretched from the Gulf of Mexico to Lower California.[42]

The central purpose of Napoleon III's Grand Design was to undermine the power of the United States and in its wake build a second and much larger French empire in the Americas that would have a global military and economic impact. For that reason, he sought a return to the halcyon days of his uncle, Napoleon I, who had briefly owned the vast lands west of the Mississippi River known as the Louisiana Territory but sold them to the United States in 1803 to finance a resumption of his war with England. Napoleon III wanted this area back and more. His consular officials in both Texas and Virginia had already unsettled the Richmond government in the fall of 1862 by their almost identically worded inquiries about the wisdom of the Confederacy's keeping Texas. His interest in Louisiana would soon raise more concerns among Confederate leaders who, as Kelly shows in his essay, had only temporarily set aside their own expansionist aims—one of which was northern Mexico.[43]

Given Napoleon's grandiose dreams, it is certain that the "Louisiana" he envisioned was not the state admitted to the union in 1812 but the entire area encompassed in the Louisiana Purchase of 1803, which in passing to the United States more than doubled its size. The door appeared open for this argument. After the negotiations in Paris, the U.S. representatives, Robert Livingston and future president James Monroe, asked the French foreign minister, Charles Talleyrand, what the boundaries were. "I can give you no direction," he cagily replied. "You have made a noble bargain for yourselves, and I suppose you will make the most of it."[44]

Napoleon III took advantage of these ambiguities over Louisiana to plan a much larger French empire than his uncle could ever have imagined: a southern border that incorporated all of Texas by following the Rio Grande from the Gulf of Mexico and then running west to the Pacific; an eastern border that began at the Mississippi River emptying into the Gulf of Mexico (or perhaps including West Florida) and moved north to its headwaters— also making a northern border vague, because no one had pinpointed the location of the headwaters of the Mississippi River; and a western border that was equally uncertain—somewhere in the mountains. Napoleon III's new Mexican ally would facilitate the expansion of the French empire into *all* the Americas and, as Jay Sexton shows, achieve a prime objective—the upper hand in the European balance of power.[45]

This was the Confederacy's friend in Europe. While the French emperor maintained a veneer of politeness in dealing with the Richmond government, he privately intended to bottle up the Confederacy and reduce its size. He never *demanded* either Louisiana or Texas—apparently thinking the Confederacy would give them up in appreciation for his help in winning its independence.[46]

The Lincoln administration could not have been aware of the magnitude of Napoleon's aims, but fortunately for the United States—and the entire American republic—General William T. Sherman's "March to the Sea" drove home the reality of imminent Confederate defeat and convinced the emperor to give up his imperial dream in the Western Hemisphere. Shortly after Lee's surrender at Appomattox in April 1865, General Ulysses S. Grant spoke for a nation when exclaiming to his aide, "Now for Mexico!" In January of the following year, Napoleon decided to withdraw his troops from Mexico and began the process in November. He had abandoned his Grand Design when realizing that to hold onto it meant war with the United States.[47]

In one final misguided decision, Maximilian chose to remain on the throne even while his own imperial hopes collapsed. His major support came to an end in February 1867 when the final contingent of French troops left Mexico. About four months later, President Benito Juárez's victorious republican troops captured Maximilian in Querétero and, after a court-martial, found him guilty of what Pani termed "usurpation" and "filibustering," sentenced him to death by firing squad in June.[48]

Perception had proved stronger than truth in this instance, for it now is clear that Napoleon's objectives were unrealistic and posed no real threat to the United States or anyone else deemed important to his Grand Design. First and foremost, he lacked widespread support at home. Critics warned of a debilitating drain on the nation's resources at the same time it became entangled in expansionist problems almost certain to undermine its prestige. France already had nearly 150,000 troops spread out among Mexico, Rome, and Algeria, and it faced growing trouble over Prussian expansion in Europe. The Latin American states strongly opposed Napoleon's vision of a new empire in the Western Hemisphere in which they were to become pawns on his make-believe global chess board. Although a monarchy, Brazil did not support the French emperor's plan; nor did the republics of Argentina, Chile, and Peru.[49] And, as Kelly shows, the French diplomatic corps was correct in warning Napoleon that a postwar Confederacy had its own expansionist interests in Mexico and other parts of Latin America and would oppose his Grand Design.

Most telling, however, Napoleon's plan attracted little support in Mexico. The execution of Maximilian sent a stern message to the French that a post-Civil War Mexico would also have opposed the French presence, along with any other power threatening to expand in the hemisphere. According to the

French minister in Washington, Jules Berthemy, the execution was "first of all a defiance of Monarchical Europe from Republican America."[50]

IN LIGHT OF THIS intricate and complex story, it is necessary to modify the long-accepted claim that Lincoln had prevented British and French intervention by steering the war into an antislavery direction. Slavery was not the essential consideration for either country as so often depicted in accounts of this period. Instead, the battle of Antietam had combined with the Emancipation Proclamation to temporarily *heighten* the danger of foreign intervention by both England and France, the first because of the growing horrors of the war and its destructive impact on commerce, and the second because Napoleon felt free to pursue his imperial dream.

Not until a month after Lincoln had announced the Emancipation Proclamation did both nations realize that his action would help the United States win the war and abolish slavery. But unlike the British, who celebrated its death as a potential achievement of the war, Napoleon saw the opportunity to recognize the Confederacy without fear of a popular backlash at home over slavery. Lewis's realpolitik had altered Palmerston's thinking about intervention, while public opinion strongly favored the Emancipation Proclamation and made it politically impossible for the ministry to do anything detrimental to the Union. The British decision against intervention came from the same sense of self-interest that propelled the French. War with the Union would endanger both the British and French empires, making the threat of war with the United States the key to understanding why London and Paris decided against intervention.[51]

The impact of the Civil War was not confined to North America; its implications affected spectator nations worldwide and became an important part of international history. At the center of the conflict in America, of course, was North against South or Union against Confederacy, but it was also a Southern rebellion against the continued growth of a strong central government in Washington that exemplified the concerns of many peoples watching these events from afar. To those on the outside, the Confederacy had launched a revolution that could provide a model for their own aspirations. How does a struggling people place limits on a government's sovereignty and thereby protect self-determination and the rights of states and individuals? Can there be a balance between the two great protagonists of positive law and property rights on the one side and natural law and natural rights on the other? The American Civil War lay at the epicenter of a timeless and heavily entangled global battle between liberty and authority.[52]

Suggested Readings

Blackett, Richard J. M. *Divided Hearts: Britain and the American Civil War*. Baton Rouge: Louisiana State University Press, 2001.

Case, Lynn M. and Warren F. Spencer. *The United States and France: Civil War Diplomacy*. Philadelphia: University of Pennsylvania Press, 1970.

Crook, David P. *The North, the South, and the Powers, 1861–1865*. New York: Wiley, 1974.

Ferris, Norman B. *Desperate Diplomacy: William H. Seward's Foreign Policy, 1861*. Knoxville: University of Tennessee Press, 1976.

———. *The Trent Affair: A Diplomatic Crisis*. Knoxville: University of Tennessee Press, 1977.

Hanna, Alfred J. and Kathryn A. Hanna. *Napoleon III and Mexico: American Triumph over Monarchy*. Chapel Hill: University of North Carolina Press, 1971.

Jenkins, Brian. *Britain and the War for the Union*, 2 vols. Montreal: McGill-Queen's University Press, 1974, 1980.

Jones, Howard. *Abraham Lincoln and a New Birth of Freedom: The Union and Slavery in the Diplomacy of the Civil War*. Lincoln: University of Nebraska Press, 1999.

———. *Blue and Gray Diplomacy: A History of Union and Confederate Foreign Relations*. Chapel Hill: University of North Carolina Press, 2010.

———. *Union in Peril: The Crisis over British Intervention in the Civil War*. Chapel Hill: University of North Carolina Press, 1992.

Merli, Frank J. *The Alabama, British Neutrality, and the American Civil War*. Edited by David M. Fahey. Bloomington: Indiana University Press, 2004.

———. *Great Britain and the Confederate Navy, 1861–1865*. Bloomington: Indiana University Press, 1970, 2004.

Owsley, Frank L. *King Cotton Diplomacy: Foreign Relations of the Confederate States of America*. Revised by Harriet C. Owsley. Chicago: University of Chicago Press, 1959. Reprint, Tuscaloosa: University of Alabama Press, 2009.

Saul, Norman E. *Distant Friends: The United States and Russia, 1763–1867*. Lawrence: University Press of Kansas, 1991.

Sexton, Jay. *Debtor Diplomacy: Finance and American Foreign Relations in the Civil War Era, 1837–1873*. Oxford, UK: Clarendon Press, 2005.

Warren, Gordon H. *Fountain of Discontent: The Trent Affair and Freedom of the Seas*. Boston: Northeastern University Press, 1981.

Notes

1. Confederate leaders, according to Davis' wife, thought recognition "an assured fact." Varina H. Davis, *Jefferson Davis: A Memoir by His Wife*, 2 vols. (New York: Belford Company, 1890), 2:165. For Seward's earlier warnings to England, see Seward to Adams, April 10, 27, May 21, 1861, U.S. Department of State, *Papers Relating to Foreign*

Affairs, Accompanying the Annual Message of the President to the Second Session of the Thirty-Seventh Congress, 1861 (Washington, DC: Government Printing Office, 1861), 1:71–80, 82–83, 87–90 (hereafter *FRUS*). Seward quote in William H. Russell (*Times* of London news correspondent in United States), *My Diary North and South*, ed. Eugene H. Berwanger (Philadelphia: Temple University Press, 1988), entry for July 4, 1861, 227–28. For an excellent study of Seward's aggressive actions, see Norman B. Ferris, *Desperate Diplomacy: William H. Seward's Foreign Policy, 1861* (Knoxville: University of Tennessee Press, 1976).

2. France declared neutrality on June 10, 1861, and by August so did the Netherlands, Spain, Belgium, Portugal, Brazil, and Hawaii. I thank Don Doyle for this information.

3. Palmerston to Queen Victoria, January 1, 1861, in Jasper Ridley, *Lord Palmerston* (New York: E. P. Dutton, 1971), 548; Russell to Richard B. Lyons, British minister to United States, January 10, November 2, 1861, Russell Papers, Public Record Office 30/22/96 (Kew, England); Howard Jones, *Union in Peril: The Crisis over British Intervention in the Civil War* (Chapel Hill: University of North Carolina Press, 1992), 22–24.

4. Howard Jones, *Blue and Gray Diplomacy: A History of Union and Confederate Foreign Relations* (Chapel Hill: University of North Carolina Press, 2010), 71–72.

5. For Vattel, see Charles G. Fenwick, translator, *Le droit des gens, Translation of the edition of 1758* [Emmerich de Vattel, *The Law of Nations or the Principles of Natural Law*] (Washington, DC: Carnegie Institution of Washington, 1916), book 2, ch. 1, sec. 4, 114–15. See also Emmerich de Vattel, *The Law of Nations; or, Principles of the Law of Nature Applied to the Conduct and Affairs of Nations and Sovereigns* (Philadelphia: Abraham Small, 1817. Originally published in 1758), book 2, ch. 1, sec. 4, 135–36. For this theme of collateral damage, see Jones, *Blue and Gray Diplomacy*, 71–72, 218–19.

6. Jones, *Blue and Gray Diplomacy*, 72.

7. Ibid.

8. Alfred J. Hanna and Kathryn A. Hanna, *Napoleon III and Mexico: American Triumph over Monarchy* (Chapel Hill: University of North Carolina Press, 1971), xiii–xiv, 4, 19, 78, 79, 199, 303; Nancy N. Barker, "Monarchy in Mexico: Harebrained Scheme or Well-considered Prospect?" *Journal of Modern History* 48 (March 1976): 59, 63, and "The French Legation in Mexico: Nexus of Interventionists," *French Historical Studies* 8 (Spring 1974): 411, 423.

9. Jones, *Blue and Gray Diplomacy*, 88.

10. Ibid., 107–9; Adams to Richard Henry Dana (friend), Feb. 6, 1862, CFA Letterbook, Adams Family Papers, Massachusetts Historical Society (Boston).

11. Palmerston to Russell, September 14, 1862, Russell Papers, PRO 30/22/14D; Russell to Palmerston, September 17, 1862, General Correspondence/Russell/728, Palmerston Papers (University of Southampton, England).

12. *Times* of London, September 16, 1862, 6; *London Morning Post* and *Morning Herald*, both September 16, 1862, the first paper cited in and the second paper quoted in Brian Jenkins, *Britain and the War for the Union* (Montreal: McGill-Queen's University Press, 1974–1980), 2:151; ibid., 167; Jones, *Blue and Gray Diplomacy*, 215.

13. Palmerston to Russell, Sept. 22, 23, 1862, Russell Papers, PRO 30/22/14D; Russell to Palmerston, September 22, 1862, GC/Russell/729, Palmerston Papers (U. of Southampton).

14. James M. McPherson, *Battle Cry of Freedom: The Civil War Era* (New York: Oxford University Press, 1988), 500, and *Tried by War: Abraham Lincoln as Commander in Chief* (New York: Penguin Press, 2008), 4–5, 269. For a public expression of Lincoln's thinking on slavery already under way for months, see his "Reply to Emancipation Memorial Presented by Chicago Christians of All Denominations," September 13, 1862, in *The Collected Works of Abraham Lincoln*, ed. Roy P. Basler (New Brunswick, NJ: Rutgers University Press, 1953–55), 5:419–25 (hereafter *CWL*).

15. Lincoln quoted in Howard K. Beale, ed., *Diary of Gideon Welles: Secretary of the Navy under Lincoln and Johnson* (New York: W. W. Norton and Co., 1960), 1:70–71 (July 13, 1862); last quote from the Preamble to the U.S. Constitution. See also Eric Foner, *The Fiery Trial: Abraham Lincoln and American Slavery* (New York: W. W. Norton, 2010), 217–20.

16. Gary W. Gallagher, "A Civil War Watershed: The Richmond Campaign in Perspective," in *The Richmond Campaign of 1862: The Peninsula and the Seven Days*, ed. Gary W. Gallagher (Chapel Hill: University of North Carolina Press, 2000), 3–27; Beale, ed., *Diary of Gideon Welles*, 1:70–71; Lincoln, "Emancipation Proclamation—First Draft," July 22, 1862, in *CWL*, 5:226–37; Benjamin P. Thomas and Harold M. Hyman, *Stanton: The Life and Times of Lincoln's Secretary of War* (New York: Alfred A. Knopf, 1962), 238–40; Howard Jones, *Abraham Lincoln and a New Birth of Freedom: The Union and Slavery in the Diplomacy of the Civil War* (Lincoln: University of Nebraska Press, 1999), 86–87; William H. Seward, *Autobiography of William H. Seward from 1801–1834: With a Memoir of His Life, and Selections from His Letters from 1881 to 1846*, ed. Frederick W. Seward (New York: D. Appleton, 1877), 3:74 (first Seward quote); McPherson, *Battle Cry of Freedom*, 505 (second Seward quote); Glyndon G. Van Deusen, *William Henry Seward* (New York: Oxford University Press, 1967), 328–29.

17. McPherson, *Battle Cry of Freedom*, 545, 569. For the most balanced account of this battle, see James M. McPherson, *Crossroads of Freedom: Antietam* (New York: Oxford University Press, 2002).

18. Seward to Adams, September 8, 1862, *FRUS, December 1, 1862* (Washington, DC: Government Printing Office, 1863), 188; Seward to Adams, circular, September 22, 1862, ibid., 195; David Donald, ed., *Inside Lincoln's Cabinet: The Civil War Diaries of Salmon P. Chase* (New York: Longmans, Green, 1954), 149–51 (September 22, 1862); Lincoln, "Preliminary Emancipation Proclamation," September 22, 1862, in *CWL*, 5:434; Jones, *Blue and Gray Diplomacy*, 229–30.

19. Stuart to Lyons, September 23, 1862, Russell Papers, PRO 30/22/36; Stuart to Russell, September 23, 26, October 7, 10, 1862, ibid.

20. Richard A. Heckman, "British Press Reaction to the Emancipation Proclamation," *Lincoln Herald* 71 (Winter 1969): 150–53; *Times* of London, October 7, 1862, 8, October 21, 1862, 9; *Spectator* (London), n.d., quoted in Arnold Whitridge, "British

Liberals and the American Civil War," *History Today* 12 (October 1962): 694; "The Crisis of the American War," *Blackwood's Edinburgh Magazine* 92 (November 1862): 636; London *Punch*, October 18, 1862, 43:161.

21. For French views, see George M. Blackburn, *French Newspaper Opinion on the American Civil War* (Westport, CT: Greenwood Press, 1997), 65–66, 95. Conservative papers cited included the *Pays*; among the liberal papers was the *Temps*. For a breakdown of the French newspapers by political affiliation, see ibid., 9.

22. Jones, *Blue and Gray Diplomacy*, 278–79; Henry Adams quoted in John Hope Franklin, *The Emancipation Proclamation* (Garden City, NY: Doubleday and Co., 1963), 125. For British worker sentiments, see Richard J. M. Blackett, *Divided Hearts: Britain and the American Civil War* (Baton Rouge: Louisiana State University Press, 2001). See also *London Morning Star*, October 6, 1862, quoted in Allan Nevins, *War Becomes Revolution* (New York: Charles Scribner's Sons, 1960), 270.

23. H. C. G. Matthew, ed., *The Gladstone Diaries* (Oxford, UK: Clarendon Press, 1978), 6:152 n. 6; *Times* of London, October 8, 1862, 7, October 9, 1862, 7–8; Ridley, *Palmerston*, 558.

24. Jones, *Blue and Gray Diplomacy*, 236–40.

25. Gilbert F. Lewis, ed., *The Letters of the Right Hon. Sir George Cornewall Lewis* (London: Longmans Green, 1870), vi, viii–ix, xi; Lewis to W. Twistleton (a friend), January 21, 1861, ibid., 391–92; Lewis to Sir Edmund Head (governor of Canada), March 10, 1861, ibid., 393; Lewis to Head, May 13, September 8, 1861, ibid., 395, 402; Charles F. Adams, Jr., "The Crisis of Foreign Intervention in the War of Secession," in *Massachusetts Historical Society Proceedings* (Boston: MHS, 1914), 2–54; Jones, *Blue and Gray Diplomacy*, 243.

26. George Cornewall Lewis, "Memorandum on the American Question," October 17, 1862, Gladstone Papers, Additional Mss. 44, 595, DX (British Library, London, England). Lewis's quote was a loose rendition of Hamlet's words in William Shakespeare's play, *The Tragedy of Hamlet, Prince of Denmark*, act 3, scene 1.

27. Russell memo for Foreign Office, October 23, 1862, Gladstone Papers (Brit. Lib.).

28. Palmerston to Russell, October 23, 24, 1862, Russell Papers, PRO 30/22/14 D.

29. Russell to Sir George Grey (Home Office), October 28, 1862, in G. P. Gooch, ed., *The Later Correspondence of Lord John Russell, 1840–1878* (London: Longmans, Green, 1925), 2:332.

30. Slidell to Judah P. Benjamin, October 28, 1862, U.S. Department of the Navy, *Official Records of the Union and Confederate Navies in the War of the Rebellion* (Washington, DC: Government Printing Office, 1894–1927), ser. 2, vol. 3, 575–76; Lynn M. Case and Warren F. Spencer, *The United States and France: Civil War Diplomacy* (Philadelphia: University of Pennsylvania Press, 1970), 356–57, and Frank L. Owsley, *King Cotton Diplomacy: Foreign Relations of the Confederate States of America*. Revised by Harriet C. Owsley. (Chicago: University of Chicago Press, 1959. Reprint with new introduction by Howard Jones. Tuscaloosa: University of Alabama Press, 2009), 333–36.

31. Russell to Grey, October 28, 1862, in Gooch, ed., *Later Correspondence of Lord John Russell*, 2:332.

32. David P. Crook, *The North, the South, and the Powers, 1861–1865* (New York: Wiley, 1974), 226–27; Frank A. Golder, "The American Civil War through the Eyes of a Russian Diplomat," *American Historical Review* 26 (April 1921): 454, 456–57; E. A. Adamov, "Russia and the United States at the Time of the Civil War," *Journal of Modern History* 2 (December 1930): 596–97; Norman E. Saul, *Distant Friends: The United States and Russia, 1763–1867* (Lawrence: University Press of Kansas, 1991), 321–23, 331; Albert A. Woldman, *Lincoln and the Russians* (Cleveland, OH: World, 1952), viii, 40, 125, 127–30; Stoeckl to Gorchakov, September 25, 1862, in Kinley J. Brauer, "The Slavery Problem in the Diplomacy of the American Civil War," *Pacific Historical Review* 46 (August 1977): 463; Gorchakov cited in Ephraim D. Adams, *Great Britain and the American Civil War* (New York: Longmans, Green, 1925), 2:45 n. 2.

33. Jones, *Blue and Gray Diplomacy*, 238–43, 268–70; George Cornewall Lewis, "Recognition of the Independence of the Southern States of the North American Union," Nov. 7, 1862, Gladstone Papers, Add. Mss., 44, 595, DX (British Library, London, England). The original draft (though incomplete) is in the archives of the National Library of Wales in Aberystwyth. See Lewis Papers, War Office and India, 3509, 3510, and 3514. On Historicus, see A. G. Gardiner, *The Life of Sir William Harcourt* (New York: George H. Doran, 1923), 1:125, 127, 132–37; letter dated Nov. 4, 1862, *Times* of London, Nov. 7, 1862, pp. 6–7; letter reprinted in William V. Harcourt, *Letters by Historicus on Some Questions of International Law* (London: Macmillan, 1863), 3–15; Historicus, "Neutrality or Intervention," ibid., 41–51.

34. G. C. Lewis, "Recognition of Independence."

35. Ibid.

36. Ibid.

37. Ibid.

38. Ibid.

39. Lewis to Clarendon, Nov. 11, 1862, Clarendon, Fourth Earl of (George William Frederick Villiers), Papers (Bodleian Library, Oxford University, Oxford, England); Jones, *Blue and Gray Diplomacy*, 270–72.

40. Russian letter in *Journal of St. Petersburg*, Nov. 15, 1862, published in *Times* of London, Nov. 17, 1862, 12, and encl. in CFA to Seward, Nov. 15, 1862, *FRUS 1863*, 3. See also Saul, *Distant Friends*, 334–35, and Woldman, *Lincoln and the Russians*, 133–35.

41. Lincoln quoted in McPherson, *Battle Cry of Freedom*, 574.

42. Case and Spencer, *U.S. and France*, 399–401; Owsley, *King Cotton Diplomacy*, 441, 513–14; Crook, *The North, the South*, 264–65, 335–36; Jones, *Blue and Gray Diplomacy*, 294; Kathryn A. Hanna, "The Roles of the South in the French Intervention in Mexico," *Journal of Southern History* 20 (February 1954): 9–10; Hanna and Hanna, *Napoleon III and Mexico*, 60–64, 80–81, 90, 117–18, 118 n. 8; Thomas Schoonover, "Napoleon Is Coming! Maximilian Is Coming? The International History of the Civil War in the Caribbean Basin," in *The Union, the Confederacy, and the Atlantic Rim*, ed. Robert E. May (Gainesville: University Press of Florida, 2013. Revised Introduction.

Original publication, West Lafayette, IN: Purdue University Press, 1995), 115–44; Adam Arenson and Andrew R. Graybill, eds., *Civil War Wests: Testing the Limits of the United States* (Oakland: University of California Press, 2015), introduction.

43. Hanna and Hanna, *Napoleon III and Mexico*, 118.

44. Ibid., xv–xvi, 4; Dexter Perkins, *A History of the Monroe Doctrine* (Boston: Little Brown, and Co., 1940, 1955), 117–18; Talleyrand quoted in Alexander DeConde, *This Affair of Louisiana* (New York: Charles Scribner's Sons, 1976), 174.

45. See Jay Sexton, *The Monroe Doctrine: Empire and Nation in Nineteenth-Century America* (New York: Hill and Wang, 2011), 140.

46. Jones, *Blue and Gray Diplomacy*, 315–16, 369–70; Hanna and Hanna, *Napoleon III and Mexico*, 118.

47. Hanna and Hanna, *Napoleon III and Mexico*, 270–72, 277–78, 296; Jones, *Blue and Gray Diplomacy*, 319–20. For Grant's remark, see essay by the acting adjutant on Grant's staff, Corporal M. Harrison Strong of the 72nd Illinois Regiment, in Hamlin Garland Papers, Doheny Library, University of Southern California. For Strong's quote, see the Ulysses S. Grant Homepage at www.granthomepage.com/instrong.htm. See also William B. Hesseltine, *Ulysses S. Grant: Politician* (New York: Dodd, Mead, 1935), 53, and William E. Hardy, "South of the Border: Ulysses S. Grant and the French Intervention," *Civil War History* 54 (March 2008): 63–86.

48. Jones, *Blue and Gray Diplomacy*, 320; Hanna and Hanna, *Napoleon III and Mexico*, 296, 299–300. I thank Erika Pani for explaining the charges against Maximilian that led to his execution.

49. Hanna and Hanna, *Napoleon III and Mexico*, 144–45, 303.

50. Ibid., 303.

51. Jones, *Blue and Gray Diplomacy*, 228, 235. For the traditional argument about Antietam, see McPherson, *Battle Cry of Freedom*, 545, 556–57; Stephen W. Sears, *Landscape Turned Red: The Battle of Antietam* (New York: Ticknor and Fields, 1983), 334; Owsley, *King Cotton Diplomacy*, 347.

52. On many of these issues, see Adam Arenson's introductory essay in Arenson and Graybill, eds., *Civil War Wests: Testing the Limits of the United States*, 1–14, and Stephen Sawyer, "Emancipation and the Creation of Modern Liberal States in America and France," *Journal of the Civil War Era* 3 (December 2013): 457–500. In this volume, Matt D. Childs, Rafael Marquese, and Christopher Schmidt-Nowara show that the collapse of slavery in the United States ignited national debates in both Brazil and Cuba over whether to legislate an end to the institution in their own countries before they faced similar violence. On the Civil War as a global event, see the pathbreaking study by Don H. Doyle, *The Cause of All Nations: An International History of the American Civil War* (New York: Basic Books, 2015). See also Thomas Bender, *A Nation Among Nations: America's Place in World History* (New York: Hill and Wang, 2006), 175; C. A. Bayly, *The Birth of the Modern World, 1780–1914: Global Connections and Comparisons* (Malden, MA: Blackwell Publishing, 2004), 161–62; and Douglas A. Egerton, "Rethinking Atlantic Historiography in a Postcolonial Era: The Civil War in a Global Perspective," *Journal of the Civil War Era* 1 (March 2011): 79–95.

CHAPTER THREE

The Cat's-Paw

Confederate Ambitions in Latin America

Patrick J. Kelly

In the decade before the U.S. Civil War, slaveholders in the American South dreamed of creating a vast slave-based empire that would encompass Spanish Cuba, portions of northern Mexico, and Central America.[1] They also envisioned an alliance with the Empire of Brazil to create what Richard K. Meade, a Southern nationalist acting as U.S. minister to Brazil, called "a grand Pro-Slavery alliance."[2] As they considered secession, Southern slaveholders believed that the creation of a tropical empire for slavery in the Americas was inevitable once their region separated from the antislavery forces of the U.S. North. "As Americans in the 1850s," one historian concludes, "and as Confederates in the 1860s, the masters of the slave South aimed not to escape the modern world, but to command it."[3] Despite this prewar optimism, however, the South's plans to expand its territorial space into the tropics, an issue that until the eve of the Civil War seemed a matter of existential importance in guaranteeing the future power and prosperity of this region, came to an abrupt halt following secession.

After hostilities broke out between the North and South, the anticipated alliance between the Confederate nation and slaveholding Brazil never materialized. Under the cautious leadership of Emperor Pedro II, Brazil recognized the Confederacy as a belligerent power but maintained its neutrality during the Civil War. Through its control of Cuba, Spain was one of the last major slave powers in the Americas. Optimistic about its ability to create a proslavery alliance with Spain—a collaboration that Southern officials hoped would begin with Madrid's diplomatic recognition of their insurgency as an independent nation—the Confederate government renounced the antebellum South's desire to annex Cuba. In July 1861, the Confederate Secretary of State, Robert A. Toombs, instructed Charles J. Helm, the Confederacy's commissioner to Havana, to inform Spanish authorities that the Confederacy favored Spain's continued control of Cuba.[4] Despite this assurance, General Francisco Serrano, Spain's captain-general in Havana, disappointed Confederate president Jefferson Davis by declaring the Spanish government's policy of "strict and severe" neutrality in the war between the Union and Confederacy.[5]

In an attempt to establish favorable relations with the government of neighboring Mexico, during the first months of the Civil War the South also renounced the desire of antebellum slaveholders to incorporate the Mexican north into the Confederacy. The following year, soon after Napoleon III deployed the French army to Mexico as part of his scheme to establish a European monarch in Mexico City, Richmond went to great lengths to assure French officials that Southern slaveholders had abandoned any plans to annex portions of Mexican territory.

The antebellum South's expansionist dreams are familiar to all. Yet historians have neglected to explain fully this region's repudiation of territorial growth in the Americas after breaking from the Union. Was Richmond's promise to foreign governments that it had abandoned its prewar expansionism a tactical move designed to buy time until the Union Army could be defeated and Southern independence assured? Or, flying as it did in the face of the antebellum South's expansionist ambitions, did Confederate officials develop a new geopolitical strategy that would seek alliances rather than conquest in order to secure the future of slavery in the Americas?

In the months after secession, the Confederate government insisted on the latter explanation. Its envoys in Madrid, London, and Mexico City were instructed to deliver the same message concerning territorial expansion as the one offered to French officials by John Slidell, the Confederacy's minister in Paris. "Heretofore," Slidell's instructions stated, "the South has desired the annexation of territory suitable to the growth of her domestic institutions in order to establish a balance of power within the Government that they might protect their interests and internal peace through its agency." After secession, Slidell continued, "this reason no longer exists, as the Confederate States have sought that protection by a separation from the union in which their rights were endangered."[6] James Mason, the South's envoy to Great Britain, informed London that as a "new member of the family of nations" the "Southern Confederacy would have every reason to preserve peace both at home and abroad, and would be prevented both by its principles and interests from the intervention in the domestic affairs and governments of other nations."[7] In September 1861 John T. Pickett, Richmond's envoy to Mexico City, declared to the government of Benito Juárez that as the "Confederate States have now more territory than they can cultivate and people for a century to come," the South no longer coveted any portion of the Mexican republic.[8] It remains unclear if the Confederacy's official renunciation of hemispheric expansion was only a cynical ploy, or if it indicated a genuine belief that, once separated from the United States, the South had no need for further territorial acquisitions to maintain the necessary balance of political power between the slaveholding and free soil regions of North America.

In attempting to explain the curious disavowal of Southern expansion in the New World during the Civil War scholars often focus their attention on the diplomatic correspondence of Confederate authorities, or by attempting to gauge the thinking of Richmond's political class. By looking at the South from the inside out, it is plausible to conclude that immediately after secession Richmond decided that expansion in the tropics, at least in the short run, was unnecessary and perhaps even counterproductive. Southerners might well have believed that the best way to secure the immediate future of slavery was not through outward expansion, sure to anger potential European allies such as Spain and France, but through the increased exploitation of land they already controlled, or the capture of territory from the United States.

Privileging the historical record left by Confederate diplomats and political figures, however, ignores the South's fundamental weakness in the Americas. Confident of their ability to command events in the hemisphere, Confederate officials never comprehended that the South's break from the Union resulted in the creation of a regional rebellion that, despite its military successes against the Union Army, possessed strikingly little ability to deploy its power beyond its southern borders into Latin America and the Caribbean. Richmond may have believed it was seizing control of its own destiny when it renounced the antebellum desire of slaveholders to expand into the tropics. In reality, however, during its short life the Confederate nation lacked the military capacity to expand territorially in the New World and, in addition, could ill afford to arouse the hostility from Old World powers that was sure to result from any land grabs in Mexico, Cuba or any other territory in the Caribbean and Latin America.

The limits of Confederate power in the Americas become especially apparent when we shift our view from Richmond and examine the wartime South by looking northward from Havana and Mexico City. Spanish colonial officials believed that the South was far weaker outside of the Union than as a politically powerful region within the United States, and thus the Confederacy did not pose a threat to Spain's control of Cuba. The relationship between the Confederacy and Mexico City suggests that the government of President Benito Juárez also calculated that the slaveholding region that had broken from the United States lacked the capacity to expand south of the Rio Grande, even if expansion remained the long-term and secret goal of Confederate officials.

The South's wartime relationship with the government of Mexico is especially revealing. Mexico and the Confederacy shared a contact zone along the Rio Grande. Before the war, Southerners made no secret of their desire to annex northern Mexico. In 1858 Mississippi Senator Albert Gallatin Brown declared, "I want Tamaulipas, Potosi, and one or two other Mexican states; and I want them all for the same reason—for the planting and spreading of slavery."[9] The sudden emergence of the Confederate nation as its northern neighbor seemingly posed an imminent threat to the territorial integrity of the Mexican nation, but the Juárez administration showed little concern about post-secession Southern expansionism. Instead of placating the rapidly coalescing Confederate government, Juárez dispatched his envoy to the United States, Matías Romero, to Springfield, Illinois, to meet with the U.S. president-elect Abraham Lincoln with the goal of establishing an alliance between Mexico and the United States. In his meeting with Lincoln, held on January 19, 1861, Romero stressed the common republican principles shared by the constitutionally elected governments of Mexico and the United States, and stressed the desire of Mexican Liberals to "maintain the most intimate and friendly relations with the United States."[10] Ideologically in tune with the liberal nationalism of Abraham Lincoln and regarding the Union, not the Confederacy, as a hemispheric "sister republic," Juárez refused to recognize the Confederacy or even accord it the status as a belligerent power.[11] Adding insult to injury, in the fall of 1861 Juárez expelled the South's minister to Mexico City, John T. Pickett, from his country.

Relations between the Confederacy and the republican government of its southern neighbor were further poisoned by Napoleon III's decision to deploy the French army into Mexico in early 1862. The Confederacy refused to denounce the French emperor's planned overthrow of the Juárez government and his forced imposition of Archduke Maximilian of Austria on the Cactus Throne in Mexico City. Anticipating that Napoleon III's "Grand Scheme" would force Paris to recognize the Confederacy, Confederate diplomats instead offered private words of encouragement for the French intervention to top government officials in Paris and to the emperor himself. Much to the surprise, anger and frustration of Southerners, however, Richmond's support of Napoleon III's Mexican adventure failed to result in the French recognition of the Confederate nation.[12] By aligning with an Old World monarchy against the democratically elected government of neighboring Mexico without gaining any sort of diplomatic or territorial reciprocity from Paris, the Confederacy exposed itself as a pawn in hemispheric affairs and, at the same time, revealed an antipathy toward democratic government in the New World that alienated the Southern rebellion from the Spanish-speaking republics in Latin America.

Viewing the Confederacy from the perspective of Mexico and Cuba reveals the stark geopolitical realities facing the post-secession South in the Americas. After separating from the United States the Southern rebellion proved too weak internationally to capture any new hemispheric territory or gain the foreign recognition it sought in order to operate as a sovereign state in the family of nations. As they left the Union, white Southerners were confident that their region would constitute a powerful nation-state destined to build a modern and prosperous slave empire dominated by the American South. Far from expanding into the Americas, however, these slaveholders found themselves playing the role of "servants rather than the masters of New World geopolitics."[13] In an ironic twist, secession marked the death knell of the slave South's dream of creating an empire for slavery in the Western Hemisphere.

DURING THE SECESSION WINTER of 1860–61, the South's ambitions to expand in the tropical Americas seemed to remain largely intact. The Crittenden Compromise, a last-ditch effort to head off the collapse of the Union, fell apart in January 1861. The failure of this proposal came in large part because Southerners demanded the legalization of slavery in any new territory "hereafter acquired" by the United States south of the old Missouri Compromise Line (reintroduced in this proposal and extended to California). Understanding that Senator Crittenden's plan opened the door to expansion of the United States into Mexico, Cuba, and elsewhere in Latin America, Lincoln ordered the compromise proposal killed by Congressional Republicans.[14] In March 1861, the Confederate Congress adopted a constitution that specifically stated that the new nation "may acquire new territory," and that slaveholders would enjoy the same legal rights to own slaves in newly incorporated land as currently existed in Southern states.[15] Even as post-secession Southerners continued to push publically for hemispheric expansion, however, Confederate diplomats were quietly sending a message to government officials in Cuba, Spain, and Mexico that explicitly disavowed the South's desire to seize territory in the Americas.

Southern slaveholders had long believed that their region and Spanish-controlled Cuba shared a commitment to plantation-style economies in which slaves produced valuable commodities such as cotton and sugar for world markets. Southerners optimistically believed that Spain was, as the *Richmond Examiner* argued, the Confederacy's "natural ally" due to a shared interest in protecting the future of slavery in the New World.[16] The Confederate Secretary of State, R. M. T. Hunter, predicted that Spain would "observe with pleasure the growth in power and influence of a State bound to them by this great common interest, and they would earnestly desire to see the nations thus bound together armed with the means to protect their common interest."[17] Hoping to gain an alliance with this Old World power, Southern diplomats in Havana and Madrid were instructed to signal to Spanish authorities that the Confederacy acknowledged Spain's sovereignty over Cuba. In February 1861 Hunter's predecessor, Robert A. Toombs, asked Martin Crawford, a member of the Confederate Peace Commission in Washington, to meet with the Spanish ambassador to the United States to assure him of "the sincere wish of this [Confederate] Government to cultivate close and friendly relations with Spain." Crawford was instructed to convey the message that Confederate officials "are fully sensible of the importance of a Great European Power possessing slave holding colonies in our Neighborhood."[18] Despite Crawford's efforts, in June 1861, following the example of Great Britain and France, Madrid recognized the Confederacy as a belligerent power but declared its neutrality in the U.S. Civil War.[19]

Spain refused to recognize the Confederacy for a number of reasons. Most importantly, Madrid did not dare recognize the South as a sovereign nation unless Great Britain and France, much stronger European powers, acted first. One other reason Spain kept its distance from the Confederacy, however, was the continued suspicion in Madrid that, despite its protestations to the contrary, the South had not abandoned its prewar goal of annexing Cuba. Spaniards had not forgotten that the antebellum Democratic Party, controlled by Southern slaveholding interests and their Northern allies, had pushed hard for the incorporation of Cuba into the United States, and that in the late 1850s important Confederate leaders such as President Jefferson Davis had loudly advocated the incorporation of Cuba into Southern territory. In a famous speech before the Mississippi Democratic State Convention in July 1859, Davis, then a U.S. senator, had demanded the "acquisition of Cuba, as advantageous to the Union as it is, and as especially necessary in the event of the formation of a Southern Confederacy."[20]

One result of the outspoken Southern expansionism of the 1850s was that government officials in Spain welcomed the election of the Republican Party candidate, Abraham Lincoln, to the presidency of the United States in 1860. William Preston, the U.S. envoy in Madrid, reported to his superiors in Washington that Spaniards believed that Lincoln's rise to the White House would halt the determined efforts of previous U.S. administrations, dominated by expansionist Democrats, to capture Cuba.[21] The secession of the South from the United States after Lincoln's election reinforced the belief among Spaniards that Cuba was safe from the expansionist aims of Southern slaveholders. Officials in Madrid believed that even if Richmond still quietly harbored plans to capture Cuba, the new Confederate nation was "weak and easier to stop than the previous giant had been."[22] By leaving the Union, for instance, Southerners forfeited the control of the U.S. Navy they had maintained since the 1840s, and they were forced to create a new maritime force largely from scratch.[23] The absence of a powerful Confederate navy patrolling international waters severely hampered Southern interests in Cuba and elsewhere in the hemisphere. The perception that the slaveholders had dramatically weakened their region on the hemispheric stage by breaking from the United States played a key role in shaping the diplomacy of Madrid toward the Confederate rebellion during the Civil War.

The belief among Spanish officials that Cuba had little to fear from Southern expansion allowed Madrid to toy with Confederate diplomats seeking diplomatic recognition after secession. Pierre Rost was the Confederacy's envoy to Spain. During Rost's only official meeting with Spanish officials in March 1862, Foreign Minister Calderón Collantes taunted Rost by repeating the statement by William Seward, the U.S. Secretary of State: "No private expeditions had ever sailed from [northern] ports for the invasion of Cuba, but invariably from those of the South; and that if the Confederate States become hereafter a strong government, their first attempt at conquest would be upon that island."[24] Madrid's goading about the Confederacy's continued desire for Cuba forced Richmond into the obsequious position of constantly reassuring Spanish authorities that the South had surrendered any plans to expand its territory in the Caribbean.

In August 1861 Confederate Secretary of State Hunter appointed Rost as the Confederacy's envoy to Spain and urged him to "proceed with all convenient speed to Madrid." Alone among the "great powers in Europe," Hunter wrote, "Spain . . . is interested through her colonies in the same social system which pervades the Confederate States." Hunter instructed Rost to negotiate with Spain for diplomatic recognition of the Confederacy. In seeking an alliance with Spanish officials, the Confederate Secretary of State felt compelled to reassure Madrid that the post-secession South no longer desired Cuba. Repeating what was quickly developing into Richmond's key talking point about expansion, Hunter asked Rost to inform the Spanish government: "If a party was found in these states during their connection with the former Union who desired the acquisition of Cuba, it was for the purpose of establishing something like a balance of power in a Government from whose dominate majority they feared oppression and injury."[25] Now that the South had separated from the Union, Hunter continued, Southern acquisition of Cuba was no longer necessary or even desirable. As late as May 1863, Judah Benjamin, then Confederate Secretary of State, instructed John Slidell, his envoy in Paris, to reassure the Spanish government through diplomatic channels that "The interests of the Confederate States . . . render it particularly desirable that the island [Cuba] should remain a colonial possession of Spain." "Desirous ourselves of no extension of our boundaries," Benjamin insisted, the wartime South sought "our safety and happiness solely in the peaceful development of our own ample resources."[26]

Richmond's repeated attempts to assuage Spanish concerns about Confederate expansion into Cuba revealed its weakness as a hemispheric power. Antebellum Southern slaveholders argued that their region's capture of Cuba was essential for the goal of creating a great slave empire in the Americas. Immediately after secession, however, Southern diplomats abandoned any talk about the seizure of Cuba in the hope that Madrid would recognize the Confederacy as an independent nation and enter into a formal slave-holding alliance with their rebellion against the United States. Neither occurred. Spanish officials in Madrid and Havana believed that secession had so weakened this region internationally that it no longer posed a threat to Cuba, and saw no compelling strategic reason to enter into a formal diplomatic alliance with the Confederacy. Spain did accord the Confederacy the status as a belligerent and, with the approval of the Spanish colonial government, Havana served as an important port utilized by Southern commercial agents and blockade runners. While access to Havana during the Civil War bolstered the economy of the Confederacy, Southern hopes for an alliance between Richmond and Madrid remained as unrealized as the fanciful belief of prewar Southerners that after leaving the Union they would inevitably absorb the Pearl of the Antilles into a tropical empire for slavery.

The South's wartime renunciation of its claims to Spanish Cuba was matched by its disavowal of any aspiration to annex regions of neighboring Mexico. Much like officials in Spain, during the first months of the U.S. Civil War the government of President Benito Juárez regarded the South's recantation of expansion with great suspicion. Mexican officials realized that the slaveholders that controlled the powerful antebellum Democratic Party were largely responsible for policies that promoted U.S. territorial growth in the tropics. The Juárez government shared the enormous relief of Spanish officials about Abraham Lincoln's victory in the 1860 U.S. Presidential election. Mexico City understood that the Democratic Party expansionists who dominated Washington during the 1850s had lost control of the office of the U.S. presidency with the election of Lincoln. In December 1860, Melchor Ocampo, Juárez's minister of interior, wrote to Matías Romero expressing the official view of the Mexican government that the expulsion of Democrats from the White House would result in a new era of improved relations between Washington and the Spanish-speaking republics of the New World.[27]

Reflecting on the profound shift in U.S. foreign relations created by Lincoln's election, Romero later wrote to William Seward, "Happy for the cause of humanity, the people of the United States withdrew their confidence in 1860 from that [Democratic] political party, by which act they showed that they disapproved of its ideas and tendencies, and confided their destinies to men who proclaimed very different principles." Romero believed that the repudiation of the expansionist policies of the Democratic Party marked a watershed moment in the history of the Western Hemisphere. "The American nations," the envoy wrote Seward, "have regarded with the highest satisfaction the change which occurred in [the United States] in March, 1861, because it is the equivalent to the abandonment and condemnation of a policy which threatened the absorption of all. . . . Fortunately," the ambassador continued, "the change in policy toward Mexico operated in the United States brought up a consequent change in the feelings of my country to yours."[28] Much to Mexico City's relief, the demographic landscape of U.S. electoral politics revealed by the 1860 election showed that Southern slaveholders, the political interest most responsible for advancing the idea of expansion into Mexico, the Caribbean, and Central America, had lost the powerful grip they had held on the U.S. federal government, especially the presidency, during the previous decade.

After war erupted in the United States, the Juárez government understood that many of the Southerners who had strongly advocated for expansion into Mexico before secession were now top officials in the Confederate government. In 1859, for instance, Jefferson Davis advocated reopening the African slave trade as necessary in supplying the labor force for "any new acquisitions to be made south of the Rio Grande."[29] Juárez strongly suspected that these Southerners continued to covet Mexican territory after splitting their region from the Union. These suspicions were reinforced by the stream of reports from Romero describing the expansionist language of the Crittenden Compromise and the Confederate Constitution, as well as the disastrous decision of the Davis administration to appoint the Kentuckian John T. Pickett, an unrepentant expansionist, as its envoy to Mexico City.

Davis appointed Pickett as envoy to Mexico in May 1861. In his letter of instructions to Pickett, Confederate Secretary of State Toombs explained that the Confederacy was not seeking "formal recognition of the independence of the Confederate States by Mexico," only Mexican neutrality in the U.S. Civil War and official recognition of the status of the Confederacy as a belligerent power. Anxious to establish close relations with Mexico if Juárez was receptive to that idea, Toombs continued, "Should the Mexican Government express any desire to form an alliance with the Confederate States you will assure them of the readiness of this Government to conclude a treaty of amity, commerce, and navigation with the Republic on terms equally advantageous to both countries."[30] Toombs also offered to "send a Minister to Mexico and receive a representative of that Republic here."[31] Striking a conciliatory tone, Toombs' instructions indicated the importance the new Confederate government placed on good relations with its southern neighbor. Unfortunately for the South, it soon became clear that the wrong diplomat had been entrusted to smooth the suspicions of Mexican officials about the expansionist intentions of the Confederate nation.

Pickett arrived in Mexico City during the summer of 1861. In his formal communications with the Mexican minister of foreign affairs, Manuel Zamacona, the envoy utilized Richmond's standard diplomatic talking point that the South, having acquired a political balance of power through secession, had renounced expansion into Mexico. After its withdrawal from the Union, he argued, the "policy of extension of territory on the part of the South ceases to exist—in fact dies a natural death."[32] Pickett's public reassurances about Confederate expansion, however, were belied by his private correspondence that continued to advocate for the capture of Mexican territory. An incompetent diplomatic operative, Pickett did not realize that Mexican agents were intercepting his confidential correspondence and reporting its content to Mexican officials, including Benito Juárez himself.[33] Immediately after writing Zamacona to assure the minister it "is not the desire of the Confederate States to acquire more Mexican territory," for instance, Pickett wrote to Toombs, explaining, "It must not be supposed from the expression ... of the foregoing diplomatic language that I am not fully impressed with the fact that 'manifest destiny' may falsify the foregoing disclaimer. No one is more impressed than the writer with the great truth that, *Southward* the Star of Empire takes its way."[34] Pickett's indiscreet calls for

Southern expansion into Mexico fatally undermined the credibility of the Confederate government, never very strong to begin with, among Mexican officials.

Regarded by the Juárez administration with deep suspicion, frustrated by the complete refusal of Juárez to enter into any sort of alliance with his government, and fearing that Mexico City was on the verge of authorizing transit rights allowing Union troops to land at Guaymas for an attack on Arizona, in October 1861 Pickett went on the diplomatic offensive. Hoping to pressure the Mexican president into a more conciliatory policy toward the South, the envoy began meeting with members of the Conservative Party, church officials, and other Mexicans hostile to the Juárez regime. In a letter intercepted by Juárez's agents and immediately brought to the attention of Mexican officials, Pickett suggested the Confederacy position troops on the Rio Grande, march on Monterrey, and capture northeastern Mexico.[35] Soon after writing this incendiary letter, Pickett assaulted John A. Bennett, an American businessman and friend of Mexico's foreign minister. Tired of his antics, the Mexican government arrested, jailed, and then summarily expelled Pickett from Mexico.[36] The envoy returned to Richmond with the relations between the Confederacy and the government of Benito Juárez in complete shambles. After Pickett's unseemly departure from Mexico, Richmond never again succeeded in posting a diplomatic envoy to Mexico City.

The rough treatment awarded the Confederate government's agent to Mexico City suggests that Juárez's government had determined that it had little to fear from its new northern neighbor along the Rio Grande. For Mexicans, the danger posed by the South had been far more perilous during the previous decade, when this politically powerful slaveholding region fashioned the foreign policy of the United States. Romero noted in a speech given in New York in 1864 that antebellum U.S. expansionists, dominated by Southern slaveholders and their Northern allies in the Democratic Party, continued to "set their eyes on the sunny regions of Mexico." "I will not conceal from you, gentlemen," Romero candidly admitted, "the fact that we have looked with deep apprehension upon such an aggressive policy, which threatened to deprive us of our independence and nationality—the highest and most precious rights that man can enjoy on earth."[37] After secession the suspicions of Mexican officials that Southerners continued plotting to capture portions of Mexico were seemingly confirmed by the seizure of the Pickett letters, documents that offered damning evidence that, despite Richmond's expressions to the contrary, top Confederate officials maintained the dream of expanding south of the Rio Grande. Instead of showing any apprehension about the danger posed by the Confederacy, however, the diplomatic stance adopted by Mexico City toward the wartime South and its diplomatic agent was one of barely concealed disdain.

Pickett did succeed in having Juárez, who wanted to avoid provoking an unnecessary war with the Confederacy, scrap any notion of offering the Union transit rights through Guaymas into Arizona Territory. Outside of that one concession, however, during the Civil War Mexico City declined to offer the Confederacy any sort of diplomatic alliance or moral support. Juárez did maintain neutrality between the North and South, but eagerly pursued good relations with the Lincoln administration and Washington's ambassador to Mexico City, Thomas Corwin. The Mexican president, on the other hand, rebuffed the South's attempts to create friendly relations with his government, including the Confederate government's offer to exchange diplomatic envoys. Juárez refused to consider the South's request that Mexico City accord the Confederacy the rights of a belligerent power and, as we have seen, his government did not hesitate to spy on and then expel the South's diplomatic agent in Mexico.[38]

Juárez was also aware that the cross-border cotton trade between Confederate Texas and the neighboring states of the Mexican northeast that developed immediately after secession provided an important source of war materiel and consumer goods for the South, and he tried to put a stop to it. In June 1862, at the urging of the U.S. Ambassador Corwin, the Mexican president ordered the governors of the northern Mexican states to "cease all intercourse with the Confederate States, under whatever circumstances."[39] Writing in November 1862, a Confederate Army officer in Texas acknowledged Mexico City's antipathy to the South by complaining: "Through the influence of Mr. Corwin, United States minister to Mexico, the tone of the Juárez Government in Mexico has been hostile to our cause, and at his dictation various measures have been initiated calculated to annoy and injure us."[40] Acting without any fear of diplomatic repercussions from Richmond, the hostile stance adopted by the Juárez regime toward the South after its separation from the United States indicates that Mexico City had determined that the Confederate rebellion lacked the military power to endanger the territorial integrity of the Mexican nation.

Having failed to gain an alliance with the Juárez regime, the South did succeed in creating a trading partnership with the fiercely independent *caudillo* Santiago Vidaurri, the powerful federalist governor known as the Lord of the North. Vidaurri was the governor of Nuevo León and Coahuila, a combination of states he had created against the wishes of the Mexican government in 1856. Vidaurri also enjoyed great influence in neighboring Tamaulipas, including Matamoros, northeastern Mexico's most important port and, after the Union blockaded Southern ports, the lifeline into the Confederate States of America.[41]

Relations between Vidaurri and Confederate authorities grew so friendly that by the late summer of 1861 it appeared that the antebellum dreams of Southern expansion into northern Mexico might come true, and far more quickly than Confederate officials had expected. In June 1861, Richmond dispatched the Cuban-born José Quintero to Monterrey to serve as its diplomatic envoy to the powerful governor. A few months later, on August 19, Quintero reported to his superiors in a confidential memo that during secret meetings the *caudillo* had suggested that the Confederacy annex Nuevo León and Coahuila.[42] The context of Quintero's memo arose from the long-standing tensions between the federalist Vidaurri and the nationalist Juárez. The struggle between Monterrey and Mexico City greatly intensified at almost exactly the same moment the U.S. Civil War erupted. In early 1861, soon after his victory in the War of Reform, Juárez attempted to reestablish the authority of his government in the Mexican northeast by appointing inspectors loyal to his administration to man the customs houses along the Rio Grande border, an area that served as a major source of revenue for Vidaurri. Juárez also deployed government troops to patrol the northeastern frontier of Mexico and secure control of the region.[43] Both of these efforts were bitterly resisted by Vidaurri. Tensions between the two rose even further when, due to the Union blockade of Southern ports, the Rio Grande borderlands became a major conduit for international trade to the South. After Juárez forbid state governors in the Mexican north from trading with the Confederacy, Vidaurri, realizing that the Mexican president lacked the power to enforce this proclamation, continued to facilitate the profitable exchange of goods, especially Southern cotton, across the Rio Grande.[44]

In his August 19 memo to Richmond, Quintero reported that the *caudillo* had grown so alienated from the central government in Mexico City that he contemplated the peaceful annexation of northern Mexico into the Confederacy. Quintero wrote that Vidaurri "said that the world knew he had been for years anxious to establish the Republic of Sierra Madre to be composed of the Mexican States on our border, but that the birth of the Southern Confederacy had made him change his mind and he was now in favor of annexation to the Confederate States." Quintero continued, "He [Vidaurri] said to me that if the President would appoint an agent—he would immediately enter into negotiations with our Government . . . New Leon and Coahuila being annexed, the balance of the frontier would soon follow."[45] To this day Mexican historians puzzle over what Vidaurri hoped to achieve by this extraordinary proposal. At the time, however, as the exultant tone of Quintero's memo to Richmond makes clear, the Confederate envoy believed the governor was completely sincere in his willingness to transfer the sovereignty of the states of northern Mexico under his direct control to the Confederacy. Just months after secession, a large area of the Mexican northeast, an area long-desired by Southerners, seemed to have miraculously fallen into the lap of the Confederate nation.

Despite Quintero's enthusiastic assurances about Vidaurri's willingness to join his territory to the South, Jefferson Davis refused to consider the governor's unexpected offer to negotiate the immediate Confederate annexation of Nuevo León and Coahuila. In his carefully worded response, Davis instructed Quintero to inform the governor that while it was "manifestly to the interest of both people that intimate social and commercial relations should subsist between them . . . the President is of the opinion . . . that it would be imprudent and impolitic in the interest of both parties to take any steps at present in regard to the proposition made by Governor Vidaurri in his confidential communications with you in reference to the future political relations of the Confederate States with the northern Provinces of Mexico."[46] The Confederate government thus refused the chance to expand into northern Mexico, a region greatly desired by Southern expansionists in the decade before the Civil War, and an objective that Davis himself had publicly supported as late as 1859.

Davis's refusal to negotiate with Vidaurri revealed the limits of the Confederate strategic position in Mexico. As Frank Owsley argued, the Confederate president rebuffed Vidaurri's offer because Davis and his cabinet were "acutely aware of the European aspect of the Mexican question." The Richmond government, Owsley maintained, judged that the South's "attempt to acquire territory in Mexico at this time would incur the displeasure of the intervening powers, especially France."[47] Davis's refusal to consider Vidaurri's offer of annexation is perhaps the earliest indication of how the French intervention, at that point still in its planning stages, would fundamentally undermine the possibility of any future expansion of Confederate territory south of the Rio Grande.

Shrugging off the news that Richmond refused to consider his offer of annexation, Vidaurri continued to facilitate the enormous trade between Confederate Texas and northeastern Mexico. The opening of the Rio Grande borderlands trade was the most important success that Southern diplomacy had enjoyed in Mexico and, arguably, the entire Western Hemisphere. Yet it is important to note that the relationship between northeastern Mexico and the Confederacy was not one marked by Southern territorial growth, but was instead a mutually beneficial economic alliance between coterminous regions violently resisting the consolidating power of their respective national governments in Washington and Mexico City. The network of trade that developed between Texas and the states of the Mexican northeast offered enormous benefits to those living on both sides of the Rio Grande. During the Civil War Vidaurri was happy to forge an alliance with the Confederates across the river, but like Juárez the governor was far from overawed by the military power of the South. Willing to sell to the Confederate Army the raw materials necessary to make ammunition—lead, powder, niter (potassium nitrate), and sulfur—all of which were in abundant supply in northeastern Mexico, the *caudillo* refused to allow Southern agents to purchase weapons from the territory under his control. As Quintero explained, Vidaurri was "unwilling to part with any part of his own armaments because of his precarious relations with the Federal government of Mexico."[48] After Davis's polite refusal of Vidaurri's offer of annexation, there was no further discussion of the South peacefully incorporating northeast Mexico. In the spring of 1864, Juárez deposed Vidaurri and entered Monterrey. A few months later, the French army occupied Nuevo León and forced the Mexican president to flee to the borderlands area of Chihuahua across from El Paso. Despite this political upheaval, the economic cooperation between the Mexican northeast and the Confederacy continued without interruption until the end of the Civil War.

Beyond the success of its economic relationship with northeastern Mexico, the South's otherwise striking lack of influence in the rest of Mexico was confirmed by the failed attempt by Confederate diplomats to turn the French intervention to their nation's advantage. By the time that the Confederate envoy to France, John Slidell, arrived in Paris in early 1862, French troops had already landed in Mexico. Aware that the South's prewar expectations that King Cotton would force France to recognize the Confederacy had proved mistaken, Slidell formulated a different strategy for diplomatic recognition that focused around the South's support for French designs in Mexico. In a July 1862 note written to the French minister of foreign affairs, Édouard Antoine Thouvenel, Slidell explained that the South had disowned its prewar ambition to capture territory in the Americas. Singing from the same diplomatic hymnal as Richmond's envoys in Madrid and

Mexico City, Slidell argued that the post-secession balance of power precluded the need for the Confederacy to expand in the Americas.[49]

In addition to renouncing Southern expansion, Slidell's July note to Thouvenel also signaled a radical shift in the attitude of wartime Southerners toward the Monroe Doctrine. Before the Civil War, both the Northern and Southern regions of the United States opposed any European interference in the New World. By January 1862, however, about the time French troops were landing in Veracruz, the *Charleston Mercury* declared without regret that the "Monroe Doctrine is dead for all time to come."[50] As if proving the point made by this influential newspaper, Slidell declared to the minister of foreign affairs that the French action in Mexico "will be regarded with no unfriendly eye by the Confederate States."[51] A few days later, Napoleon III received the Confederate envoy at the French resort of Vichy. Slidell reported that the emperor declared his "sympathies had always been with the South" and that he "considered the reestablishment of the Union impossible and final separation a mere question of time." Broadening the conversation to include the French conflict in Mexico, the Confederate envoy declared to Napoleon III that as the "Lincoln Government was the ally and protector of his enemy Juárez, we could have no objection to make common cause with him against a common enemy."[52] This transparent attempt to leverage Napoleon III's Mexican scheme as a means of persuading France to recognize the Confederacy failed. Napoleon maintained that he would not recognize the Confederacy without the cooperation of Great Britain.[53] The result of Slidell's July 1862 negotiations with Thouvenel and Napoleon III failed to secure French recognition of the Confederacy, his intended goal. Instead, by the summer of 1862 the Confederate States of America found itself in the position of freely acquiescing, without any reciprocal agreements from France, to Napoleon III's "Grand Scheme" to install a European monarch on the Cactus Throne.

During the next year, Slidell continued to meet with senior French officials. In his June 1863 meeting with Napoleon III the Confederate envoy reemphasized that the South supported Paris's effort to replace the republican government of Juárez with a European monarch and did not object to the French army's occupation of Mexico. Meeting with the emperor just a few weeks prior to the French occupation of Mexico City, Slidell declared, "There could be no doubt of the bitterness of the Northern people at the success of his arms in Mexico, while all our sympathies were with France." He then "urged" upon the emperor "the importance of securing the lasting gratitude and attachment of a people already so well disposed [as] there could be no doubt that our Confederacy was to be the strongest power of the American Continent, and that our alliance was worth cultivating."[54] Napoleon III offered a friendly but noncommittal response to Slidell's assertion concerning the hemispheric clout of the Confederacy, but Richmond's acquiescence to the French occupation of its southern neighbor was welcome news in Paris. Slidell's continued signal of support for his Mexican adventure was one reason that Napoleon III continued to tantalize Richmond with the possibility that the French might soon unilaterally recognize the Confederacy.

Slidell's promise that the Confederacy had eschewed territorial growth in Mexico, and his comments backing the French intervention, demonstrated the ways in which Napoleon III's Grand Design for Mexico had upset the South's calculations about the inevitability of its post-secession expansion in the Americas. After the French intervention, Southerners found their rebellion geographically surrounded by a hostile Union to its north, suspicious Spaniards in Cuba, and a powerful French military occupation in neighboring Mexico. The most promising opportunity for expansion available to Southerners, Vidaurri's offer to negotiate with Richmond for the Confederate annexation of northeastern Mexico, had been quickly declined by the Davis administration as "imprudent and impolitic." By the second year of the Civil War the possibility of Southern expansion in the New World, whether Confederate leaders recognized it or not, had evaporated into thin air.

The French intervention and the continued refusal of Paris to offer the Confederacy diplomatic recognition convinced at least some Southerners that their rebellion was playing a distinctly subservient role in the hemisphere. A few months before the French army occupied Mexico City in June 1863, the legendary Texan Sam Houston admitted that the French emperor had demolished any Confederate plans for future expansion in Mexico. "Napoleon III," Houston declared in March 1863, "steps forward to grasp the prize, which is beyond our reach; and we who are the most interested have but to make the best of it."[55] In September of that same year, a Houston paper described the position of the South in Mexico by using a popular phrase that described a national entity hoodwinked by the government of a more powerful country. Explaining that the cunning emperor had duped the Confederacy into favoring his Mexican scheme by flirting with Richmond about the possibility of French recognition of the South, this newspaper argued that Napoleon III was "quite willing to make a cats-paw of the Southern Confederacy and any other power upon earth."[56] By the time Maximilian was crowned emperor of Mexico, in June 1864, it became painfully clear to Confederate officials that they had been outmaneuvered by Napoleon III at every turn.

Expecting friendly relations with the government of Maximilian, in January 1864 Richmond appointed William Preston as its diplomatic envoy to Mexico City. Judah Benjamin instructed Preston to inform Maximilian that "the future safety of the Mexican empire is inextricably bound to the safety and independence of the Confederacy."[57] After arriving in Mexico, however, Maximilian refused to grant Preston, who was waiting in Havana, permission to assume his post in Mexico City. The reason for this, as the Confederate envoy in Brussels, Dudley Mann, reported to furious Confederate officials in March, was that "Louis Napoleon has enjoined upon Maximilian to hold no official relations with our commissioner to Mexico."[58] Realizing that the Confederacy's acquiescence to Maximilian's ascent to the Cactus Throne would not award the South either diplomatic recognition by Napoleon III or any significant role in Mexico, in August 1864 Slidell and Preston, who was in Europe to meet the Mexican diplomats representing Maximilian's government in London and Paris, attempted a more aggressive diplomatic approach.

That summer, as Slidell explained to Benjamin, rumors were sweeping Europe that the Confederacy would soon make peace with the United States based upon a mutually agreed separation of the North and South. Taking advantage of these rumors, Slidell and Preston hatched a plot that indicated their belated understanding that foreign governments viewed the South as much more powerful when its interests were projected through an alliance with the United States, rather than as an independent nation acting on its own. Slidell reported to Benjamin that the spurned Preston "hinted" to Maximilian's envoys "that one of the conditions of our peace with the North, now considered not very remote, may probably be a treaty of alliance, offensive and defensive, for the establishment of an American policy on our continent, which will result in the suppression of monarchical institutions in Mexico. . . . I have thought it politic to throw out similar suggestions," Slidell continued, "from which they will be likely to reach the Emperor and Mr. Drouyn de Lhuys," France's current minister of foreign affairs.[59] The Confederacy's inconsistent policy on the French occupation of Mexico—veering as it did from embracing the French intervention early in 1862 to threatening a joint U.S.-Confederate attack on the French expedition by the summer of 1864—failed to impress French officials. Instead, it illustrated the

geopolitical reality that the South's influence in the New World was fundamentally linked to the military and diplomatic power of the United States.

As Slidell's proposal for a possible joint North-South invasion of Mexico
indicated, the behavior of the French in Mexico had forced the South to
come full circle on the Monroe Doctrine. Realizing that the French intervention had undermined the Confederacy's influence in Mexico without
resulting in the hoped-for recognition by Napoleon III, important voices in
Richmond revived the idea of protecting the New World from predatory
European powers. In February 1865, Davis sent three commissioners, including his vice president, Alexander Stephens, to negotiate with Lincoln
and Seward behind Union lines at Hampton Roads, Virginia. Davis's decision to send Southern commissioners to the negotiating table was based
largely on the proposal of Francis Preston Blair, Sr., a political ally of Lincoln, that the two sides declare a truce and create an expeditionary force,
commanded by Jefferson Davis, to enter Mexico and drive Maximilian and
the French army out of Mexico. "After the Monroe Doctrine is restored
to the continent," Blair declared, "the two sides could sit down in common
victory to work out a peace."[60] At the Hampton Roads Peace Conference
Stephens, who had been briefed about Blair's proposal by Davis and Benjamin, indicated support for the idea for a combined North-South invasion of
Mexico to be followed by peace talks designed to resolve the issues between
the two warring parties. Lincoln, however, firmly rejected the idea of a Mexican expedition, informing Stephens that Blair had acted on his own and that
the U.S. federal government would not enter into a truce with the Confederacy until the national authority was reestablished throughout the South.[61]

As the position adopted by the Confederate vice president concerning
the creation of a joint Union-Confederate expedition designed to oust Maximilian and his French protectors from Mexico demonstrated, by the end of
the Civil War it had become apparent to many Southern leaders that the
ability of the South to achieve its interests in the Americas depended upon
a close alliance with the United States. The growing recognition of the
South's dependence on U.S. power was apparent in January 1865, when D. C.
DeJarnette, a Confederate congressman, discussed the Monroe Doctrine in
a speech to the Confederate House of Representatives. DeJarnette, who
might have gotten wind of Blair's proposal to Davis, envisioned an independent South working in concert with the United States against common European rivals in the New World.

What is most interesting about the scenario posed by DeJarnette is the
secondary role the South would have played to the United States in such an

alliance. Any hemispheric clout the South might enjoy, in fact, was contingent upon the strength and influence of the United States. Much like Slidell and Blair, DeJarnette argued for the separation of the North and South followed by an allied "union of arms with ours for the expulsion of ... France from the continent of North America." DeJarnette, however, took his scenario one step further: "From the union of arms proposed to be brought about by the resolution I have offered," he continued, "the United States will become possessed of the scepter of commercial power, and the commercial center of the world will be changed from London to New York. The South, in the peaceful enjoyment of her independence, will devote herself to agriculture, and thus furnish food and clothing for the world, and the North with ships and factories will realize the fact that agriculture is the handmaid of commerce."[62] Shorn of any fantasy of independence, DeJarnette's vision of Southern power was not radically different than what actually unfolded after the defeat of the Confederacy. As for the people of Latin America and the Caribbean, after the Confederate surrender its citizens could only wonder what the reentry of the South into the United States would mean for future relations between the newly united "Colossus of the North" and its neighbors in the New World.

Suggested Readings

Barker, Nancy N. "Monarchy in Mexico: Harebrained Scheme or Well-Considered Prospect?" *Journal of Modern History* 48 (March 1976): 51–68.

Guterl, Matthew Pratt. *American Mediterranean: Southern Slaveholders in the Age of Emancipation.* Cambridge, MA: Harvard University Press, 2008.

Irby, James. *Backdoor at Bagdad: The Civil War on the Rio Grande.* El Paso: Texas Western Press, 1977.

Kelly, Patrick J. "The North American Crisis of the 1860s." *Journal of the Civil War Era*, September 2012, 337–68.

Lavalle, Gurza. *Una Vecindad Efímera: Los Estados Confederados de America y su Politica Exterior hacia Mexico, 1861–1865.* México, D.F.: Instituto Mora, 2001.

May, Robert E. *Slavery, Race and Conquest in the Tropics: Lincoln, Douglass and the Future of Latin America.* New York: Cambridge University Press, 2013.

Sanders, James E. *The Vanguard of the Atlantic World: Creating Modernity, Nation, and Democracy in Nineteenth-Century Latin America.* Durham, NC: Duke University Press, 2014.

Schoonover, Thomas. *Dollars over Domination: The Triumph of Liberalism in Mexican- United States Relations, 1861–1867.* Baton Rouge: Louisiana State University Press, 1978.

Schoonover, Thomas B., ed., *Mexican Lobby: Matías Romero in Washington 1861–1867.* Lexington, KY: University of Kentucky Press, 1986.

Thompson, Jerry. *Cortina: Defending the Mexican Name in Texas*. College Station: Texas A&M University Press, 2007.

Tyler, Ronnie. *Santiago Vidaurri and the Southern Confederacy*. Austin: Texas State Historical Association, 1973.

Notes

1. Among the many books on this topic, see Robert E. May, *The Southern Dream of a Caribbean Empire, 1854–1861* (Baton Rouge: Louisiana State University Press, 1973), and *Slavery, Race and Conquest in the Tropics: Lincoln, Douglass and the Future of Latin America* (New York: Cambridge University Press, 2013); Matthew Pratt Guterl, *American Mediterranean: Southern Slaveholders in the Age of Emancipation* (Cambridge, MA: Harvard University Press, 2008); Amy Greenberg, *Manifest Manhood and the Antebellum American Empire* (New York: Cambridge University Press, 2005).

2. *New York Times*, February 16, 1858.

3. Matthew Karp, "The World the Slaveholders Craved: Proslavery Internationalism in the 1850s," in *The World of the Revolutionary American Republic*, ed. Andrew Shankman (New York: Routledge, Taylor and Francis Group, 2014), 414–32, quote on 426.

4. Robert A. Toombs to Charles J. Helm, July 22, 1861, in James D. Richardson, ed., *A Compilation of the Messages and Papers of the Confederacy Including the Diplomatic Correspondence 1861–1865* (Nashville: United States Publishing Company, 1905), 2:48. (Hereafter *Messages and Papers of the Confederacy*, vol. 2).

5. General Francisco Serrano quoted in Wayne S. Bowen, *Spain and the American Civil War* (Columbia: University of Missouri Press, 2011), 70.

6. R. M. T. Hunter to John Slidell, September 23, 1861, quoted in *The War of the Rebellion: A Compilation of the Official Records of the Union and Confederate Navies in the War of the Rebellion* (Washington, DC: Government Printing Office, 1894–1922), ser. 2, vol. 3, 271. (Hereafter cited as *ORN*).

7. R. M. T. Hunter to James Mason, September 23, 1861, quoted in *ORN*, ser. 2, vol. 3, 262.

8. Quoted in Mary Wilhelmine Williams, "Letter from Colonel John T. Pickett, of the Southern Confederacy, to Senor Don Manuel De Zamacona, Minister of Foreign Affairs, Mexico," *Hispanic American Historical Review* 2, no. 4 (November 1919): 611–17, quote on 614.

9. Quoted in James McPherson, *Battle Cry of Freedom: The Civil War Era* (New York: Oxford University Press, 2003), 106.

10. Quoted in *Mexican Lobby: Matías Romero in Washington 1861–1867*, ed. Thomas B. Schoonover (Lexington: University of Kentucky Press, 2014), 2.

11. For a discussion of the New World liberalism of Spanish-speaking republic and their conception of the United States as a "sister republic," see James E. Sanders, *The Vanguard of the Atlantic World: Creating Modernity, Nation, and Democracy in Nineteenth-Century Latin America* (Durham, NC: Duke University Press, 2014).

12. See Patrick J. Kelly, "The North American Crisis of the 1860s," *Journal of the Civil War Era* (September 2012): 337–68; Nancy N. Barker, "Monarchy in Mexico: Harebrained Scheme or Well-Considered Prospect?" *Journal of Modern History* 48 (March 1976): 51–68.

13. Robert Bonner, *Mastering America, Southern Slaveholders and the Crisis of American Nationhood* (New York: Cambridge University Press, 2009), 301.

14. McPherson, *Battle Cry of Freedom*, 115.

15. Avalon Project at Yale Law School, "Confederate Constitution," Article IV, Clause 3, http://avalon.law.yale.edu/19th_century/csa_csa.asp.

16. Quoted in Bowen, *Spain and the American Civil War*, 1.

17. R. M. T. Hunter to William L. Yancy, A. Dudley Mann, Pierre A. Rost, August 24, 1861, quote in *ORN*, ser. 2, vol. 3, 250–51.

18. Robert A. Toombs quoted in Don Doyle, *The Cause of All Nations: An International History of the American Civil War* (New York: Basic Books, 2015), 113.

19. Bowen, *Spain and the American Civil War*, 58.

20. Davis quoted in Henry Mills Alden, *Harper's New Monthly Magazine* 19, nos. 109–14 (June–November 1859): 694–95.

21. Peter J. Sehlinger, *Kentucky's Last Cavalier, General William Preston, 1816–1887* (Lexington: University of Kentucky Press, 2004), 114.

22. Quoted in Bowen, *Spain and the American Civil War*, 70.

23. For the South's prewar influence on the U.S. Navy see Matthew J. Karp, "Slavery and American Sea Power: The Navalist Impulse in the Antebellum South," *Journal of Southern History* 77 (May 2011): 283–324.

24. Pierre Rost to R. M. T. Hunter, March 21, 1862, quoted in *ORN* ser. 2, vol. 3, 368.

25. R.M.T. Hunter to William L. Yancy, Pierre A. Rost and A. Dudley Mann, August 24, 1861, quoted in ORN, ser. 2, vol. 3, 250.

26. Judah P. Benjamin to John Slidell, May 9, 1863, quoted in *ORN* ser. 2, vol. 3, 763.

27. Thomas Schoonover, *Dollars Over Domination: The Triumph of Liberalism in Mexican-United States Relations, 1861–1867* (Baton Rouge: Louisiana State University Press, 1978), 13.

28. Matías Romero to William Seward, October 2, 1862, quoted in U.S. Congress, House, *The Conditions of Affairs in Mexico* House Ex. Doc. No. 54, 205 (hereafter cited as *House Ex. Doc. 54*).

29. Quoted in *Harper's New Monthly Magazine* 19, nos.109–14 (June to November 1859): 694–95.

30. Toombs to John T. Pickett, May 17, 1861, quoted in *ORN*, ser. 2, vol. 3, 203, 204.

31. Toombs to John T. Pickett, May 17, 1861, quoted in *ORN*, ser. 2, vol. 3, 204.

32. Quoted in Williams, "Letter from Colonel John T. Pickett," 613–14.

33. Schoonover, *Dollars over Domination*, 31.

34. Quoted in Williams, "Letter from Colonel John T. Pickett," 614.

35. Schoonover, *Dollars over Dominion*, 42.

36. Ibid., 42–43.

37. Romero speech, March 29, 1864, quoted in U.S. Congress, Senate, *Message from the President of the United States*, 38th Cong., 2nd sess., Sen. Ex. Doc. 11, 411–12 (hereafter cited as *Senate Ex. Doc. 11*).

38. John Bassett Moore, *History and Digest of the International Arbitrations to Which the United States has been a Party* (Washington, DC, Government Printing Office, 1898), 2888.

39. Juárez order quoted in Ronnie Tyler, *Santiago Vidaurri and the Southern Confederacy* (Austin: Texas State Historical Society, 1973), 82. For the cotton trade into Mexico, see James Irby, *Backdoor at Bagdad: The Civil War on the Rio Grande* (El Paso: Texas Western Press), 1977.

40. Brig. Gen. H.P. Bee to Lt. Col. S.S. Anderson, November 30, 1862, quoted in *The War of the Rebellion: A Compilation of the Official Records of the Union and Confederate Armies*, 128 vols. (Washington, DC: Government Printing Office, 1880–1901), ser. 1, vol. 15, 881.

41. See Artemo Benavides Hinojosa, *Santiago Vidaurri: Caudillo Del Noreste Mexicano 1855–1864* (México, D.F.: Tusquets, 2012.)

42. Ronnie Tyler, *Santiago Vidaurri and the Southern Confederacy* (Austin: Texas State Historical Society, 1973.), 50–51.

43. See Gerardo Gurza Lavalle, *Una Vecindad Efímera: Los Estados Confederados de America y su Politica Exterior hacia Mexico, 1861–1865* (México, D.F.: Instituto Mora, 2001.), esp. 74–77.

44. Frank Lawrence Owsley, *King Cotton Diplomacy: Foreign Relations of the Confederates States of America*, 2nd ed. (Chicago: University of Chicago Press, 1959), 112.

45. José Quintero to Robert M. T. Hunter, August 19, 1861, "Confidential," *Records of the Confederate States of America*, vol. 58, roll 32.

46. Wm. M. Browne to Quintero, September 3, 1861, *Messages and Papers of The Confederacy*, 78.

47. Owsley, *King Cotton Diplomacy*, 117.

48. Quintero to Wm. M Browne, August 22, 1861, *Records of the Confederate States of America*, vol. 58, roll 32.

49. John Slidell to Édouard Antoine Thouvenel, July 21, 1862, *ORN*, ser. 2, vol. 3, 474.

50. Quoted in Bonner, *Mastering America*, 301. See also Jay Sexton, *The Monroe Doctrine: Empire and Nation in Nineteenth-Century America* (New York: Hill and Wang, 2012.)

51. John Slidell to Édouard Antoine Thouvenel, July 21, 1862, *ORN*, ser. 2, vol. 3, 475.

52. John Slidell, "Enclosed Memorandum," *ORN*, ser. 2, vol. 3, 484.

53. John Slidell, "Enclosed Memorandum," *ORN*, ser. 2, vol. 3, 482–87.

54. John Slidell, "Memorandum of an Interview with the Emperor at the Tuileries on Thursday, 18th June 1863," *ORN*, ser. 2, vol. 3, 813.

55. Quoted in Adrian Robert Brettle, "The Fortunes of War: Confederate Expansionist Ambitions During the American Civil War" (PhD Dissertation, University of Virginia, 2014), 272.

56. *Houston Tri-Weekly Telegraph*, September 23, 1863.

57. Judah P. Benjamin to William Preston, July 7, 1864, quoted in *ORN*, ser. 2, vol. 3, 989.

58. Dudley Mann to Judah P. Benjamin, March 11, 1864, quoted in *ORN*, ser. 2, vol. 3, 1057.

59. John Slidell to Judah P. Benjamin, August 8, 1864, quoted in *ORN*, ser. 2, vol. 3, 1187.

60. Francis P. Blair, Sr., quoted in Eli N. Evans, *Judah P. Benjamin, the Jewish Confederate* (New York: Free Press, 1988), 277.

61. See Doyle, *The Cause of All Nations*, 286–88.

62. "The Monroe Doctrine. Speech of Hon. D. C. DeJarnette, of Virginia to the Confederate House of Representatives, 30 January 1865": http://digilib.usm.edu/cdm/ref/collection/rarebook/id/3584.

CHAPTER FOUR

Manifest Dominion

The British Empire and the Crises of the Americas in the 1860s

Richard Huzzey

The crises of the 1860s tested the reality of Britain's presumed and assumed power across the Americas. Debates over the continents' future turned on how American peoples and nations might form part of a global system of British preeminence. Besides the fates of formal colonies in Canada and the Caribbean, the tumult of this decade tested a broader presumption of political, economic, and military power around the globe. British writers and politicians generally agreed on the desirability of their country's influence beyond the Atlantic. Beyond this broad goal, they differed on how far particular causes or countries might prove to be vehicles for British interests, particularly when it came to the question of whether the "manifest destiny" of the United States might be embraced or rejected as part of their own Anglo-Saxon mission. The rise or demise of the errant American republic was an arresting crisis of this period, but it can only be understood in the context of British calculations regarding the threat of French and Spanish imperialism in Latin America, the postemancipation policies of Britain's supposedly "antislavery empire," and the internal crises of their own colonies. Together, these imperial puzzles challenged Britons to imagine how their own manifest dominion should be realized in the later nineteenth century.

Of course, Britons did not think or speak with consistency about events across the Americas; their responses reflected differences within Britain as much as they extended the realities of "new world" conflicts into the old world. Such complex divisions sustained a voluminous public literature on events overseas. As one author quipped, in travel writing, "Scarcely any two travelers agree in their general impressions; the consequence is, that they wax warm in support of the cause they espouse, and that always amuses the world at large."[1] By tracing the patterns of anxieties and excitement in travel literature, partisan pamphlets, and the popular press, it is possible to reconstruct the fault lines in British responses to these crises.

Throughout five regions of the world—progressing from the Mosquito Coast in Central America, to Cuba, the Confederacy, Mexico, Jamaica, and, finally, to Canada—the crises of the 1860s emerged as part of broader debates about the means and ends of British power. Recent histories of the Empire paint officials and statesmen as buffeted by financial or commercial lobbies of varied influence; episodic eruptions of outrage from an oft-distracted public; and a cautious preference for influencing existing polities rather than invading and subjugating them. This adds up to a differential equation for imperial expansion, not the unwavering policies of an "official mind" or the raw determinism of economic interests.[2] In such a spirit, we may examine the low politics of imperial strategy, testing the ambitions, dreams, and fears of authors selling books or selling policies to their metropolitan readers. And, crucially, we will see that decentering the American Civil War and assessing broader British thinking about the Americas helps to illuminate many of these complexities. In such a spirit, we may begin to trace the crises of the 1860s in the demise of the Republic of Nicaragua, not the birth of the Confederate States of America.

IN SEPTEMBER 1860, as Abraham Lincoln's campaign for the U.S. presidency entered its final months, a shot was heard around the Atlantic world: Honduran soldiers executed William Walker, the American filibuster. He had been handed over by the Royal Navy, who caught Walker and his confederates in the midst of their latest expedition to conquer modern Belize and Nicaragua, where he ruled briefly in his self-proclaimed Republic of Nicaragua.[3] Walker's demise marked the end, not the beginning, of a crisis in Central America. However, his efforts were part of a broader, long-running contest for influence across this region, where Britons and Americans both calculated the benefits of cooperation or competition.[4] British assessments of Walker's death underline the uncertainty over how American expansionism should be greeted.

Voicing the views of policymakers, the *Times* concluded that Honduran retribution should meet "universal satisfaction," since Walker "broke into States as ordinary burglars break into houses" and "by promising to establish slavery in those parts, he either conciliated the goodwill or secured the connivance of those who were anxious to see another slave State introduced into the American system."[5] The *London Review* concluded that "no pitying tear has fallen on the grave of Walker," since he was one of "that dangerous class, the impoverished whites of the southern states, paupers in means and aristocrats by caste, who are the most rabid advocates of slavery." The failure of Walker's allies to foment an "anti-English excitement" struck the author as a good omen for sober and peaceable relations with the United States in the future.[6] As Patrick Kelly shows in his chapter of this volume, Walker was only the most prominent and active of those antebellum southerners who dreamt of a tropical empire despite the official policies of the U.S. government. A decade earlier, Britain and the United States renounced territorial possessions along the route of a possible interoceanic canal in the Clayton-Bulwer Treaty of 1850. Each fearing the domination of Pacific trade routes by the other, the two governments agreed that any canal would be neutral and they would not acquire formal colonies.[7]

While Walker's filibustering endangered this prosperous accommodation, not all Britons saw him as a piratical renegade threatening Central American allies. The eccentric traveler Laurence Oliphant accompanied the early stages of an 1857 filibustering expedition in support of Walker.[8] In defending the reputation of his American compatriots against widespread British contempt for them, Oliphant begged readers to remember that it was "not likely that we should have cared more for the liberties of Nicaraguans, who were generally without any government at all" if Britons had "not feared that the country itself was likely to be annexed to the United States." This, he argued, was never Walker's plan nor the desire of American statesmen. Rather, "an Anglo-Saxon government" in Central America would mean "we should find a counterpoise to the Northern Republic, and hear no more of its aggressive designs" and avoid "the regime of the blacks" in an independent state.

Oliphant's was an unusual interpretation of how "Central American questions, as between this country and the United States," would be "set at rest for ever," but it illustrates the British debate as to how to mediate the ambitions of the United States and desires for a balance of power in the Americas.[9] What mattered most, in regions such as Central America, was that "viewing the present disorganized state and retrograde condition of these states, the spread of the Anglo-Saxon race would be desirable; at the same time, it is absolutely essential that the Transit Route should be kept open to the public generally."[10] Debates over Walker's life and death encapsulated Britons' anxieties, recurring in later crises of the Americas, over future domination of the Pacific world, the fraternity of race, and whether the United States was a rival or agent of British power.

INDEED, IN THE 1860s, during the Civil War, Union propagandists still appealed to Walker's villainy in convincing Britons that an independent

Confederacy would be an aggressive proslavery empire.[11] Generations of scholars have considered the Anglo-American aspects of the Civil War, but the bewildered and bewildering range of British responses can only be appreciated in light of the diverse considerations—and geographies—entangled in it. Studies of both elite and popular opinion in Britain have confirmed little succor for Southern fantasies of intervention; confusion, indifference, and horror characterized British responses.[12] Ambitions to interfere were remarkably rare and undeveloped in practice, with the cabinet only considering interference seriously during the autumn of 1862, as Howard Jones's chapter in this volume shows.

Contemporary Northerners and historians since have tended to focus on the inconsistency of British antislavery sentiment and admiration for the slaveholding Confederacy. In fact, British foreign policy had long sought suppression of the international slave trade as the proper channel for anti-slavery diplomacy, rather than directly promoting foreign emancipations.[13] Focusing on this continental struggle over the slave trade moves our attention away from the cotton bundled on the docks of Charleston and towards the waters off the coast of Cuba. Just before the war, in 1858, Foreign Secretary Lord John Russell and Prime Minister Viscount Palmerston dispatched British gunboats to patrol close to the shores of Cuba. This provoked public outrage on both sides of the Atlantic, since the Royal Navy's desire to visit ships to prove they were not flying false flags from the United States awoke the outrages of the War of 1812, which had been spurred by an asserted right of search on neutral shipping.[14] An Anglo-American treaty to encourage slave-trade suppression had been scuppered in 1842, in large part thanks to Lewis Cass, Duff Green, and anglophobic Southerners aligned with the Tyler administration.[15] Despite the 1808 ban on the international slave trade, American citizens provided the capital and vessels for the slave trade to Cuba. In 1859, approximately eighty-five slave ships had left New York on slaving voyages, and the Royal Navy deferred to American sensitivities when patrolling so close to Florida.[16] By the last years of the 1850s, this last branch of the transatlantic slave trade grew rapidly as a result of Cuban sugar planters' demand for African labor. Antebellum British diplomats delicately sought to steer a path that would both guarantee effective Spanish suppression of this illicit traffic and deter Cuban annexation by the United States.[17]

As the British mill owner Henry Ashworth warned working men in Bolton, in a lecture following his 1860 visit to Cuba, "Every class in Havana, ladies as well as gentlemen," subscribed to high-profit slaving voyages, with "no sort of concealment in regard to their success." Typical of Cobdenite free traders, Ashworth insisted that while the Spanish colonial authorities "are corrupt from the head downwards" and "share the spoil with their slavers," still "the progressive intelligence of Cubans themselves" was more effective than British militancy in forcing effective abolition.[18] This criticism of hectoring diplomacy and naval enforcement placed Ashworth at odds with the belligerent anti-slave-trade policies championed by Viscount Palmerston and sustained by his Conservative rivals. In all questions of British foreign policy—from suppression to the Civil War—Britons were divided on how far state power and military force could or should achieve national interests, just as much as they debated what those national interests really were.[19]

In the months leading up to the U.S. Civil War, Palmerston and Russell were focused on a new slave-trade treaty with the Buchanan administration; despite growth in the Cuban slave trade, their hopes were dashed when it came to the submission of American-flagged ships to search by the Royal Navy.[20] The pamphleteer Frederick Milnes Edge, who had lived five years in America, predicted during the 1860 election campaign that Lincoln would immediately "reverse the foreign policy of the Slave power, and render the Slave-trade impossible," which would mean that Britain's "expensive fleets on the coast of Africa and in the Mexican Gulf" could be withdrawn.[21] Edge and others would be disappointed in his predictions of Lincoln's immediate priorities, however.

On the floor of the House of Commons, in February 1861, Palmerston insisted that "no doubt Spain has given us good cause for war, if we had thought proper to avail ourselves of it," in failing to arrest the traffic. Denunciations of Spanish failure and defiance led to British public discussion of new, aggressive measures to enforce slave-trade suppression.[22] However, Palmerston and other politicians could never act on such threats without risking war with the United States or provoking American annexation of Cuba, both of which would represent disasters for British power in the Americas. As the Republicans took office in March 1861, Anglo-American relations remained engulfed in the dynamics of antebellum conflicts.

Long-term debates about the fate of slavery and the influence of Britain in the Americas help explain the muted impact of short-term pressures, such as the Lancashire "cotton famine" prompted by the closure of British access to the South's exports.[23] As recent work highlights, the search for new sources of cotton drove British agents to Egypt, India, and to the slave plantations of Brazil.[24] However, we can understand the subtle balance of competing British interests—and the consequential kaleidoscope of interpretations of the Civil War—as part of a web of continental and global pressures on the British Empire. If Britons adopted bewildering stances on the American conflict, they did so because they saw different things in the contests of ideologies, national interests, or moral principle. The importation crisis over slave-grown cotton did not prompt military intervention in the United States by Great Britain, not least because war with the Union offered more, not less, commercial disorder and crisis by risking imports of Northern grain.[25] If the Civil War damaged British interests, Anglo-American war would threaten British commerce and influence on the continent even more. Strategically, a pro-Southern stance would prompt such a war and imperil Canada, where Palmerston deployed 11,000 British troops from 1861–64.[26] Hence, British distaste for an expensive and disruptive conflict with the U.S. government, in the 1860s, mirrored deference to the U.S. government over Cuban patrols in 1858.

This balance of fears restrained the policy of Her Majesty's Government in Britain's greatest crisis of the Civil War. In December 1861, British and Union newspapers whipped up jingoistic fervor over the removal of Confederate envoys from the British mail steamship *Trent*. In Britain, this appeared to be a gross breach of "English hospitality," because the men, Slidell and Mason, had been travelling on a neutral vessel under the British flag. A pro-Union newspaper such as the *Birmingham Daily Post* could balance patriotism and American sympathies by celebrating that "in defence of a principle . . . England was prepared to take up arms" while still condemning the Confederate diplomats as representatives of "a slaveholding community" where "some of the Southern leaders . . . desire to re-establish the direct importation of negroes from Africa."[27]

Britain came closest to intervention during the summer and autumn of 1862. The baldest calls for intervention came from the zealous MP William Schaw Lindsay; during the July 1862 debate that he initiated in the House of Commons, he insisted that he "desired the disruption of the American Union, as every honest Englishman did, because it was too great a Power and England sh'd [sic] not let such a power exist on the American continent."[28] On the other hand, many British elites feared transatlantic war even if the Confederacy succeeded: Palmerston suspected the loss of Southern states would encourage Northerners to invade Canada, and his U.S. ambassador, Lord Lyons, felt that "three quarters of the American people are eagerly longing for a safe opportunity of making war with England."[29] Rather, as part of a united front with the Great Powers of Europe, Palmerston and Russell hoped to offer mediation and cow the Union from responding with a declaration of war.[30] This focus on international arbitration only serves to underline British politicians' disinclination for war. After Russia stood aloof, Garibaldi threatened war on Rome, the French government fell, and the British cabinet retreated from a formal intervention in October. In the end, any action seemed too costly—while inaction reinforced international legal precedents, which generally favored British influence around the world.[31]

Principles, as well as realpolitik, deterred British confrontation with the Union. The preliminary emancipation proclamation of September 1862 was directly motivated by U.S. anxieties about European interference in the war. The measure certainly did persuade, perhaps belatedly, the British and Foreign Anti-Slavery Society, the country's leading abolitionist group, to declare its sympathies with the Union in contradiction of its previous policy of neutrality and pacifism.[32] The society's reasons are telling, since they cited as final proof of the North's virtue not just the proclamation but progress on the slave-trade question. Indeed, Lincoln's emancipation policies formed part of a broader package of official and unofficial antislavery diplomacy in 1861–63. As his private correspondence makes clear, Palmerston had long wished to see a slave-trade suppression treaty as the principal proof of the Union's moral purpose in the Civil War. Approaching the Lincoln administration discreetly and giving them public credit for the initiative, Palmerston won the mutual right of search and established mixed commission courts to try suspected slavers in New York and Sierra Leone. The Lyons-Seward Treaty of 1862 offered further proof that the Union's emerging antislavery pretensions were sincere by breaking the Anglo-American-Spanish impasse over the traffic of enslaved Africans to Cuba.[33]

Wartime emancipation—for the slaves of rebels alone—did not impress British antislavery opinion as much as the northerners hoped.[34] Nor should the Lyons-Seward Treaty be given a prime causal role in British debates about the Civil War or the Palmerston ministry's response to it. Rather, the issue helps to illustrate Richard Blackett's conclusion that British public opinion fostered a multiplicity of explanations for the causes of disunion, hopes for promoting antislavery, and judgments of how to secure a peaceful, orderly return to transatlantic prosperity.[35]

Even after Lincoln's preliminary emancipation proclamation, British supporters saw Southern radicals' antebellum efforts to restore the slave trade from Africa as the best possible proof of Confederate immorality. Guarding against such accusations, a ban on the Atlantic slave trade in the Confederate constitution had sought to seduce British observers as well as Virginian slave-dealers.[36] However, in November 1862, the Irish economist John Elliot

Cairnes took to the pages of the *Daily News* to suggest that a victorious Confederate States of America would reopen the slave trade. Quickly, George McHenry, a delegate to the North Carolinian secession convention, responded that the cited discussion of reopening the slave trade had been met with laughter, not applause, by his fellow attendees; he sought to assure British readers that the Confederacy was every bit as committed to preventing the Atlantic slave trade as the United States.[37] The slave trade issue was a constant embarrassment to Southern propagandists, and in January 1863, two weeks after the Emancipation Proclamation was enacted, Confederate Secretary of State Judah P. Benjamin took action. He instructed his envoy L. Q. C. Lamar to explain to European powers that Southerners could not follow suit in freeing slaves because their constitution denied such powers to the executive branch. Intercepted by the United States, this memorandum was eagerly published as evidence of a Southern plot to delude Britons.[38] While this intrigue changed little in the realm of high politics, it strengthened pro-Northern efforts to paint Confederates as part of a vast pro-slavery conspiracy across the Americas.[39]

Whatever Benjamin's efforts, the conclusion of the Lyons-Seward Treaty made the slave trade issue a further liability for the Confederacy. As well as healing wounds inflicted over the *Trent* controversy, Seward's initiative helped remove a longstanding source of strain in Anglo-American relations before the 1860s. Within the Spanish Empire, a complex mix of domestic and metropolitan pressures turned elites against the slave trade, which Spain finally banned in 1867 after a rapid decline in the years beforehand.[40] While the Reformist party in Havana saw abolition as part of a larger project of free trade and democratic reform, the Marquis of Castell-Florite, captain-general of Cuba, enforced Spanish law with new zeal after his appointment in 1862.[41] None of these factors, involving Cuban or Spanish developments, registered in triumphant Anglo-American celebrations of a belated end to both the Atlantic slave trade and slaveholding within the United States.[42]

While the resolution of long-running arguments about slave-trade suppression removed a recurring cause of tension between Britain and the United States, it did nothing to resolve the broader tensions over influence in Latin America. The Civil War did not end the designs of the United States on Cuba and Central America, as British commentators such as Frederick Milne Edge and Ernest Jones predicted when they blamed aggression on proslavery interests. Rather, it removed the stigma of sectionalism from the ambitions William Walker had embodied.[43] Meanwhile, European meddling in Mexico during the early 1860s had further underscored the challenges of creating a balance of power favorable to British influence; the same hesitancy that marked official and popular responses to the Civil War also characterized Britons' attitudes to the Confederacy's southern neighbors.

American disunion allowed Anglo-Franco-Spanish intervention in Mexico without the usual fears of reprisal from Washington. Whatever the Monroe Doctrine meant, the Civil War muted it.[44] The Convention of London, in October 1861, declared Mexican failure to meet foreign loan repayments as the *casus belli*, but Palmerston admitted in private that "I do not know any arrangement that would be more advantageous for us" than stopping "the North Americans whether of the Federal or the Confederate States in their projected absorption of Mexico."[45] Hence, the invasion and promotion of regime change seemed to offer both stability and a counterbalance to American hegemony.[46] The famous explorer Richard Francis Burton was typical of British observers when he condemned Mexico in 1861 as "a miserable caricature of the Anglo-American federal Union."[47] As Nancy Barker has argued, monarchy—particularly under a European ruler—suited British, French, and Spanish politicians, who doubted a republic of "*les races latines*" could ever prosper internationally or defend themselves from North American neighbors. While a similar scheme for a coup, presented to Lord Clarendon in 1856, had seemed too provocative to win British backing, Mexico's crisis and America's distraction seemed to make action less risky.[48]

The invasion of republican Mexico did not represent an unambiguous victory for British plotting. Intervention was attractive as a way to counterbalance American aggression and the long-term concerns generated by the U.S. annexation of Texas.[49] However, it is fair to conclude that the 1861 London Convention "was designed only to limit Britain's risks and liabilities, not to hamper Napoleon's scheme."[50] The Mexican expedition reflected delicate, controversial judgments over which imperial anxieties or foreign concerns should reign paramount; British readers following the crisis in their newspapers doubtless had just as much trouble as politicians and editors in keeping straight the latest calculation of national interest. While bondholders pressed their personal interests, there was a wider, strategic context.[51] Some commentators had immediately rejected, on principle, this "offence against the law"; they took delight in declaring it "a blunder" when the extent of France's ambitions and deceptions became plain.[52]

Most Britons initially accepted their nation's role in the venture, but the sympathies of British newspapers faltered in early 1862 when rumors circulated that Napoleon had offered Austrian Archduke Maximilian the throne of Mexico. The radical *Reynolds's Newspaper* spoke for a broader constituency in wishing that "if the English people shall witness the perpetration of this gigantic crime without protesting against it, they deserve to get a Hapsburg or a Bourbon to rule over them."[53] Still, even after Britain had quit the tripartite alliance in April 1862, commentators took different views of whether their nation's influence in Mexico was better advanced alongside French or American interests. The *Ipswich Journal* welcomed France's gambit since "it cannot harm us to see France established in Mexico, and not on good terms with the North American Republic."[54] Meanwhile, Charles Lempriere, travelling in Mexico on a mission from financier Moses Montefiore during the invasion, warned his fellow Britons that they had "blundered out as we blundered into" the "foolish" and "fraudulent convention" of London. His pamphlet concluded that "England can safely and profitably build up trade and commerce" through the Mexican Liberals, whereas "the success of the Church or Monarchical party will seriously compromise the well-being of the United States" and French victory "must bring us into hostile collision, not only with Mexico, but with one or more of the great powers."[55]

SUCH A DISPUTE was typical of Britons' capacity to create new crises of authority whenever they addressed current dilemmas: seeking a counterbalance to one rival might easily prompt a new threat. Matthew Macfie, writing in 1865 about the prospects of British dominion in the Pacific, warned that the "erection of a barrier against the application of the Munro [sic] doctrine by the United States, and the development of the boundless resources of Mexico, are but subordinate acts" to be assayed against Napoleon III's railway "in progress from Vera Cruz in the Gulf of Mexico, and now rapidly approaches the city of Mexico." For him, the pleasure of confounding American power in Mexico weighed little against the threat from "rival European Powers multiplying means of communication with that [Pacific] ocean and busily laying foundations of future empires."[56]

However much observers differed in balancing French and U.S. influence in the Americas, they rarely showed much respect for Mexicans' political institutions or national sovereignty. In large part, racial contempt and anglophone prejudice left Britons with little faith in independent Latin American governance.[57] In 1868, the historian Lord Acton, lecturing at the Bridgnorth Literary and Scientific Institution, voiced this widespread contempt for "the degraded millions of the [Mexican] Indian race" who could not "overcome the mental incapacity, the want of enterprise, the want of combination." He looked back on the disastrous affair in Mexico and warned that an "ancient rivalry between France and England was expanded into the rivalry of the Latin with the Anglo-Saxon race." In welcoming the United States as "the children of our race" and anticipating "the time when the whole continent shall be theirs," Acton differed from those contemporaries with a more skeptical view of the errant republic. However, in thinking about Mexico and other crises of the 1860s in terms of continental dominion, racial solidarity, and British preeminence, he was far more typical.[58]

THIS PRESUMPTION OF EUROPEAN superiority and white rule also marked Britain's greatest colonial crisis of the 1860s, when the brutal massacre of black Jamaicans triggered a crisis of imperial authority and metropolitan outcry. Since the British emancipation of slaves in the West Indies in 1834–38, efforts to restrict "the amount of land the negro population has been able to secure for squatting" led to black resentment.[59] Land and labor laws framed the terms of emancipation, directing black Britons into plantation cultivation for exports and so ensuring that they only used their liberty as the Colonial Office had intended.[60] In 1865, the secretary of the Baptist Missionary Society, Edward Underhill, raised the concerns of his fellow pilgrims with Colonial Secretary Edward Cardwell, blaming the island's "stupid legislature". When asked to prepare a response, the civil servant Henry Taylor blamed the black population, not the white-dominated assembly or Governor Edward Eyre, for the commonplace poverty, ill health, and resentment in the once-prosperous colony. Fatefully, Taylor's advice that "it is from their own industry and prudence in availing themselves of the means of prosperity that are before them" was adapted by Eyre for publication as "Queen's Advice" and promulgated throughout Jamaica.[61]

The effect was incendiary, framing the response of black Jamaicans to a local confrontation in the town of Morant Bay, St. Thomas parish. A local court case over land tenure escalated rapidly when magistrates issued arrest warrants for those protesting against restrictions on black farming. On October 11, 1865, soldiers opened fire on the preacher Paul Bogle and a crowd of supporters who were challenging the orders for his arrest. In the subsequent reprisals, "Soldiers and militiamen seem to have regarded all blacks in the affected areas as enemies and subject to immediate retribution," killing more than 400 and burning a thousand homes.[62] When news of these recriminations reached Britain, Governor Eyre and his apologists blamed missionaries such as Underhill, but particularly Charles Gordon, a black assembly member with whom he had frequently clashed. In arresting Gordon, taking him into an area of martial law, and executing him, Eyre won widespread condemnation. A famous "war of representation" over the events in Jamaica drew a host of celebrities into debate conflict, including Charles Dickens and Thomas Carlyle, who were defending Eyre, and J. S. Mill and John Bright, who were prosecuting him. This created drama for the British public. Black Jamaicans reportedly believed that "the Queen is angry, and that all the officials who, in the suppression of the riots, treated them with so much severity, will be hanged."[63] Indeed, the government declined to bring charges against Eyre, and in 1868 the "Jamaica Committee" failed in their final effort to bring a private prosecution against Eyre, who retired on his government pension.[64]

In these metropolitan debates the rule of law loomed larger than any particular interest in Jamaicans. For years afterwards, British elites shared rumors that the insurrection was pre-meditated and that "the white women were to be distributed among the blacks." The virulence and violence of Eyre and his defenders tapped into old fears of slave insurrections and fears that nearby Haiti offered a template for black Jamaicans to take independence by force. Indeed, Haitians associated with the exiled Emperor Soulouque were spuriously blamed as "chief instigators" of the unrest.[65] For his defenders—in Britain and Jamaica—the governor's decisive action had prevented another Haitian revolution and confirmed their belief that the common man in Jamaica was not yet "a black Anglo-Saxon" ready for civilized, consensual government.[66]

INDEED, IF EYRE's detractors and defenders disagreed on the morality or legality of his actions, then they differed remarkably little in their expectations for black Jamaicans and their capacity for self-government. British controversy over Morant Bay ran in parallel with American debates about black suffrage and citizenship after emancipation.[67] The Colonial Office did not follow America's example by enhancing the representation of black or mixed-race politicians such as the late Charles Gordon in the House of Assembly, where candidates were restricted to wealthy—and for the most-part white—elites, even if the electorate was majority black. Rather, the Colonial Office abolished the representative chamber altogether.[68]

"I look upon the abolition of that body, which acted as a clog on every good measure that was proposed, as a turning-point in the history of the colony," the Marquess of Lorne concluded from his visit shortly afterward.[69] In fact, the British government's abolition of the assembly and return to direct crown rule won widespread support. Henry Clarke, a curate in Westmoreland, Jamaica, wrote to the Paris Anti-Slavery Conference of 1867 to share his diagnosis that "emancipation ought to be dated from 1865, not 1834, for while an oligarchy of old slave-owners held the supreme power, it was ridiculous to call the people free."[70] The humanitarian Secretary to the Royal Commission, Charles Savile Roundell, argued that "an elective representative assembly is, in fact, the conflict of the white and coloured races, an oligarchic tyranny veiled in a popular dress." However, he fully endorsed "the necessity of measures for preventing vagrancy, for regulating native settlements, for encouraging settled industry," and so differed from Jamaican planters in the means and degrees, not the ends, of his prescription.[71]

Britons remained divided over whether the former planters or the former slaves had proven to be the real "savages" in the rebellion, but this crisis of the 1860s fixed a surprising consensus against self-government in black majority colonies.[72] An opponent of Governor Eyre, and an enthusiastic pro-Union advocate, such as the Oxford Regius Professor of History Goldwyn Smith, felt—in America or Jamaica—that there could not be "political equality without social fusion" nor could there be "social fusion while the difference of color and the physical antipathy remain." While, in one of Britain's American colonies, metropolitan authority was strengthened, politicians supported the very opposite in another. The reinforcement of white rule in the British West Indies marked an important moment in "drawing the global colour line" since the same period saw new enthusiasm for colonial self-rule in white Canada.[73]

WHEN NEWS OF THE Morant Bay uprising reached Europe in November 1865, warning that "negroes are committing characteristic atrocities on the whites," it was accompanied by reassurance that British military "reinforcements from Halifax," Nova Scotia, were en route to quell the rebellion. The immediate role of British troops from Canada in restoring "order" mirrored a long-term disjuncture in metropolitan views of British North America and the former slave colonies.[74] Indeed, at the same time that representative institutions were abolished in multiracial Jamaica, Parliament acknowledged new freedoms for white Canadians (even though a minority, regrettably, spoke French rather than English). A crisis of colonial government in Canada was prompted not by rebellion but anxieties over the colony's prospects in comparison (or competition) with the United States. Before the Civil War, Henry Ashworth warned that Americans would "run away with an undue share" of the commerce, energy, and emigration that "could have been retained to Canada" without serious liberal reforms.[75] For his part, the travelling sportsman Grantley Berkeley in 1861 predicted the disintegration of the Union and celebrated evidence that Canadian fields were "better laid out and fenced . . . and as to sheep, the superiority of breed was at once observable."[76]Authors boosting the attractions of emigration to the United States or Canada for readers back home naturally disagreed for more practical and less cerebral reasons.[77]

Traditionally presumed to be a pragmatic response to governance crises within Lower and Upper Canada and fears about American invasion or Fenian Raids, the July 1, 1867, Confederation of Canada has generated a rich and lively historiographical debate in recent years.[78] Scholars now approach the creation of Britain's first "dominion"—formed from Canada West and Canada East, Nova Scotia, and New Brunswick—as an ideological choice, though they identify radically different motives.[79] Peter J. Smith proposes that confederation was forged from *laissez-faire* commercial pressures rather than bureaucratic inevitability or defensive paranoia.[80] Andrew Smith, following the "gentlemanly capitalism" approach to British imperialism, sees the politics of confederation eased by the pressure of financial interests in London and Canada. The interests of lobby groups such as the British North American Association complemented ideological concerns for a "constitutional political economy" that would support prosperity.[81] What these interpretations share is an emphasis on a contest of metropolitan and colonial concerns in light of larger continental and imperial anxieties.[82]

What remains certain is that the American Civil War created a brief and rare period when British migrants to North America headed for Canada rather than the United States. This aberrant period, though, confirmed long-term imperial insecurities about Canada's inferiority to the peacetime United States.[83] In debating and imagining a future for Canada, metropolitan Britons confronted their uncertainties over whether the United States would be an ally or rival in the sustenance of British power across the continent. William Barrington feared American "consciousness of immense national strength, coupled with the natural pride of having proven to the world that by that strength they are both able and determined to maintain their national unity." This, he suspected, might lead the United States to support Fenian conspiracies, cloaked in the same neutrality behind which Confederate supporters had operated in Britain during the Civil War.[84] More concretely, the suspension of the Reciprocity Treaty of free trade with America, in 1865, focused Britons on both sides of the Atlantic on a slow-burning crisis of Canada's comparative under-development.[85] Hence, many advocates of confederation hoped it would create a dynamic, self-governing polity to rival the republicans to the south.[86]

From a very different point of view, the Liberal MP Charles Dilke was, at the time of confederation, engaged in a journey that "followed England round the world: everywhere I was in English-speaking, or in English-governed lands." As Duncan Bell suggests, Dilke's best-selling travelogue and manifesto, *Greater Britain*, was emblematic of broader fancies of future world dominance by Britons and the pretension that "through America, England is speaking to the world"—though Dilke's contradictions are as representative as his consistencies.[87] Writing shortly after the 1867 U.S. purchase of Alaska from Russia, he noted with alarm that "a map of North America has been published in which the name of the Great Republic sprawls across the continent from the Behring Straits to Mexico, with the 'E' in 'United' ominously near Vancouver Island, and the 'T' actually planted upon British territory."[88] Suspicions of William Seward's desires to acquire British Columbia would lead to its confederation into Canada in 1871.[89] Yet, by contrast, Dilke's preferred solution was to make Canadians truly independent and encourage rapprochement, not rivalry, with the prodigal United States. Declaring that "we are no more fellow-countrymen of the Canadians than of the Americans of the North or West," he concluded that the progress of the British immigrants leading both countries was hampered by American jealousy and Canadian conceit at the prospect of Old World interference in North America.[90]

Radical thinkers, such as Goldwyn Smith, similarly imagined joint U.S.-Canadian citizenship in a reunited North America. However, this view was roundly mocked by Secretary for the Colonies Edward Cardwell when he presented the Canadian confederation plan to Parliament.[91] The key division among these Britons lay in how far the political dominion of formal empire hindered or fostered imperial power across the continent. The Canadian confederation stirred metropolitan anxieties and official concerns on this question, and historians have grown increasingly alert to this contemporary debate and the strength of real—rather than imagined—community. Scholars can trace an "Anglosphere" that extended across and beyond the borders of the Empire, with the United States as part of—or partner in—the nineteenth-century "British world," thanks to the ties of family, culture, and language—perhaps an "Honorary Dominion" in Tony Hopkins's playful phrase.[92] These scholarly interpretations mirror Victorian political discussion of the 1860s; the reality of social, economic, linguistic, and cultural intercourse challenged Britons to resolve how far their power would be advanced under the stars and stripes. Discussion of the future of Latin America, the British West Indies, and the "Anglo-Saxon" peoples of North America all raised questions about the future and the form of British dominion.[93] As Gary Magee and Andrew Thompson conclude, "The sense that America was a part of the British diaspora was real, but it was also ambivalent, open to dispute by contemporaries, and it eroded over time."[94]

The divisive matter of Canadian-American relations turned on global, as well as continental, questions of British influence. Anticipation of the Pacific coast's potential to carry commerce into Asia shaped, as we have seen, perspectives on the Mosquito Coast and the invasion of Mexico. For Foster Barham Zincke, an East Anglian vicar, educational reformer, and Jamaican planter's son, the future domination of the Pacific by the United States meant that the "the circuit of the world has been completed." He traced for readers of his 1867 travelogue how Aryans, originating in India, became "the grandest race the world had seen" in England, so that "America is peopled with that which is most enterprising and progressive in that race in which these qualities had been mostly highly developed." For Zincke, "The hardy, the inventive, the go-ahead American looks out on the Pacific and towards that side of the old continent from which his first ancestors started on the long career which in his person is consummated."[95]

This racial myth was also deployed by those who doubted whether the United States was the vehicle for Anglo-Saxon domination of the Pacific world. The Congregationalist minister Matthew Macfie demanded a transcontinental railroad through Canada because "the tide of human migration that has since the creation of our race been rolling westward from Asia, still advances restlessly towards the lands of the setting sun, undeterred by the turbulent waters of the Atlantic or the lonely wilds of the great American continent."[96] Though his mission to the Pacific coast had been most notable for his exclusion of black settlers from full participation in worship, Macfie's book instead focused on his ambitions for international cooperation under British leadership.[97] He promised Britons back home, in his 1865 account of five years on the Pacific coast, that the "free-port system" in Victoria, "taken in connection with our exports of timber and fish, which meet with a profitable and increasing market in China," promised "a vast emporium for Eastern commerce."[98]

In harking back to the origins of Caucasians in Asia, Zincke and Macfie played on the powerful myths of "Anglo-Saxon" racial supremacy, developed from the Comte de Gobineau's Aryan myths published in the 1850s.[99] This circumlocution of the globe by an ever-more-perfect race differed on whether the United States was a renegade rival or energetic subcontractor for such ambitions. This division, over how far imperial power was safely outsourced, signaled a fundamental division between Britons studying the crises of the 1860s. Zincke and Macfie agreed that Canadians were "not yet a people" and "unlike their neighbours, they are not possessed with the idea, that if they will only give themselves the trouble to attempt it, they can make anything bear its proper fruit."[100] Where they disagreed was in Zincke's further claim that "[a]n Englishman cannot feel towards Americans as he does towards Italians or Frenchmen. Wherever in America he sees a piece of land being cleared and settled, or a church or a school being built, he looks as if something were being done by and for his own countrymen."[101]

While British audiences split between these two extremes, over whether Canada should be developed or abandoned, there was little political appetite for financing the infrastructure and ambition necessary to develop Pacific Canada.[102] The delicate negotiations over confederation obscured the reality that, as Thomas Rawlings suggested in 1867, "the interests and future welfare of the British Crown" depended on uniting "our noblest sisterhood by tying them together with iron bands, and making them one in the great object they seek to obtain" of traversing the continent.[103] Rather than building new solidarities, Britain's transfer of Rupertsland from the Hudson Bay Company to the new Canada, in 1869, provoked the "Red River Rebellion" by mixed-heritage Métis fearing Ontarian migrants would pass through their intervening territory in a rush west.[104] Colonel Wolseley's subsequent expedition to subjugate the Francophone rebels "carried and asserted the power of Great Britain to the far west while opening up a virgin soil for her sons in a distant land," as one British officer told his audience at the Royal United Services Institute after his return to London. However, while the 1870 absorption of the Red River territory, as Manitoba, certainly "added yet another province to that Empire on which the sun never sets," it did not secure Canadian supremacy over the continent.[105]

UNCERTAIN BRITISH DESIGNS for Canadian confederation and Pacific expansion reflect the messy patterns in policies towards American upheavals of the 1860s, as the crises of the Americas coincided with Britain's crises of empire in the Americas. More broadly, confederation left unresolved the competing visions for Canada's relationship with the United States, just as British debate and elite policymaking struggled to balance the Empire's broader interactions with the errant former colony. Duncan Bell fruitfully suggests that dreams of a "Greater Britain" and resistance to it reflected broader anxieties about "the way in which both Britain and the empire were conceived (through a reconsideration of the relationship between the two), and in so doing they challenged the boundaries, language, and traditions of British political thought."[106] We might broaden this conclusion to note how discussion of international challenges in the 1860s revealed divergent ambitions and ideologies, though the desirability of British political and commercial influence was a consistent presumption.[107]

British strategies and fantasies of influence in the Americas—from Honduras to Havana, from Virginia to Veracruz, and from Morant Bay to Montreal—revealed disagreements over means and, to a lesser extent, the ends of foreign policy. Crises in these different theatres revealed tensions between British anxieties to preserve dominion—meaning preeminence and prosperity—and pluralist pressures on the boundaries of race, territory, and authority within the British Empire. The lure of Pacific riches meant that the various crises we have examined were marked by concerns that a rival power would monopolize transcontinental routes, be they by canal or rail.[108] This complemented a broader interest in maintaining British influence by diluting the power of any particular rival.

Yet, in the cacophony of British views, we may trace the impossibility of balancing contradictory impulses to preserve prosperity, peace, and power in the Americas. Encouraging the revival of European empire in Mexico, welcoming the Confederacy as rival to the Union, or supporting Spanish rule in Cuba did not make for complementary strategy; in navigating crises tactically, the British government and their opinionated citizens made an art of stumbling inconsistency and inadvertent self-harm. If Britons divided over each of the crises we have studied, they did not divide consistently along ideological, partisan, or geostrategic lines. On the Mosquito Coast, in Cuba, in the Civil War, in Mexico, in Jamaica, and in Canada, Britons found different questions at stake and hence came to very different answers as to how their nation should respond.

At the same time that the cotton famine and military incidents, such as Confederate raids on Vermont from Canada, the *Trent* affair, and the *Alabama* controversy, generated crises in Anglo-American relations, deference and indecision during the Civil War underlined the long-term weakness of British influence in the Western Hemisphere.[109] In the 1860s, we can trace a dim awareness of "the undoubted supremacy of one great power with the actual independence of many lesser ones" across the continents. More and more, Britons queried how, not if, their nation's power could complement or direct American preeminence.[110] Subsequent decades saw "inter-imperialism" underpinned by "capacious cultured depth—based in language, literature, and race—that could accommodate interconnected empires."[111]

The 1867 invention of a Dominion of Canada reflected the reality that British dominion over the continent was waning. The contrasting experiences of Canada and Jamaica underline a dilemma over how empire would flourish in the Americas. Resisting black rule in Jamaica and encouraging dynamic nation building in Canada, the British Empire struggled to accommodate those forces of democracy and racial supremacy that the republican form of government, as Americans proved, was so adept at sustaining. Crises, while apparently averted, did not defuse the larger challenges for each of the multiracial, multinational empires of Britain and the United States, constricted in their development both by the exclusionary prejudices of hierarchical authority and the responsive desire for political consent. Pulled in these directions and uncertain of how to sustain white rule after abolishing slavery, the projection and illusion of British political power in the Americas was dimming even as commercial links, especially to the United States and Brazil, brightened.[112] Britain's manifestly partial dominion over the Americas diverged from the "manifest destiny" of the United States in achievement rather than the challenges it faced in the 1860s. The decade confirmed and accelerated the waning influence of a monarchical, European empire and the rising power of the republican, American empire.

Suggested Readings

Blackett, Richard. *Divided Hearts: Britain and the American Civil War*. Baton Rouge: Louisiana State University Press, 2001.

Bourne, Kenneth. *Britain and the Balance of Power in North America, 1815–1908*. Berkeley: University of California Press, 1967.

Campbell, D. A. *English Public Opinion and the American Civil War*. Woodbridge, Suffolk: Boydell, 2003.

Hall, Catherine. *Civilising Subjects: Metropole and Colony in the English Imagination, 1830–1867*. Oxford: Polity, 2002.

Heuman, Gad. *"The Killing Time": The Morant Bay Rebellion in Jamaica*. London: Macmillan, 1994.

Huzzey, Richard. *Freedom Burning: Anti-Slavery and Empire in Victorian Britain*. Ithaca, NY: Cornell University Press, 2012.

Jones, Howard. *Blue & Gray Diplomacy: A History of Union and Confederate Foreign Relations*. Chapel Hill: University of North Carolina Press, 2010.

Magee, Gary B. and Andrew S. Thompson. *Empire and Globalisation: Networks of People, Goods and Capital in the British World, c. 1850–1914*. Cambridge: Cambridge University Press, 2010.

May, Robert J., ed. *The Union, the Confederacy, and the Atlantic Rim*. West Lafayette, IN: Purdue University Press, 1995.

Notes

1. Laurence Oliphant, *Patriots and Filibusters, or Incidents of Political and Exploratory Travel* (Edinburgh and London: Blackwood, 1860), 133.

2. See John Darwin, *The Empire Project: The Rise and Fall of the British World-System* (Cambridge: Cambridge University Press, 2010), 24–60.

3. Regis A. Courtemanche, "The Royal Navy and the End of William Walker," *The Historian* 30 (1968): 350–65; Robert E. May, *Manifest Destiny's Underworld: Filibustering in Antebellum America* (Chapel Hill: University of North Carolina Press, 2002), 244–48.

4. Thomas Schoonover, "Napoleon Is Coming! Maximilian Is Coming?" in *The Union, the Confederacy, and the Atlantic Rim*, ed. Robert J. May (West Lafayette, IN: Purdue University Press, 1995), 101–30, at 105–11.

5. As quoted by *Glasgow Herald*, October 19, 1860, 6.

6. *London Review*, October 20, 1860, 365; *London Review*, October 27, 1860, 386.

7. Kenneth Bourne, *Britain and the Balance of Power in North America, 1815–1908* (Berkeley: University of California Press, 1967), 176–77; Richard W. Van Alstyne, "British Diplomacy and the Clayton-Bulwer Treaty, 1850–60," *Journal of Modern History* 11 (1939): 149–83.

8. Oliphant, *Patriots and Filibusters*, 190.

9. Ibid., 208–9.

10. Ibid., 221–22.

11. See, for example, Sargent Fitzwilliam, *England, the United States, and the Southern Confederacy*, 2nd ed. (London: Hamilton, Adams, and Co, 1864), 63, and *Report of the Speeches of the Rev. Ward Beecher, Delivered at Public Meetings in Manchester, Glasgow, Edinburgh, Liverpool, and London* (Manchester: Union and Emancipation Society, 1864), 57.

12. For diplomatic aspects, see Howard Jones, *Abraham Lincoln and a New Birth of Freedom: The Union and Slavery in the Diplomacy of the Civil War* (Lincoln: University of Nebraska Press, 1999), 65–67; Howard Jones, *Blue & Gray Diplomacy: A History of Union and Confederate Foreign Relations* (Chapel Hill: University of North Carolina Press, 2010); Jay Sexton, *Debtor Diplomacy: Finance and American Foreign Relations in the Civil War Era 1837–1873* (Oxford: Oxford University Press, 2005). The best general analyses of British opinion and the Civil War are Richard Blackett, *Divided Hearts: Britain and the American Civil War* (Baton Rouge: Louisiana State University Press, 2001), and D. A. Campbell, *English Public Opinion and the American Civil War* (Woodbridge: Boydell, 2003).

13. Richard Huzzey, *Freedom Burning: Anti-Slavery and Empire in Victorian Britain* (Ithaca, NY: Cornell University Press, 2012), 57.

14. Richard Fulton, "The London *Times* and the Anglo-American Boarding Dispute of 1858," *Nineteenth-Century Contexts* 17 (1993): 133–44.

15. Richard Huzzey, "The Politics of Slave-Trade Suppression," in *British Suppression of the Transatlantic Slave Trade: Policies, Practices and Representations of Naval*

Coercion, ed. Robert Burroughs and Richard Huzzey (Manchester: Manchester University Press, 2015), 17–52, at 24.

16. Douglas R. Egerton, "Rethinking Atlantic Historiography in a Postcolonial Era: The Civil War in a Global Perspective," *Journal of Civil War Era* 1 (2011): 79–95, at 86.

17. David Eltis, *Economic Growth and the Ending of the Transatlantic Slave Trade* (Oxford: Oxford University Press, 1987), 210–13.

18. Henry Ashworth, *A Tour in the United States, Cuba, and Canada: A Course of Lectures Delivered Before the Members of the Bolton Mechanics' Institution* (London and Manchester: Bennett, Pitman and Heywood, 1861), 62–66.

19. Huzzey, *Freedom Burning*, 120–28.

20. Huzzey, "Politics," 38–43.

21. Frederick Milnes Edge, *Slavery Doomed, or, The Contest between Free and Slave Labour in the United States* (London: Smith, Elder and Co., 1860), 223, see vii on residence.

22. As quoted by David R. Murray, *Odious Commerce: Britain, Spain and the Abolition of the Cuban Slave Trade* (Cambridge: Cambridge University Press, 1980), 300.

23. Huzzey, *Freedom Burning*, 24–30.

24. Sven Beckert, "Emancipation and Empire: Reconstructing the Worldwide Web of Cotton Production in the Age of the American Civil War," *American Historical Review* 109 (2004): 1405–38; Egerton, "Rethinking Atlantic Historiography," 83–84.

25. James McPherson, *Battle Cry of Freedom: The Civil War Era* (Oxford: Oxford University Press, 1988), 386.

26. W. L. Morton, "British North America and a Continent in Dissolution, 1861–71," *History* 47 (1962): 139–56, at 148.

27. *Birmingham Daily Post*, January 31, 1862, 2.

28. As quoted by Jones, *Abraham Lincoln and a New Birth of Freedom*, 81.

29. As quoted by Bourne, *Britain and the Balance of Power*, 257.

30. Howard Jones, *Blue and Gray Diplomacy*, 204–5; Don H. Doyle, *The Cause of All Nations: An International History of the American Civil War* (New York: Basic Books, 2015), 221–26.

31. Peter Thompson, "The Case of the Missing Hegemon: British Nonintervention in the American Civil War," *Security Studies* 16 (2007): 96–132; Doyle, *Cause of All Nations*, 231–36.

32. *The Crisis in the United States* (London: British and Foreign Anti-Slavery Society, 1862), 2.

33. Huzzey, "Politics," 38–43; Eugene H. Berwanger, *The British Foreign Service and the American Civil War* (Lexington: University Press of Kentucky, 1994), 33–34.

34. Jones, *Blue and Gray Diplomacy*, 207.

35. R. J. M. Blackett, *Divided Hearts: Britain and the American Civil War* (Baton Rouge: Louisiana State University Press, 2001).

36. Huzzey, *Freedom Burning*, 56–57.

37. Their letters are collected in *The Southern Confederacy and the African Slave Trade* (Dublin: McGlashan and Gill, 1863).

38. *The African Slave Trade: The Secret Purpose of the Insurgents to Revive It* (Philadelphia: Sherman, Son & Co., 1863).

39. "An American," *England, the United States, and the Southern Confederacy* (London: Hamilton, Adams, and Co., 1863), 24–29.

40. Christopher Schmidt-Nowara, *Empire and Antislavery: Spain, Cuba, and Puerto Rico, 1833–1874* (Pittsburgh: University of Pittsburgh University Press, 1999), 102–3.

41. Vanessa Michelle Ziegler, "The Revolt of 'the Ever-faithful Isle': The Ten Years' War in Cuba, 1868–1878," PhD thesis, University of California, Santa Barbara, 11–12, 110; Murray, *Odious Commerce*, 325–26.

42. Richard Huzzey, "Minding Civilisation in 1867: A Case Study in British Imperial Culture and Victorian Anti-Slavery," *Journal of Imperial and Commonwealth History* 40 (2012): 807–25.

43. Edge, *Slavery Doomed*, 207; Ernest Jones, *The Slaveholder's War: A Lecture Delivered in the Town Hall, Ashton-Under-Lyne* (Ashton-Under-Lyne: Union and Emancipation Society, 1863).

44. Jay Sexton, *The Monroe Doctrine: Empire and Nation in Nineteenth-Century America* (New York: Hill and Wang, 2011), 140–51; Jones, *Blue and Gray Diplomacy*, 75–80.

45. As quoted by Bourne, *Britain and the Balance of Power*, 255.

46. Schoonover, "Napoleon Is Coming!" 117–18.

47. Richard Francis Burton, *The City of the Saints, and Across the Rocky Mountain to California* (London: Longman, 1861; New York: Harper, 1862), 501.

48. Nancy Barker, "Monarchy in Mexico: Harebrained Scheme or Well-Considered Prospect?" *Journal of Modern History* 48 (March 1976): 51–68, at 60, 63–65.

49. Lelia M. Roeckell, "Bonds over Bondage: British Opposition to the Annexation of Texas," *Journal of the Early Republic* 19 (1999): 257–78.

50. Bourne, *Britain and the Balance of Power*, 256.

51. Richard Garde, *A Letter to the Right Honourable Earl Russell, on the Absolute Right of the Mexican Boldholders, Who Are Subjects of Her Most Gracious Majesty* (London: Letts, Son & Co., 1861); Barbara A. Tenebaum, "Merchants, Money, and Mischief, The British in Mexico, 1821–1862," *The Americas* 35 (1979): 317–39.

52. *Dundee Courier and Argus*, January 30, 1862, 2.

53. *Reynolds's Newspaper*, February 16, 1862, 3. See also *Leeds Mercury*, January 29, 1862, 2; *York Herald*, February 8, 1862, 8; *Leeds Mercury*, February 13, 1862, 2; *Examiner*, February 15, 1862, 1.

54. *Ipswich Journal*, May 24, 1862, 5.

55. Charles Lempriere, *Notes in Mexico: In 1861 and 1862; Politically and Socially Considered* (London: Longman, 1862), 389–90, 420–21. See A. T. S. Goodrick, rev. H. C. G. Matthew, "Charles Lempriere," in *Oxford Dictionary of National Biography*, ed. Laurence Goldman (Oxford: Oxford University Press, 2004–14), http://www.oxforddnb.com/view/article/34493 (accessed 25 Aug. 2014).

56. Matthew Macfie, *Vancouver Island and British Columbia: Their History, Resources and Prospects* (London: Longman, 1865), 366–68.

57. Nancy N. Barker, "The Factor of 'Race' in the French Experience in Mexico, 1821–1861," *Hispanic American Historical Review* 59 (1979): 64–80, at 76–78.

58. Lord Acton, "The Rise and Fall of the Mexican Empire" (1868) in *Historical Essays and Studies*, ed. John Neville Giggis and Reginald Vere Laurence (London: Macmillan, 1907), 144–45, 151.

59. Marquess of Lorne, *A Trip to the Tropics and Home Through America* (London: Hurst and Blackett, 1867), 33.

60. Thomas C. Holt, *The Problem of Freedom: Race, Labor, and Politics in Jamaica and Britain, 1832–1938* (Baltimore: Johns Hopkins University Press, 1992); Richard Huzzey, "Concepts of Liberty: Freedom, Laissez-Faire and the State after Britain's Abolition of Slavery" in *Emancipation and the Remaking of the British Imperial World*, ed. Catherine Hall, Nicholas Draper, and Keith McClelland (Manchester: Manchester University Press, 2014), 149–71.

61. As quoted by Catherine Hall, *Civilising Subjects: Metropole and Colony in the English Imagination, 1830–1867* (Oxford: Polity, 2002), 243–44.

62. Gad Heuman, *"The Killing Time": The Morant Bay Rebellion in Jamaica* (London: Macmillan, 1994), quotation at 38; Bernard Semmel, *Jamaican Blood and Victorian Conscience: The Governor Eyre Controversy* (Westport, CT: Greenwood Press, 1976 [1962]), 41–48; Holt, *Problem of Freedom*, 302.

63. Lorne, *Trip*, 75.

64. Hall, *Civilising Subjects*, 107–9; Catherine Hall, "The Economy of Intellectual Prestige: Thomas Carlyle, John Stuart Mill, and the Case of Governor Eyre," *Cultural Critique* 12 (1989): 167–96; Semmel, *Jamaican Blood and Victorian Conscience*, 167–68.

65. Ibid., 5–6.

66. Hall, *Civilising Subjects*, 256.

67. Richard Huzzey, "British Liberties, American Emancipation, and the Democracy of Race" in *The American Experiment and the Idea of Democracy in British Culture, 1776–1914*, ed. Ella Dzelzainis and Ruth Livesey (Aldershot, UK: Ashgate, 2013), 121–34.

68. Huzzey, "British Liberties," 131–33.

69. Lorne, *Trip*, 145.

70. *Special Report of the Anti-Slavery Conference, Held in Paris* (London: British and Foreign Anti-Slavery Society, 1867), 74. See also Thomas Harvey and William Brewin, *Jamaica in 1866: A Narrative of a Tour through the Island* (London: A. W. Bennett, 1867), 73.

71. Charles Savile Roundell, *England and Her Subject-Races, with Special Reference to Jamaica* (London: Macmillan and Co., 1866), 31–32.

72. Huzzey, "Minding Civilisation."

73. As quoted by Marilyn Lake and Henry Reynolds, *Drawing the Global Colour Line: White Men's Countries and the International Challenge of Racial Equality* (Cambridge: Cambridge University Press, 2008), 55.

74. *Dundee Courier and Argus*, November 11, 1865, 2.

75. Ashworth, *Tour*, 166–67.

76. Grantley Berkeley, *The English Sportsman in the Western Prairies* (London: Hurst and Blackett, 1861), 2, 390, 430–32.

77. William Hancock, *An Emigrant's Five Years in the Free States of America* (London: T. C. Newby, 1860), 233; William Fraser, *The Emigrant's Guide: Or, Sketches of Canada, with Some of the Northern and Western States of America* (Glasgow: Porteous Brothers, 1867), 39–47.

78. Robin W. Winks, *The Civil War Years: Canada and the United States* (Baltimore: Johns Hopkins University Press, 1960; Montreal and Toronto: McGill-Queens University Press, 1998), 338–58; Andrew Smith, "Toryism, Classical Liberalism, and Capitalism: The Politics of Taxation and the Struggle for Canadian Confederation," *Canadian Historical Review* 89 (2008): 1–25, at 4–5.

79. Philip Buckner, "The Maritimes and Confederation: A Reassessment," *Canadian Historical Review* 71 (1990): 1–30, at 24.

80. Peter J. Smith, "The Ideological Origins of Canadian Confederation," *Canadian Journal of Political Science* 20 (1987): 3–29.

81. Andrew Smith, *British Businessmen and Canadian Confederation: Constitution Making in an Era of Anglo-Globalization* (Montreal: McGill-Queens University Press, 2008), esp. 3–7, 27–31, 47–49.

82. Ged Martin, *Britain and the Origins of Canadian Confederation, 1837–67* (Vancouver: University of British Columbia Press, 1995), 126–34, 293–95.

83. Ibid., 85, 88.

84. William Barrington, *Reflections on Some of the Results of the Late American War* (Dublin: R.D. Webb and Son, 1866), 36.

85. Thomas Rawlings, *The Confederation of the British North American Provinces: Their Past History and Future Prospects* (London: Sampson Low, Son and Marston, 1865), 138–48.

86. Smith, *British Businessman*, 53–59, 64–70.

87. Charles Dilke, *Greater Britain: A Record of Travel in English-Speaking Countries during 1866 and 1867*, 2 vols. (London: Macmillan, 1869), quotations from vol. 1, vii–viii; Duncan Bell, *The Idea of Greater Britain: Empire and the Future of World Order, 1860–1900* (Princeton, NJ: Princeton University Press, 2007).

88. Dilke, *Greater Britain*, 1:73.

89. David E. Shi, "Seward's Attempt to Annex British Columbia, 1865–1869," *Pacific Historical Review* 47 (1978): 217–38.

90. Dilke, *Greater Britain*, 1:80.

91. As quoted by Fraser, *Emigrant's Guide*, 56–57.

92. James Belich, *Replenishing the Earth: The Settler Revolution and the Rise of the Anglo-World* (Oxford: Oxford University Press, 2009), esp. 65–67; Gary B. Magee and Andrew S. Thompson, *Empire and Globalisation: Networks of People, Goods and Capital in the British World, c. 1850–1914* (Cambridge: Cambridge University Press, 2010); A. G. Hopkins, "The United States, 1783–1861: Britain's Honorary Dominion?" *Britain and the World* 4 (2011): 232–46. They are more subtle than the "Anglo-globalisation"

posited by Niall Ferguson, *Empire: How Britain made the Modern World* (London: Penguin, 2003), xxii.

93. For the "Anglo-Scandinavian" as an alternative, see Burton, *City of the Saints*, xi.

94. Thompson and Magee, *Empire and Globalisation*, 19.

95. F. Barham Zincke, *Last Winter in the United States, Being Table Talk Collected during a Tour through the Late Southern Confederation, the Far West, Rocky Mountains &c.* (London: John Murray, 1868), 28–29.

96. Macfie, *Vancouver Island*, 335.

97. R. W. Winks, *The Blacks in Canada*, 2nd ed. (Montreal: Queens-McGill Press, 1997), 281–82.

98. Macfie, *Vancouver Island*, 335–36.

99. Penelope Edwards, " 'I Followed England Round the World': The Rise of Trans-Imperial Anglo-Saxon Exceptionalism, and the Spatial Narratives of Nineteenth-Century British Settler Colonies of the Pacific Rim," in *Re-Orientating Whiteness*, ed. Leigh Boucher, Jane Carey, and Katherine Ellinghaus (New York: Palgrave, 2009), 99–118; Gregory Blue, "Gobineau on China: Race Theory, the 'Yellow Peril', and the Critique of Modernity," *Journal of World History* 10 (1999): 93–139, at 100–103. Many thanks to Stuart Semmel for suggesting the influence of Gobineau on this common motif.

100. Zincke, *Last Winter*, 273. He referred to Upper Canada.

101. Ibid., 297.

102. On the failure of settling the Canadian West, see Belich, *Replenishing the Earth*, 406–9.

103. Rawlings, *Confederation*, 135–37.

104. Darwin, *Empire Project*, 149.

105. G. L. Huyshe, "The Red River Expedition," *Royal United Services Institution Journal* 15 (1871): 70–84.

106. Duncan Bell, "The Victorian idea of a Global State," in *Victorian Visions of Global Order: Empire and International Relations in Nineteenth-Century Political Thought*, ed. Duncan Bell (Cambridge: Cambridge University Press, 2007), 159–85, at 177–78.

107. See Darwin, *Empire Project*, 60–61.

108. Schoonover, "Napoleon Is Coming!", 119; see, for example, John Collinson, "Explorations in Central America, Accompanied by Survey and Levels from Lake Nicaragua to the Atlantic Ocean," *Proceedings of the Royal Geographical Society* 12 (1867): 25–48.

109. See Peter J. Hugill, "The American Challenge to British Hegemony, 1861–1947," *Geographical Review* 99 (2009): 403–25.

110. Morton, "British North America," 156.

111. Stephen Tuffnell, "Anglo-American Inter-Imperialism: U.S. Expansion and the British World, c. 1865–1914," *Britain and the World* 7 (2014): 174–95, at 195.

112. Sexton, *Debtor Diplomacy*, 250–53; P. J. Cain and A. G. Hopkins, *British Imperialism, 1688–2000*, 2nd ed. (Routledge: Abingdon, 2013 [2002]), 261–65.

CHAPTER FIVE

France's Grand Design and the Confederacy

Stève Sainlaude

The early 1860s opened for France a series of distant ventures abroad. Having focused on the European theater earlier, Napoleon III now turned the ambitions of the Second Empire outside the continent. First Africa captured the emperor's attention, beginning with the campaigns of Faidherbe in Senegal. Then his gaze turned toward the Middle East, when France became involved in the construction of the Suez Canal in Egypt and intervened in Syria. Finally, his attention was drawn to the Far East where France established an imperial foothold in Cochinchina and Cambodia.

It was within this global imperial context that the most famous expedition of the Second Empire would occur, that of Mexico, which began in 1862 and came to its ignominious end in 1867. It was a military adventure that many historians of Anglo-Saxon background ironically refer to as the "Grand Design," but the French called it *La Grande Pensée du règne* (the grand thought of the reign). This expression, originally used by French statesman Eugène Rouher, speaking before the legislature early in 1864, was a pretentious phrase that became famous, especially among the liberal opposition who used it to mock Napoleon III's grand disaster in Mexico.[1]

By whatever name, the Grand Design or *Grande Pensée*, the importance of the Napoleonic project in Mexico to the foreign policy of the Second Empire was undeniable. Rouher, and through him the emperor, considered the intervention in Mexico a higher priority, for example, than Russia in the Crimea or the Italian question. French policy on Mexico must, therefore, be understood as a major element of imperial strategy, and it was central to French foreign policy because it held such an important place in the mind of Napoleon III. Since the 1840s, the emperor had focused closely on the fate of the New World and had been fascinated with the idea of a canal through Nicaragua as a passage between the Atlantic and Pacific and the vast commercial worlds surrounding these two oceans. The Mexico project was also important because, unlike his uncle Napoleon I, Napoleon III embraced a vision of truly global dimensions. At a time when developments in transportation and communication were shrinking the world, Napoleon III was thinking on a global scale. He wanted France to become, once again, a major European power, a counterbalance to Great Britain. To accomplish this he pursued an aggressive foreign policy of grand designs that would undo the treaties of Vienna in 1815, which had reduced France's power after the failure of his uncle's first French empire.

In 1848 Louis-Napoleon was elected president of the second French republic (he would become known as Napoleon III in 1852 after conducting a coup d'état and proclaiming the Second Empire). He already was concerned by the emerging position of the United States on the world stage, and this led him to become interested in Mexico. He saw in Mexico the possibility of thwarting the ambitions of the United States for territory and influence. It was therefore the policy of France not toward *Mexico* but *toward the United States*, that inspired his Grand Design for Mexico. Thus in the early 1860s the histories of the French, the United States, and Mexico became entangled in Napoleon's *Grande Pensée*.

All that remained was the determination of when to implement the plan. The American Civil War suddenly neutralized the United States, which opposed European interference on the American continent, and presented France with the possibility of an independent Confederacy hostile to the United States. It was an ideal opportunity for "the Grand Design" to be launched.

THE FEAR OF U.S. territorial expansion originated before Napoleon III came to power. During the reign of Louis-Philippe (1830–48), François Guizot, the foreign minister, conducted a policy aimed at stemming the expansion of the United States. Guizot, and later Napoleon III, defended an old idea of French diplomacy, which sought to maintain a balance of power on all continents. With regard to America, Guizot strongly supported an independent Republic of Texas to stem the territorial expansion of the United States.[2]

After Guizot, the major turning point for France was President Polk's provocation of war with Mexico in 1846. French observers feared that once it reached the Pacific Ocean the United States would become a dangerous global power. They were frightened that the conquests of the war against Mexico would constitute a first step in the conquest of territories south of the Rio Grande.

The advent of the Second Empire in 1851–52 coincided with the resumption of French fears concerning Mexico. The election of James Buchanan as president of the United States in 1856 coincided with Mexico's growing tensions between Liberals and Conservatives, which resulted in a bitter civil war that raged from 1858 to the end of 1860. Buchanan had never hidden his expansionist aims, and his inaugural speech indicated that Mexico would become the objective of a new expansionist impulse in his administration.[3] Napoleon III and his imperial government feared Buchanan would be a new Polk. For the very able French minister in Washington, Eugène de Sartiges, arguably the best diplomat sent to the United States during the Second Empire, Buchanan's victory unleashed boisterous expansionist rhetoric.[4] The president's annual message to Congress at the end of 1858, with Mexico's Reform War raging, proposed to guarantee the border with Mexico with military posts and even establish a buffer space inside Mexico (in the north of Sonora and Chihuahua). This did nothing to put Sartiges' mind at ease or assure Napoleon III's government.[5] In November 1858, the French commander of the West Indies department of the navy received an order to proceed to Mexican coasts officially to "guarantee the respect of French interests in Mexico," but in reality it was a demonstration of French naval strength in the region.[6]

In France the press reacted strongly to Buchanan's expansionist schemes. The *Moniteur*, the mouthpiece of the imperial government, wrote on December 7, 1859, that the government of the United States concentrated considerable armed forces on the Mexican border.[7] Even the opposition Orléanist press noted the ominous signs of interference by the United States in Mexican affairs.[8]

On April 5, 1859, Robert McLane, the new U.S. minister to Mexico, extended official recognition of the government of Benito Juárez. The United States thus publicly demonstrated its support for the Liberal faction against that of the Conservatives. This was seen as both congruent with U.S. republican political traditions, but also a reply to European nations that had favored Juárez's Conservative enemies.

French diplomats kept a careful eye on McLane's negotiations in Mexico and particularly to a treaty McClane signed with Melchor Ocampo, Juárez's foreign affairs secretary, on December 14, 1859. The treaty guaranteed U.S. privileges of transit across specified Mexican trade routes and included provisions for American armed intervention should Mexico deem it necessary to protect trade routes.[9] The French minister in Mexico, Viscount Gabriac, feared that this would open the door to U.S. acquisition of all Mexico.[10]

In his annual message to Congress in December 1859, Buchanan crossed another line. After detailing the woeful situation of Mexico in the throes of civil war, he recommended that Congress vote to authorize him to use armed forces to intervene in Mexico and reestablish the constitutional government led by Benito Juárez.[11] Jules Treilhard, the French *chargé d'affaires* in Washington, and Gabriac in Mexico expressed strong disapproval on behalf of the French government.[12] The minister of foreign affairs, Édouard Thouvenel, reaffirmed his support to the Conservative leader, General Miguel Miramón, whom he thought better qualified to protect Mexico from American covetousness.[13]

The U.S. Senate refused to authorize President Buchanan to send troops into Mexico, but Buchanan's proposals of intervention worried the French, who began reaching out to Britain to devise an agreement for joint intervention in Mexico. Rather than a military intervention, the French and British diplomats preferred a diplomatic interposition offering to mediate peace between the warring parties in Mexico.[14] A plan suggested by the British was adopted by which they would first propose an armistice of six months to a year, during which time Mexico would elect a National Assembly whose mission would be to decide the form of government for the country. Meanwhile, a provisional government would deal with current affairs.[15]

However, the military successes of the Liberal faction beginning in the summer of 1860 ruled out any possibility of arbitration. By early 1861, the Liberals were in control of the capital, and in March Benito Juárez was elected president under the Liberal constitution. French anxiety over the future of Mexico was only heightened by the end of Mexico's Reform War. Juárez and the Liberal Party were favored by the United States. The French feared Juárez would either suspend the payment of foreign debts or sell Mexico's northern provinces to the United States in order to pay its debts.

NAPOLEON III WAS NOW convinced that he had to intervene and that it was high time to realize his Grand Design for Mexico. In Napoleon III's mind, France's mission was to enable Mexico to resist the expansionist attempts of the United States. He was inspired by the 1856 report of the Marquis de Radepont, entitled "Purpose for the Regeneration of Mexico."[16]

The geopolitical purpose of Napoleon III in Mexico was, first and foremost, to oppose the omnipotence of the United States in North America. His plan for Mexico was inseparable from the idea of the United States as an aggressive, imperialistic threat to the balance of power in the New World. The primary purpose of the intervention, Napoleon III wrote to his ambassador in England, Count Flahaut, was to use Mexico to contain the United States. Mexico was the Crimea of America that would block the expansion of the United States on its southern border.[17]

In a famous letter written in July 1862 to General Forey, the commander in chief of the French expedition in Mexico, Napoleon III explained that Mexico must be rescued not only to enable the preservation of its integrity but also to establish French influence in this highly coveted part of the continent. By rescuing Mexico, France would also assure a balance of power in this part of the globe. The Forey letter borrowed from Guizot's earlier scheme of an essential counterbalance that would prevent one power from dominating a region, grabbing a monopoly of trade, and imposing its will on others. Napoleon III added that it was the interest of France that the republic of the United States not take control of the Gulf of Mexico and become the only major provider of goods to the New World. Instead, if Mexico could maintain the integrity of its territory, if a strong government was put in place and defended by French bayonets, France would have created an impassable barrier to encroachments by the United States. Napoleon III proposed that France was directly concerned in this containment because it wanted to preserve the independence of its remaining colonies of the West Indies. However, France also wanted to extend its influence in the Americas and create huge economic opportunities, not least those emanating from the inter-ocean canal that Napoleon III wanted to build to connect the Atlantic and Pacific.[18]

To resist the encroachments of the United States, Mexico should not only rely on France but also be strengthened sufficiently to defend itself. Mexico's weakness, Napoleon III believed, lay in its government. The intervention was thus accompanied by a political project whose aim was not only to restore stability to Mexico by supporting the Conservative faction against the Liberals, but also to regenerate the nation and make it a powerful state. Only a monarchy, Napoleon III was convinced, could create the unity Mexico required. Had Mexico been properly governed, it would never have suffered all the amputations at the hands of the United States during the past thirteen years. Thus, the monarchical experiment in Mexico was closely associated with risk of United States encroachment. It is unlikely that Napoleon III had ever considered any solution other than the imposition of a European monarch sponsored by the French. Only that would assure that a regenerated Mexico would become a staunch ally of France against the United States. Mexico would remain favorable to France not only out of gratitude but also because their interests would naturally be in full agreement with those of France.[19]

However, Napoleon did not merely offer a model he considered best suited to Mexico. He wanted a monarchical Mexico as a challenge to the republic of the United States, and a religious as well as political challenge. Faced with a Protestant United States, Mexico's commitment to the Catholic religion must be reaffirmed, since the Liberal Party had recently stripped the church of its landed wealth and important powers involving education. Napoleon III was also concerned with regaining the sympathy of Catholics in Europe, many of whom distrusted his commitment to defend the temporal powers of Pope Pius IX in Rome and the Papal States. The defense of the Catholic faith was integral to the idea of *Latinité* or, in Spanish, *Latinidad* (Latinity), a term used frequently at the time to describe the common language, religion, and civilization binding the Latin peoples of the Old and New Worlds. Napoleon III also feared that, in case of war between France and England, American would rush to rescue their Anglo-Saxon cousins.[20] The Mexican question highlighted the idea of the "Latin races" opposed to the "Anglo-Saxon races" in both hemispheres. French contemporaries were distressed by the general decadence of Catholic and Latin countries, which were confronted with Anglo-Saxon and Protestant people who had the fate of the world in their hands. Thus, Prussia, Great Britain, and the United States were ascending while Spain, Portugal, Italy, and finally Mexico were in general decline. France alone could direct the regeneration of Mexico and lead the Latin nations in the global struggle of the races.

So prominent were these political and cultural motives that it seemed the economic and financial interests of France were secondary when Napoleon III decided to intervene in Mexico.[21] At first, the problem of Mexico's debts to French investors seemed only a convenient accessory to the Grand Design. Compared to Britain, and even Spain, Mexico owed little money to France.[22] So when, in July 1861, the new Mexican republican president, Benito Juárez, suspended for two years the payment on foreign debts, France stood to lose far less than other European powers. It was the same for the Jecker claims. Jecker, a Swiss banker, had arranged with Conservative leader General Miramón a loan of 15 million pesos, to be financed with the sale of bonds. Jecker saw to it that the Duke of Morny, half-brother of Napoleon III, and others in the imperial government had a stake in the loan, which helped set the stage for French intervention.[23] The money owed Jecker and French creditors provided a wonderful excuse for intervention, but the motives went beyond debt recovery. Several years later Empress Eugenie, who would live until 1920, confirmed this suspicion in a conversation: "I assure you that in the genesis of the project, financial speculation, debt recovery, Jecker's coupons, the mining of Sonora and Sinaloa, held no place; we were not thinking about these."[24] There was an idea, deeply rooted in the collective imagination, that a Mexican El Dorado lay waiting to be exploited. However, Mexico's wealth required peace and order before such enterprises could attract investors. Thus, the political project took precedence, if only as a precondition to the economic exploitation of Mexico's riches.

To intervene in the affairs of Mexico was not easy, however. Not least among the difficulties was that the French government feared retribution by the United States. Napoleon III was convinced that intervention would lead to war with the United States. That was why the prospect of a protracted civil war tearing the United States apart was seen in 1861 as an ideal opportunity not to be missed. Napoleon III understood that if he wanted to invest in Mexico, he should not lose a moment. He wrote to the French ambassador in Britain: "Today unforeseen events have changed the face of things. The American war has made the United States unable to interfere in the matter."[25]

We see clearly from the beginning the link between the French intervention and the weakening of the United States. This is important because it shows that, apart from the internal situation in Mexico, the success of the intervention was conditioned by external events. By the same logic, if such a political project should be realized, it was necessary that the Civil War not end too soon. The essential question was whether the South would be able to withstand a protracted war against the North, and whether the North was determined to put down the rebellion. The demonstration of Southern valor against all odds at the first battle of Bull Run in July 1861 and Lincoln's decision to mobilize a huge citizen army were decisive psychological factors for the French onlookers. Thouvenel was influenced by the reports of consul Alfred Paul in Richmond, who wrote to his minister in Washington that it was certain to become a prolonged struggle.[26]

The Grand Design could now move forward. By the end of the summer in 1861, after the Union's disastrous defeat at Bull Run, Napoleon had already selected Maximilian, the Hapsburg archduke, as his candidate for the future monarch of Mexico. The political project in Mexico was thus directly linked to the crisis tearing the United States apart.[27] As for Mexico, the pitiful state of republican armed forces led the French ambassador to Mexico, Dubois Saligny, to estimate that it would take a maximum of 2,000 men to overthrow the Juárez regime. Such optimistic reports encouraged the emperor and those gathered around him in Paris that the intervention in Mexico would be settled before Southerners and Northerners could bury the hatchet.

WHAT PLACE DID the Confederacy occupy in Napoleon's mind? At the beginning of the French expedition to Mexico, the Confederates and their sympathizers represented themselves as essential to the success of Napoleon's project. As Howard Jones notes in his essay for this volume, the Confederacy welcomed foreign allies in their quest for independence. Many times the *Index*, the propaganda organ of the Southern government in London, defended Napoleon III's Mexican project.[28] John Slidell, the Confederate emissary in Paris, made his support of the French expedition clear to Napoleon III during their private interview in July 1862.[29] Slidell went so far as to propose a military alliance between France and the Confederacy against their "common enemy," the United States.[30] In June 1863 at their third meeting, Slidell reaffirmed the sympathy of the South for the French initiative in Mexico, and he predicted that the Confederacy would displace the United States as the major power in North America and that an alliance with Mexico would, therefore, remain essential to the ongoing success of France's project.[31]

We must underscore the opportunistic nature of the Southern support for France, once the French expeditionary force actually landed in Mexico early in 1862. The Confederacy could hardly afford to alienate the French entering Mexico to the south while fighting the Union to the north. The South wanted French assistance, but at the very least, it had to have their neutrality as an occupying force in Mexico. After the loss of New Orleans in April 1862, the major commercial conduit for cotton exports to fund the war was through the port of Matamoros, located on the Rio Grande across from Brownsville, Texas. When French troops captured Matamoros in September 1864, the survival of the Confederacy depended on the goodwill of the French.[32]

Napoleon III took great delight in the ongoing fragmentation of the United States. A sensational pamphlet published in 1863 by the emperor's advisor, Michel Chevalier, entitled *La France, le Mexique et les Etats Confédérés*, revealed the close relationship between France's Grand Design and the Confederate rebellion.[33] Apparently, Napoleon III believed the Confederates were sincere in their support of the Mexican project. He suspected the North of pushing Juárez "in the path of resistance" and believed that Northerners' tenacious loyalty to the Monroe Doctrine led them to reject the French intervention.

The emperor considered the Confederates to be his natural allies and to ensure his success in Mexico, he intended to be more than a mere spectator of the struggle they waged against the Union. He wanted to recognize the Confederacy and bring the war to an end on terms of separation. The partition of the United States would create two independent and mutually hostile powers, whose ongoing animosity would help protect Mexico from attack by either party. Napoleon III feared aggression from the North more than from the South, and he expected an independent Confederacy to form a buffer state, "an intermediate balancing power between the Federals and the Hispanic-Americans."[34] The containment of American expansion and the preservation of Mexican territory thus required the splitting of the Union.

However, the archives of the French foreign ministry reveal clear opposition to Napoleon's desire to recognize the South or intervene in the American war from both of his ministers of foreign affairs during this period. We know that during the American Civil War, Thouvenel and Drouyn de Lhuys did everything possible to deter the emperor from tilting in favor of the South, even including defiant refusals to carry out his instructions in some instances. Recalling the ups and downs of American history in antebellum years and drawing on information delivered by French agents in the United States, both foreign ministers argued that a southern victory would pose a greater threat to France's Grand Design than a unified United States.

Unlike the emperor, the French ministers of foreign affairs were aware that the South supported the French project in Mexico out of necessity rather than conviction. They had not forgotten that at the beginning of the secession crisis, Southerners leaned towards Juárez, and gravitated to the Conservatives only as a result of blunders committed by John Pickett, their envoy in Mexico who ended up being expelled from Mexico.[35] It is therefore less out of conviction than pragmatism that the Southerners decided to back the Mexican Conservatives. Consequently, they found themselves practically allied with the French.

Moreover, the two ministers noted that the Southerners had not sincerely accepted the Grand Design. After speaking with Slidell, both Thouvenel and, later, Drouyn de Lhuys realized that the government of Richmond wanted to impose conditions on the establishment of a Mexican monarchy, including some evidence of popular support from Mexicans. Slidell's July 1862 message to Thouvenel, in which he applied for recognition of the Confederacy by France, made this point by saying that the Confederacy was confident that Napoleon III would not impose in Mexico a government not in accordance with the wishes of its inhabitants.[36] Thouvenel and Drouyn de Lhuys were both aware of how this condition exposed a weakness in France's design for Mexico.

French consul Alfred Paul in Richmond also alerted Paris that Confederate president Jefferson Davis, in his congressional address at the end of 1863, made a point of insisting that the Mexican people demonstrate popular support for Napoleon's project. Davis took the occasion to remind Napoleon III that he had earlier disavowed any plan that would impose a monarchy against the will of the Mexican people.[37] Davis and other Southern leaders were fully aware that Napoleon's Grand Design was not truly democratic in nature. On June 30, 1863, an assembly of 250 "notables," all selected by the Conservative Party in Mexico, voted to adopt the monarchical form of government for Mexico and to offer the throne to Maximilian, just as Napoleon III had planned. Before accepting the crown, Maximilian insisted on a plebiscite that would demonstrate to the world that the Mexican people wanted him to rule over them. The French carried out a hasty poll of local notables, but French officials understood that Maximilian's legitimacy would not rest on any real test of popular sovereignty.[38]

France's foreign ministers relied heavily on their diplomats in the United States who were alerting the French about Confederates voicing concern that the principles of the Monroe Doctrine be respected. From New York to New Orleans, French diplomats reminded Paris that the Monroe Doctrine still had strong support in the slave states, and they warned that the South would not be indifferent to the French presence in Mexico. It would not be difficult, they further warned, for the Southerners to mobilize their most eminent citizens against the French project.[39]

Since the North also manifested hostility toward the French intervention in Mexico, Napoleon III's cabinet was afraid that once peace returned to the United States, the North and South would ally against Maximilian. French diplomats in the United States were informed of the unofficial mission of Francis Preston Blair, who in January 1865, with President Lincoln's permission, attempted to negotiate a peace between the North and South and to reunite the warring sections in a joint expedition against Maximilian's regime in Mexico. Blair's negotiations led to the Hampton Roads peace conference on February 3, 1865, at which Confederate delegates took up Blair's idea of a military alliance between the North and South against the French in Mexico. The peace conference, and plans to invade Mexico, came to nothing, but it left a sharp impression on French diplomats.

These attempts at reconciliation troubled French emissaries abroad. From Washington to Mexico City, via New York, or London, they all warned that the Monroe Doctrine would eventually serve as a basis for reunification between Northerners and Southerners and provide a basis on which to carry out a foreign war against the French in Mexico.[40] The Quai d'Orsay, home of the French foreign ministry, was torn between fears of a possible coalition of former adversaries and the reassuring statements issued by agents of the federal government that the United States did not intend to interfere in Mexico.[41]

To French diplomats, the South seemed even more dangerous than the United States because it appeared to be playing a double game. It must be remembered that even as the Hampton Roads conference took place, Duncan Kenner was en route to Europe on a secret mission for the Confederate government to offer a plan for emancipating the slaves in exchange for foreign recognition of his government. News from Hampton Roads of the possibility of a joint expedition to expel the French from Mexico arrived in France before Kenner.[42] The Kenner mission reinforced the suspicions inside the Quai d'Orsay, and perhaps the emperor's mind, that the South was not a reliable ally with regard to the Mexican question. In truth, no one inside the French ministry of foreign affairs ever believed the Confederates were sincere in their support of the French intervention in Mexico, simply because their temperament and their interests vigorously defended their own right to territorial expansion in Latin America.

THOSE IN THE FRENCH government who supported the Southern cause welcomed the fragmentation of the United States as a way of curbing its expansionist impulses. Slidell, in his July 1862 interview with Thouvenel, had encouraged this notion that the South would contain the United States and that an independent South would put aside its earlier ambitions in Latin America, which had been motivated only by the rivalry with the North for congressional power.[43] But French diplomats in the United States were well aware of the continued desire for conquest that drove Southerners into the Caribbean, Mexico, and Central America.

French diplomats explained this Southern proclivity for expansion by the practical need of the cotton economy for virgin soil.[44] They also noted the enthusiasm with which Southerners applauded the incursions by William Walker in Mexico in 1853. The signing of the Gadsden Purchase that same year was also received warmly in the South. During the Mexican Reform War, the French legation in Washington noted that the political instability seizing Mexico during the Reform War invited foreign intervention from all directions.[45]

French fears had resurfaced with the election of James Buchanan in 1856. Sartiges explained that, though a native of Pennsylvania, Buchanan was deferential "to the party of the South" since it could not rely on the Northern states to support its expansion plans.[46] French agents were not the only ones to remark on Buchanan's support for southern expansion. The French liberal press that opposed Napoleon III reminded its readers of the South's ambitions in Latin America.[47] During the American Civil War, this idea of expansionism as a driving motive of the Southern slave states became a recurring theme in the liberal press.[48]

French liberals cultivated the idea that people in the northern states, because they were hostile to slavery, were more respectful of their Mexican neighbor.[49] The victory of Lincoln should have put an end to the spread of slavery, and the integrity of Mexico would therefore be respected. In retrospect, this binary view of a peaceful and respectful North and an aggressive South ready to seize Mexico on any pretext shaped French foreign policy.

In the eyes of French diplomats, Southern leaders were branded by their past aggressions in Latin America, and they blamed Southerners as main instigators of expansionist policies. During his long stay in the United States prior to the secession crisis, Sartiges drew a portrait of those leaders who now controlled the destinies of Confederacy. He never failed to present Jefferson Davis, Benjamin, or Slidell as proponents of Southern imperialism. Confederate diplomats and leaders, however, were slow to understand that the South's lingering reputation for filibustering affected French policy toward them.[50]

Union diplomats made certain that the French understood the threat posed by the South to Mexico. Secretary of State William Seward's instructions to Thomas Corwin, his minister in Mexico, written on April 6, 1861, were made public and immediately sent to Paris. In it Seward outlined the dangers faced by Mexico by rebel Southerners now operating separately from the U.S. government. Seward warned that the anarchy in Mexico would naturally seduce the Confederates to pursue the conquest of Mexico and other parts of Spanish America.[51]

Such a warning was unnecessary, for French diplomats in America realized that the birth of the Confederate States of America (CSA) posed a grave threat to the Mexican project. They understood that Southern imperialism might be temporarily set aside but that separation would actually increase the threat by allowing an independent South to expand without hindrance. Henri Mercier, the new French minister to the United States, favored the South, but he could not deny that the South's expansionist impulse would lead to aggression past the Rio Grande.[52]

Thouvenel was also well aware of the danger that would follow separation of the South. In the autumn of 1861, in a message to the French ambassador to Britain, he emphasized how a politically weakened Mexico offered a "territorial compensation" to its nearest neighbor, the Confederacy.[53] In February 1862, Thouvenel wrote again to his minister in London that the biggest challenge would be to contain the new slaveholders' republic.[54]

With the specter of Confederate aggression in mind, French government officials tried to persuade Maximilian, after he accepted the crown of Mexico, not to pursue relationships with the Confederacy. While visiting Paris on his way to Mexico in 1864, Maximilian snubbed Slidell and, after arriving in Mexico City, he also refused to meet with William Preston, the Confederate envoy to Mexico.[55] The French imperial government had successfully convinced Maximilian that the Grand Design did not require an alliance with the Confederacy. One year later, when the U.S. Civil War ended, Maximilian would rejoice at having preserved the neutrality of the Mexican Empire.[56]

THE FRENCH, WHOSE MAIN objective in Mexico for over two decades had been to contain the expansion of the United States, had realized that recognition of the Confederacy would do more to endanger than protect Mexico from aggression. We must recall that the Confederacy was born nine months before the launch of the expedition. The French government understood that a fragmented United States would not insure against territorial aggression from the North, and that the independence of the South would pose an even graver threat to Mexican territory. French diplomats also observed that Southerners refrained from setting any territorial limits to their new nation and that the spirit of the new republic remained ominously imperialist.

The danger of the Southern expansion was more important to French observers than the prospect of an independent South fragmenting and weakening the United States. The republic born in 1776 had to survive, they believed, because it would defeat the imperialist ambitions of the slave states. Not least in their calculations were the numerous threats issued by the Union that any effort to aid the Southern rebellion would bring war with the United States. The French diplomats realized that they would have to do all they could to dissuade Napoleon III from recognizing the Confederacy or doing anything to aid in its struggle for independence.

If the formal recognition of the Confederacy was not conducive to the success of the Napoleonic project in Mexico, the civil war the South ignited was absolutely essential. The South's capitulation in 1865 signaled the end of the French mission in Mexico. The prospect of a massive Union army to the north forced Napoleon III to announce the withdrawal of French troops early in 1866. The result of France's tragic intervention in Mexico was exactly opposite to the goals Napoleon III had pursued. The French withdrawal from Mexico spelled the end of an experiment in monarchical government and, instead of creating a balance of power in North America, it left the United States more powerful than before. The United States, in effect, had been able to enforce the Monroe Doctrine without firing a single shot and was left the undisputed master of the future in the North American continent.

Suggested Readings

Anceau, Eric. *Napoléon III*. Paris: Tallandier, 2008.

Avenel, Jean. *La campagne du Mexique (1862–1867): La fin de l'hégémonie européenne en Amérique du Nord*. Paris: Economica, 1996.

Barker, Nancy Nichols. "France, Austria and the Mexican Venture (1861–1864)." *French Historical Studies* 3 (1963): 224–45.

———. *The French Experience in Mexico (1821–1861): A History of Constant Misunderstanding*. Chapel Hill: University of North Carolina Press, 1979.

Blumenthal, Henry. "Confederate Diplomacy: Popular Notions and International Realities." *Journal of Southern History* 32 (May 1966): 151–71.

Case, Lynn M. *French Opinion on the U.S. and Mexico, 1860–1867: Extracts from the Reports of the Procureurs généraux*. New York: D. Appleton-Century Company, 1936.

Case, Lynn Marshall and Warren F. Spencer. *The United States and France: Civil War Diplomacy*. Philadelphia: University of Pennsylvania Press, 1970.

Cullop, Charles C. *Confederate Propaganda in Europe (1861–1865)*. Coral Gables: University of Miami Press, 1969.

Cunningham, Michele. *Mexico and the Foreign Policy of Napoléon III*. New York: Palgrave, 2001.

De Leon, Edwin. *Secret History of Confederate Diplomacy Abroad*, edited by William C. Davis. Lawrence: University Press of Kansas, 2005.

Dugast, Guy-Alain. *La tentation mexicaine en France au XIXème siècle: L'image du Mexique et l'intervention française (1821–1862); Le mythe mexicain et le courant interventionniste*. Paris: L'Harmattant, 2008, Tome II.

———. *La tentation mexicaine en France au XIXème siècle: L'image du Mexique et l'intervention française (1821–1862); Les mythiques attraits d'une nation arriérée*. Paris: L'Harmattan, 2008, Tome I.

Girard, Louis. *Napoléon III*. Paris: Fayard, 1986.

Glantz De Lopez Camara, Margarita. *Le Mexique vu par les Français (1847–1867)*. Thèse, Paris: Université de la Sorbonne, 1958.

Gouttman, Alain. *La guerre du Mexique (1862–1867): Le mirage américain de Napoléon III*. Paris: Perrin, 2008.

Hanna, Alfred Jackson and Kathryn Abbey Hanna. *Napoléon III and Mexico: American Triumph over Monarchy*. Chapel Hill: University of North Carolina Press, 1971.

Hubbard, Charles M. *The Burden of Confederate Diplomacy*. Knoxville: University of Tennessee Press, 1998.

Jones, Howard. *Blue and Gray Diplomacy: A History of Union and Confederate Foreign Relations*. Chapel Hill: University of North Carolina Press, 2010.

Lally, Frank Edward. *French Opposition to the Mexican Policy of the Second Empire*. Baltimore: Johns Hopkins Press, 1931.

Lecaillon, Jean-François. *Napoléon III et le Mexique: Les illusions d'un grand dessein*. Paris: L'Harmattan, 1994.

May, Robert E. *The Southern Dream of a Caribbean Empire (1854–1861)*. Baton Rouge: Louisiana State University Press, 1973.

McCardell, John. *The Idea of a Southern Nation: Southern Nationalists and Southern Nationalism (1830–1860)*. New York: W.W. Norton and Company, 1979.

Miller, Robert Ryal. "Arms across the Border: United States Aid to Juarez during the French Intervention in Mexico." *Transactions of the American Philosophical Society*, New Series 63, part 6 (December 1973): 4–61.

Noirsain, Serge. *La Confédération sudiste (1861–1865): Mythes et réalités*. Paris: Economica, 2006.

Owsley, Frank Laurence. *King Cotton Diplomacy: Foreign Relations of the Confederate States of America*, 2nd ed. Chicago: University of Chicago Press, 1959.

Sainlaude, Stève. *La France et la Confédération sudiste (1861–1865), la question de la reconnaissance diplomatique pendant la guerre de Sécession*. Paris: L'Harmattan, 2011.

———. *Le gouvernement impérial et la guerre de Sécession (1861–1865), l'action diplomatique*. Paris: L'Harmattan, 2011.

Schefer, Christian. *La grande pensée de Napoléon III: Les origines de l'expédition du Mexique (1858–1862)*. Paris: Marcel Rivière et Cie, 1939.

Schoonover, Thomas David. "Confederate Diplomacy and the Texas-Mexican Border, 1861–1865." *East Texas Historical Journal* 11 (Spring 1973): 33–39.

Notes

1. Some contemporaries even regarded Rouher as a "Vice-Emperor." He represented the emperor in front of the Senate and Legislative bodies.

2. French minister of foreign affairs from 1840 to 1848.

3. James Buchanan, "Inaugural Address," March 4, 1857. Online in Gerhard Peters and John T. Woolley, *The American Presidency Project*, http://www.presidency.ucsb .edu/ws/?pid=25817. Frederick Binder, *James Buchanan and the American Empire* (Selinsgrove, PA: Susquehanna University Press, 1994), 93. The Ostend manifesto encouraged the United States to purchase Cuba from Spain and declare war against Spain if it refused to sell.

4. Sartiges to Walewski, Washington, February 15, 1858, A.M.A.E. CP, EU, 118: 109. Count Eugene de Sartiges was appointed in 1851. Nine years later, he was replaced by Henri Mercier.

5. Sartiges to Walewski, Washington, December 6, 1858, A.M.A.E. CP, EU, 120: 118.

6. Walewski to Sartiges, Compiègne, November 18, 1858, A.M.A.E. CP, EU, 120: 93.

7. *Le Moniteur*, December 7, 1859.

8. *Le Journal des Débats*, May 31, 1859. Prevost-Paradol.

9. *Diccionario Porrúa, Historía, Biographía y Geographía de Mexico* (Mexico: Editorial Porrúa, 1976), 2165–67.

10. Gabriac to Thouvenel, Mexico, January 11, February 20, March 22, 1860, A.M.A.E. CP, M, 52: 257-v., 258, 345-v., 53: 54.

11. James Buchanan, "Third Annual Message to Congress on the State of the Union," December 19, 1859. Online in Peters and Woolley, *The American Presidency Project*.

12. Treilhard to Walewski, Washington, January 15, 1860, A.M.A.E. CP, EU, 123: 6. Gabriac to Thouvenel, Mexico, February 29, 1860, A.M.A.E. CP, M, 52: 376v.-377, 53: 130.

13. Thouvenel to Dubois de Saligny, Paris, May 30, 1860, A.M.A.E. CP, M, 53: 302v.-303.

14. Binder, *James Buchanan*, 247–48.

15. Christian Schefer, *La grande pensée de Napoléon III: Les origines de l'expédition du Mexique (1858–1862)* (Paris: Marcel Rivière, 1939), 55.

16. Victor Dubosc, Marquis of Radepont, made his fortune thanks to the development of a French institution in the State of Veracruz. On November 24th, 1856, he met Napoléon III. Several years later, the emperor recognized that Radepont was the main architect of his "Grand Design." Kathryn Abbey Hanna, "The Roles of the South in the French Intervention in Mexico," *Journal of Southern History* 20 (February 1954): 4–5. Alfred Jackson Hanna and Kathryn Abbey Hanna, *Napoléon III and Mexico: American Triumph over Monarchy* (Chapel Hill: University of North Carolina Press, 1971), xvi, 14; *Projet pour la régénération du Mexique*; Paris, November 26, 1856, A.M.A.E. CP, M, 46: 104–21.

17. Napoléon III to Flahaut, Compiègne, October 1861, A.M.A.E. CP, A, 720: 215 v., 218v.

18. Napoléon III to Forey, Fontainebleau, July 3, 1862, A.M.A.E. LJ, M, 191.

19. Ibid.

20. Jean-François Lecaillon, *Napoléon III et le Mexique: Les illusions d'un grand dessein* (Paris: L'Harmattan, 1994), 46.

21. Nancy Nichols Barker, *The French Experience in Mexico (1821–1861): A History of Constant Misunderstanding* (Chapel Hill: University of North Carolina Press, 1979), 193.

22. René Pillorget, "Mexique," *Dictionnaire du Second Empire* (Paris: Fayard, 1995), 815. Three million pesos for France, nine for Spain, seventy for Great Britain.

23. Shirley Black, "Napoléon III et le Mexique; un triomphe monétaire," *Revue historique* 259 (1978): 61.

24. Maurice Paleologue, *Les entretiens de l'Impératrice Eugénie* (Paris: Plon et Nourrit, 1928), 101–2.

25. Napoléon III to Flahaut, Compiègne, October 1861, A.M.A.E. CP, A, 720: 216v.

26. The ministers of foreign affairs were inspired by Alfred Paul's analysis. Thus, in December 1860, he predicted that secession would lead to a civil war, and at the

beginning of the conflict he announced the defeat of the Confederacy. Stève Sainlaude, "Alfred Paul: un diplomate français dans la guerre de Sécession," *Revue d'Histoire Diplomatique* (2011): 3–15; Thouvenel to Mercier, Paris, October 31, 1861, A.M.A.E. CP A, 720: 221.

27. The intervention was formally settled with representatives of Britain and Spain on October 31, 1861 (London Convention). Carl Bock, *Prelude to Tragedy: The Netociation and Breakdown of the Tripartite Convention of London, October 31, 1861* (Philadelphia: University of Pennsylvania Press, 1966), 122–215.

28. Charles Cullop, *Confederate Propaganda in Europe (1861–1865)* (Coral Gables: University of Miami Press, 1969), 66–84.

29. Slidell'Mémo., Slidell to Benjamin, Paris, July 25, 1862, in *The War of the Rebellion: A Compilation of the Official Records of the Union and Confederate Navies in the War of the Rebellion* (Washington, DC: Government Printing Office, 1894–1922), ser. 2, vol. 3, 479–87. (Hereafter cited as *ORN*.)

30. Slidell's confidential note, Paris, July/August, 1862, A.M.A.E. ADP, EU, 32:91. Slidell'Mémo., Slidell to Benjamin, Paris, October 28, 1862, *ORN*, ser. 2, vol. 3, 572–79.

31. Slidell'Mémo., Slidell to Benjamin, Paris, June 21, 1863, *ORN*, ser. 2, vol. 3, 812–14.

32. Jean Avenel, *La campagne du Mexique (1862–1867): La fin de l'hégémonie européenne en Amérique du Nord* (Paris: Economica, 1996), 69; Serge Noirsain, *La Confédération sudiste (1861–1865), Mythes et réalités* (Paris: Economica, 2006), 160–65. This can also be explained by France's desire to prolong the conflict: Maximilian had just taken office. There was no doubt that when the U. S. Civil War was over, France would have to take into account the pressures of Washington.

33. Michel Chevalier and Ernest Rasetti, *La France, le Mexique et les États Confédérés* (Paris: E. Dentu, 1863); Michel Chevalier, *France, Mexico, and the Confederate States*, trans. William Henry Hurlbert (New York: C. B. Richardson, 1863).

34. Michel Chevalier, *La France, le Mexique et les Etats Confédérés contre les Etats-Unis* (Paris: E. Dentu, 1863), 10–30.

35. Thomas Schoonover, "Pickett," *Encyclopedia of the Confederacy* (New York: Simon and Schuster, 1993), 3:1209–10. Fred Rippy, "Mexican Projects of the Confederates," *Southwestern Historical Quarterly* 22 (April 1919): 291–317.

36. Slidell to Thouvenel, Paris, July 21, 1862, A.M.A.E. ADP, EU, 32: 57v.

37. Paul to Drouyn de Lhuys, Richmond, December 23, 1863, A.M.A.E. CPC, EU, 15: 91-v. Jefferson Davis, Message to the Confederate Congress, December 7, 1863, https://en.wikisource.org/wiki/Jefferson_Davis'_Message_to_the_Fourth_Session_of_the_First_Confederate_Congress.

38. Egon Caesar Corti, *Maximilian and Charlotte of Mexico*, trans. Catherine Alison Phillips (New York: Alfred A. Knopf, 1928), 435; Dawson, *The Mexican Adventure*, 318, 343–44; Jasper Ridley, *Maximilian and Juárez* (New York: Ticknor and Fields, 1992), 156–57.

39. Fauconnet to Drouyn de Lhuys, La Nouvelle-Orléans, June 17, 1864; Boilleau to Drouyn de Lhuys, New York, February 7, 1865; Paul to Drouyn de Lhuys, Richmond, February 25, 1864, A.M.A.E. CPC, EU, 19: 90-91v., 180; 20: 91-v.

40. Montholon to Drouyn de Lhuys, Mexico, March 10, 1865, A.M.A.E. CP, M, 63: 124v.-125; Boilleau to Drouyn de Lhuys, New York, February 7, March 28, 1865, A.M.A.E. CPC, EU, 20: 92-v., 202–7; La Tour d'Auvergne to Drouyn de Lhuys, London, February 6, 28, 1865, A.M.A.E. CP, A, 732: 70v., 109-v.

41. Bigelow to Seward, Paris, February 14 and 22, 1865; Bigelow to Drouyn de Lhuys, Paris, February 23, 1865. Lynn Case and Warren Spencer, *The United States and France: Civil War Diplomacy* (Philadelphia: University of Pennsylvania Press, 1970), 563.

42. La Tour d'Auvergne to Drouyn de Lhuys, London, February 27, 1865, A.M.A.E. CP, A, 732: 105–6.

43. Slidell to Thouvenel, Paris, July 21, 1862, A.M.A.E. ADP, EU, 32: 56v.-57.

44. To avoid overloading the text we had to limit ourselves to some significant dispatches, but the observation is recurrent. See, for example Montholon to Drouyn de Lhuys, Richmond, March 1, 1849; Lacoste to Turgot, New York, April 12, 1852, A.M.A.E. CPC, EU, 2: 206–7, 3: 172; Sartiges to Walewski, Washington, January 5, 1858, A.M.A.E. CP, EU, 118: 26.

45. The Gadsden Purchase included lands on south of the Gila River and west of the Rio Grande, a 29,640-square-mile region. Boilleau to Walewski, Washington, September 24, 1855, A.M.A.E. CP, EU, 113: 123.

46. Sartiges to Walewski, Washington, February 8, 15, March 2, 1858, A.M.A.E. PS, 10.

47. *Le Journal des Débats*, January 7, 1860. F. Camus.

48. See for example in *La Revue des Deux Mondes* the articles of Elisée Reclus and Auguste Laugel between 1861 and 1865.

49. See for example Montholon to Thouvenel, New York, August 27, 1861, A.M.A.E. CPC, EU, 8: 61.

50. Sartiges to Drouyn de Lhuys, Washington, April 8, 1855, A.M.A.E., PS, vol. 8; Sartiges to Walewski, Washington, February 15, 1858, A.M.A.E. PS, 10; Sartiges to Drouyn de Lhuys, Washington, May 2, 1854, A.M.A.E. PS, 6.

51. *Archives diplomatiques* (Paris: Amyot, 1862), 424–27.

52. Mercier to Thouvenel, Washington, April 6, 1861, A.M.A.E. CP, EU, 124: 133.

53. Thouvenel to Flahaut, Paris, October 11, 1861, A.M.A.E. LJ, M, 154.

54. *Id.*; Paris, February 10, 1862. Louis Thouvenel, *Le secret de l'Empereur* (Paris: Calmann-Levy, 1889), 2:236–37.

55. Frank Lawrence Owsley, *King Cotton Diplomacy* (Tuscaloosa: University of Alabama Press, 2008), 521–22. Preston was waiting in Havana, Cuba, when it was confirmed that Maximilian would not meet with him.

56. Dano to Drouyn de Lhuys, Puebla, June 11, 1865, A.M.A.E. CP, M, 63: 342–43.

CHAPTER SIX

From Aggression to Crisis
The Spanish Empire in the 1860s

Christopher Schmidt-Nowara

The U.S. Civil War transformed the geopolitics and the domestic politics of the Spanish colonial empire. With the United States divided, Spanish leaders carried out a series of adventures in the Americas, the most central of which was the annexation of Santo Domingo between 1861 and 1865, the subject of Anne Eller's contribution to this volume. Intended to solidify slavery and sovereignty in Spain's last American territories, Cuba and Puerto Rico, war and occupation in Santo Domingo had the inverse effect, playing a role in the protracted crisis of Antillean slavery and Spanish dominion that would break out in 1868 when anticolonial revolts in the two islands converged with the overthrow of the Bourbon monarchy in the metropole. Thus, by the end of the 1860s, it had become clear to many Spaniards that the U.S. Civil War was not the opportunity for expansion and consolidation that it had initially appeared to be but was instead a dress rehearsal, a "broken image,"[1] for their empire's own crisis of slavery and sovereignty. This article will track the historical arc traced by the Spanish Empire during the 1860s, from aggression to crisis, by analyzing the centrality of the Cuban slave complex to Spanish colonial interests. It will also show how the foreign adventures of the early 1860s produced unforeseen blowback by the end of the decade, including heightened antislavery sentiment in the metropole, partly inspired by the war and emancipation in the United States, and the crystallization of an abolitionist movement that challenged the pillar of the colonial system.

CONTROL OF CUBA and protection of the colony's slave-worked plantation complex were the organizing principles during the 1860s. Spanish and colonial elites and officials believed that exerting military and commercial might in the Americas (and, to a certain extent, globally) would consolidate sovereignty and slavery in the imperial core. The Dominican intervention, for example, would ideally remove the filibustering threat that had menaced Cuba in the 1840s and 1850s, as proslavery adventurers and politicians from the United States clamored for annexation.[2] Spaniards, especially the military governors clustered in Havana and San Juan, always saw the unstable former colony as the jumping off point for an American invasion. The U.S. Civil War temporarily neutralized that threat, giving Spain the opening to annex Santo Domingo by diverting the Union's and the Confederate States of America's (CSA's) attention and resources away from the Caribbean. As Howard Jones and Patrick Kelly discuss in their essays for this volume, the CSA did make efforts to forge diplomatic relations with Spain and other European power, but the Spaniards were under no illusions; the southerners had always been their bitter foes and the most dangerous threat to Cuba, the colony that always preoccupied Spanish rulers. Víctor Balaguer, the minister of overseas territories (Ministro de Ultramar), summarized the island's centrality, complaining at the end of the nineteenth century that the great weight of Cuba within the colonial empire distracted his office's attention away from other colonies: "But then there is Cuba, Cuba, which . . . has monopolized all of the hours of the minister, taking control of him body and soul."[3] Why always Cuba?

Beginning in the late eighteenth century, local planters and metropolitan officials undertook legal, commercial, and fiscal reforms that culminated with the deregulation of the slave trade to the Caribbean colonies in 1789, a revolutionary innovation that broke with almost three centuries of close control of the traffic in slaves to the Spanish American settlements. In the aftermath of the Seven Years' War, during which the British seized and occupied Havana for almost a year, it became clear to economic elites, royal officials, and the military that Spain needed to enhance colonial defenses and colonial revenues. One way of creating the wealth that would pay for a new navy, more fortifications, and more troops was by emulating the Caribbean colonies of the French, British, Danish, and Dutch, where the slave trade flowed and plantation production thrived. The conjuncture of Creole demands and metropolitan policies was especially propitious, coinciding with the surge in global demand for tropical commodities like sugar, coffee, and cotton. Cuba, by far the greatest beneficiary of the deregulated slave traffic and the largest slave society in Spanish colonial history, was swept up in and helped to shape what Dale Tomich has called the "second slavery." This was an American plantation regime centered in Cuba, the United States, and Brazil with a productive capacity, spatial extension, employment of unfree labor, capital investment, and market for its goods that greatly surpassed previous iterations of the New World plantation system. By the mid-nineteenth century, Cuba was the world's largest producer of cane sugar, as hundreds of thousands of enslaved and indentured workers labored on plantations that ran cutting edge transportation and refining technology to expand the space of cultivation, increase the productivity of unfree labor, and secure access to international markets.

The colony had assumed an even greater role in Spanish colonial fortunes by the 1820s when the vast majority of the American empire successfully gained independence from the metropole. Cuba and Puerto Rico remained loyal for a variety of factors, the most central being the plantation revolutions overtaking the islands with the vast riches on offer and the threat of slave rebellion and racial conflict present in the minds of local elites and officials. For the remainder of the nineteenth century, Cuba was the core of Spain's diminished yet still prosperous overseas empire. The treasury reaped rewards from colonial taxes and customs duties, while metropolitan producers and shippers relied heavily on Cuba as a protected market for their goods and services. Meanwhile, Spanish immigrants to the Antilles were the beneficiaries of many of the planting, slaving, banking, and commercial fortunes, great and small, earned in Cuba during the nineteenth century.[4]

Defense of the colony from internal revolts and foreign invasions was thus a high priority for Spanish governments. In the mid-nineteenth century, this priority took a strange turn when the normally cautious government of Spain undertook wars in Africa, the Americas, and Asia during an era known as the Liberal Union (1856–68), so-called for the dominant political formation of the same name, which had taken shape in response to the deadlock between Spain's major political parties, the conservative Moderates and the liberal Progressives. The Liberal Union drew supporters from both parties as a way of breaking the pattern in which the Moderates and the monarch, Isabella II, sought to monopolize power and the Progressives sought to gain power through insurrections. Under the premiership of General Leopoldo O'Donnell, the Liberal Union governed between 1858 and 1863, with a brief return to power in 1865 and 1866. O'Donnell oversaw a period of economic growth in Spain, the leading sector being the railways, which were financed and constructed with French capital and expertise in the 1850s and 1860s. Though the government remained staunchly protectionist of metropolitan manufactures and agriculture and wary of joint-stock companies (banned with the exception of the railway companies), there was a period of economic euphoria as the railway network expanded and public revenues burgeoned.[5]

A counterpart to metropolitan economic growth was O'Donnell's aggressive foreign policy, financed by the economic bubble that temporarily provided surpluses.[6] The occupation of Santo Domingo in 1861 was part of a series of interventions undertaken by the Spanish state beginning in the late 1850s and continuing through the mid-1860s. These actions included a short war with the Sultan of Morocco (the Guerra de África, 1859–60), led personally by O'Donnell, during which the government sought to whip up patriotic fervor in the peninsula; a joint invasion of Cochinchina and Saigon with France (1858–62); an expeditionary force sent to Mexico with France and Britain to recoup debts (1861–62); and the seizure of insular territories and the bombardment of fortresses in Chile and Peru in the mid-1860s, which were efforts to extort reparations and favorable trade agreements, an exercise that had proven successful in Morocco. Moreover, in 1863, the government established the Ministerio de Ultramar (the ministry of overseas territories), meant to rationalize the administration of the Caribbean and Pacific possessions.[7] The period thus looks like one of confidence and innovation in foreign and colonial affairs.

Historians of Spain are turning their attention to this period, trying to understand the connections among these interventions, if there are any, and what emboldened Madrid, a normally cautious regime that sought to avoid entanglements that might threaten its small but vital and valuable overseas empire.[8] They have adduced several explanations. First, foreign wars were for domestic consumption, meant to solidify the regime of the Liberal Union, a new political formation that sought to reconcile the Spanish political class to compromise and power sharing in the constitutional monarchy, to break the cycle of military uprisings that were the mechanism of political change, and to open the metropole to greater foreign investment and modernization through the development of infrastructure, especially the railway network. Historians have treated the Guerra de África as a war that engendered widespread popular support, measured in terms of voluntary enlistments for the war and mass celebrations heralding Spanish victories in cities and towns throughout the peninsula, though there is also evidence that such demonstrations and proclamations of affiliation were orchestrated from Madrid, a topic that should be explored further.[9]

Foreign policy is another area of explanation.[10] The Liberal Union's close connection to the regime of Napoleon III forced it into a junior partner role in some of these interventions, most notably in Indochina and Mexico, and encouraged hopes that France would collaborate in the Dominican adventure by invading Haiti. France had a powerful economic influence in Spain: along with Britain, it was Spain's largest export market, while French capital, materials, and expertise were crucial to the construction of the Spanish railway network in the 1850s and 1860s. Indeed, shut out of the London credit market, the Spanish government was completely reliant on Paris for foreign loans.[11] Moreover, Spanish conservatives admired Napoleon III's combination of dictatorship and economic modernization, a formula that the Moderate Party tried out with mixed success in the middle decades of the nineteenth century. Nonetheless, the limits of French influence and partnership were soon clear: Spain took part in the Cochinchina invasion but reaped little reward, while in Mexico, the Spanish general Juan Prim y Prats withdrew Spain's expeditionary force, refusing to support the overthrow of the Mexican government and the enthronement of Maximilian.[12] The two countries clashed over the Spanish occupation of Santo Domingo, the French government warning the Spanish over the amount of force it might use against Haiti.

Finally, there is some evidence that Cuba's plantation system was the center around which these apparently disparate events circulated, not only its security but also its necessary rivers of unfree workers.[13] That the Liberal Union's dominant figure was General Leopoldo O'Donnell is significant. O'Donnell was captain-general of Cuba in the 1840s and oversaw the suppression of the La Escalera Conspiracy, a revolt of slaves and free blacks to abolish slavery, which he carried out with extreme brutality. These experiences endowed O'Donnell with two crucial views of the colonial empire: first, he could see first-hand the terrific wealth and economic dynamism of Spain's largest colony, and second, he saw that it was politically fragile both internally and regionally. Social groups in Cuba, especially the enslaved and free people of color, chafed at the authoritarianism and violence of the militarized plantation regime.[14] Meanwhile, abolitionist forces made their presence felt in the Caribbean in a variety of ways, including British pressure to abolish the slave trade and the active conspiring of British agents in Cuba, some of whom were implicated in the La Escalera Conspiracy to overthrow slavery.[15]

In assessing the centrality of the Caribbean plantation colonies, it is important to keep in mind that on the Cuban and Puerto Rican haciendas, while enslaved laborers predominated, there was a mix of workers, free and unfree.[16] Indeed, in the 1840s and well into the 1850s, there was a significant decline in the transatlantic slave trade to Cuba even though the demand for labor remained high (the traffic would spike again at the end of the 1850s and remain robust into the 1860s), while in Puerto Rico, the trade was more or less closed by 1850 for economic reasons. The state and planters were thus casting about for complementary systems of labor recruitment and control, the most important for Cuba being the large-scale traffic in Chinese indentured workers from the Portuguese port of Macao between the 1840s and the 1870s (there was also a traffic in indentured Yucatecan workers). In Puerto Rico, though proposals for renewing the slave trade or opening a traffic in indentured workers remained in play, the solution was found internally through the use of the *libreta*, a work book system, that compelled landless laborers and small holders to work on large-scale enterprises. O'Donnell was certainly familiar with this economic and political situation—the precariousness of the slave trade, the demand for forced labor, and foreign abolitionist pressures. Thus, one possible unifying principle tying together Liberal Union militarism was the effort to secure the Antillean colonies and promote flows of unfree labor, not only from Africa but also from Asia (hence the alliance with France in Cochinchina), principally to Cuba.

WHAT WE CAN SAY about Spanish actions in the Caribbean is that they were a long time coming.[17] Spain refused to recognize Santo Domingo's independence until the 1850s, hoping either to reclaim the former colony or to extract reparations, much as France did from Haiti. A renewed colonialism was an attractive option especially for the military leadership that governed Cuba and Puerto Rico in the nineteenth century because the generals in Havana and San Juan saw the island of Hispaniola as a constant source of instability in the Spanish colonies. For example, in the mid-1850s, news arrived in Madrid from San Juan and Havana that on the one hand, Haiti was preparing a large force to invade Cuba and abolish slavery, while on the other, thousands of filibusters from the United States were going to take over Santo Domingo and use it as a base from which to expel Spain from its last colonies. Since Spain had no formal relation with either country, such rumors were difficult to verify or discount. In his report to the Ministry of State, Mariano Torrente, an official who had been sent as a spy to the two countries in 1854, urged the government of Spain to organize a joint invasion with France to retake the island and bring peace to Cuba and Puerto Rico. At the time, the cabinet of ministers in Madrid rejected the plan. Minister of State Calderón de la Barca, a career diplomat with extensive experience in the United States and Mexico, argued that the United States would invoke the Monroe Doctrine and actively oppose any Spanish/Dominican attempts at annexation. However, with the outbreak of the Civil War, the possibility of reincorporating Santo Domingo looked like a real possibility.[18]

In the end, as Anne Eller shows, this course of action failed miserably, though the Spaniards arrived with much hope. One of their early and telling decisions was to locate and restore the home of Christopher Columbus in the city of Santo Domingo, a monument that would serve as a reminder of the new regime's ancient roots. Later in the century, though, Columbus would become a source not of colonial legitimacy but of national vindication against Spain when Dominican and papal officials announced that they had found the admiral's mortal remains in the Santo Domingo cathedral, a claim that supposedly had its roots in the anti-Spanish rumors and conspiracies in the capital during the occupation.[19] Moreover, the occupation, which was spearheaded from Havana, not from Madrid, by Captain-General Francisco Serrano y Domínguez, inspired some optimism and curiosity in the metropole, and not only from advocates of a militarist foreign policy. Economic and political liberals argued that Spanish rule in Santo Domingo, if implemented correctly, might serve as a model for extensive reforms in Cuba and Puerto Rico. Instead of a colonial regime based on slavery, exceptional military rule, and protectionism, liberals believed that a new system based on free labor, constitutional government, and free trade might be introduced immediately in Santo Domingo, a society without slaves, and then spread to the neighboring colonies. The result would be social and political peace and an invigorated Antillean economy that would produce ample customs and tax revenues for the metropole without the costly and counterproductive repressive apparatus of the current regime.[20] Such a perspective obviously flew in the face of vested metropolitan and colonial interests and would inspire ferocious opposition later in the decade; nor was it universally shared in reformist circles. One of the mouthpieces of Spain's Progressive Party, *El Clamor Público*, asked whether the monies expended in Santo Domingo might not be put to better use in Spain itself. Had not history shown that Spain had exhausted itself in such overseas adventures? What the country needed was more railways, canals, ports, and arsenals, not a distant territory of dubious economic value.[21]

General Juan Prim y Prats, the Count of Reus, who had led the Spanish expedition to Mexico, also criticized (indirectly) his erstwhile ally O'Donnell for the military and geopolitical problems attending his adventures in the Americas. Spanish and French ambitions in the New World were pure folly, based on ignorance of the United States and its vast military and economic prowess. After withdrawing Spanish forces from Mexico, Prim departed for the United States in 1862, eager to witness the epic battle under way in the northern republic. Two years later, writing in the Progressive paper *La Iberia*, Prim recalled meeting Abraham Lincoln and William Seward at the White House. But the bulk of his article concerned his tour of General George McClellan's Army of the Potomac, which was preparing to attack Richmond, an experience that left him deeply impressed by the military capabilities of the Union. The huge number of men, weapons and other materials, the engineering and the good order of the troops were far beyond the capacity of any of the European armies. He left no doubt that in the context of general mobilization for war, the United States was the world's premier military power, a bad omen not only for Spain as it occupied Santo Domingo, but also for France in Mexico: "Whenever the Monroe doctrine is to be defended— America for the Americans . . . woe unto those who shall dare to contend with them in America. If this article should, perchance, come to the knowledge of the statesmen of France, it is to be hoped that they will take note of this prophecy."[22]

Prim published his veiled criticism of the Liberal Union and the occupation of Santo Domingo in 1864, after the war there had turned sour for Spain because Dominicans refused to give the Army of the Antilles the warm welcome its leaders expected. By 1863 Spanish occupying forces in Santo Domingo were engaged in a ferocious guerilla war that led to thousands of casualties suffered by the Army of the Antilles and the accumulation of a huge debt charged to the Cuban treasury.[23] After withdrawing from Santo Domingo in 1865, Spain was in a weaker position in the region because the war had disrupted finances in the colonies, leading to greater internal discontent that would soon break out into the open in 1868, specifically in the Grito de Lares (Puerto Rico, September 23) and the Grito de Yara (Cuba, October 10), the uprisings against Spanish rule that would destabilize the slave regime. How to finance the extraordinary costs of combatting the Cuban insurgency became a matter of extensive and heated debate in Spain during its own revolutionary epoch, the September Revolution (1868–74),[24] during which all aspects of the colonial regime came into open contention after more than three decades of muted conversation and general adherence to the status quo. Whether to incorporate the Caribbean colonies into the new 1869 constitution, how to address the challenge to slavery coming from both the colonies and the metropole (see below), and how to defeat the separatist rebellion took center stage during the years of ferment in the metropole.[25]

The Spanish revolution was brought on by interrelated political and economic crises. On the one hand, the monarchy refused to allow the liberal Progressive Party to form a government and clung to the Liberal Union under O'Donnell before turning to its habitual partner in governance, the conservative Moderate Party. The intransigence of the Crown and the Moderates drove the Progressives, the Liberal Union, and, from the far Left, Democrats and Republicans into fervid insurrectionary plotting between 1866 and 1868. Adding to the insurrectionary mood was the concatenation of economic misfortunes, including the slowdown of railway construction and the bursting of the speculative bubble, the drying up of foreign credit, the global cotton famine brought on by the U.S. Civil War that hit Catalan manufacturing, and, in 1868, a grave subsistence crisis aggravated by the government's protectionist trade policies.[26]

Colonial politics also figured into this crisis atmosphere. The U.S. Civil War and the Dominican fiasco had put on the table urgent matters, including the fiscal burden on the Cuban treasury, the suspension since 1837 of constitutional government in the colonies, and the fate of Antillean slavery. The latter issue had new immediacy thanks to emancipation in the United States and the victory of the Union, and by the more successful persecution of the Cuban slave trade under the terms of the Lyons-Seward Treaty of 1862 that effectively removed the American flag as cover for illegal slaving to Cuba. In 1866 and 1867, the Spanish government convened in Madrid a consultative body of representatives from Cuba, Puerto Rico, and the metropole to propose a range of economic and political reforms. In 1867, the government finally abolished the slave trade, but when debate shifted to slavery itself, consensus broke down when Cuban representatives were loath to discuss the possibility of abolition in a public forum.[27]

However, after 1868 they were powerless to stop such conversations. The new government that came to power in the fall of 1868 was a democratic constitutional monarchy with mandates to liberalize the economy and to reform the colonial system. Yet, while the revolutionary coalition, made up of parties from across the political spectrum, spoke of far-reaching colonial reforms in its manifestoes, change was frequently hamstrung.[28] On one hand, the revolutionary coalition included quite conservative parties committed to maintaining the colonial order of slavery and despotism and whose leaders, such as the regent, General Francisco Serrano y Domínguez, former captain-general of Cuba and close ally of the planter class; Antonio Cánovas del Castillo, the mastermind of Spanish conservatism; and Cánovas' protégés, including Adelardo López de Ayala, the first minister of overseas territories in the revolutionary government, argued that nothing could be done in Cuba until the insurgency was thwarted, a view shared even by some political figures who cut a radical profile in peninsular debates.[29] On the other hand, the aggressive mobilization of conservative settlers against the insurgency in Cuba's great plantation zones meant that Madrid was almost powerless to dictate policy. One of the most notorious examples of this situation took place during Spain's First Republic (1873) when the minister of overseas territories traveled to the colony (the only sitting minister ever to do so) only to be virtually ignored by the captain-general and his administration. Similarly, the authorization to establish branches of the Spanish Abolitionist Society in Puerto Rico and Cuba in 1872 and 1873 was dead on arrival in Havana (but not in Puerto Rico, where abolitionism was a potent force in undermining the slave regime[30]).

Central to the pro-Spanish mobilization in Cuba were the Volunteers, irregular forces of Spaniards that held and terrorized Cuban cities. The Volunteers had their origins in the defense of Cuba against the filibustering campaigns in the 1840s and 1850s led by Spanish renegade Narciso López and his North American proslavery supporters, who were intent on annexing the island to the United States as a slave state. After being captured in 1851, López was publicly garroted and dozens of his men were shot down by firing squads; their fate foreshadowed how the Volunteers and their patrons would respond to the challenge to Spanish sovereignty in 1868.[31] Faced with an internal enemy in 1868, the Volunteers harassed, arrested, murdered, drove into exile, and confiscated the properties of suspected separatists. These properties were often substantial, as in the case of the Creole planter Miguel de Aldama from whom the government seized hundreds of slaves.[32]

The Volunteers were auxiliary forces to the massive military deployment from the Spanish peninsula to Cuba. During the course of the Ten Years' War (1868–78), Spain sent close to 200,000 troops to defend the colony against pro-independence forces, ten times the number of troops sent to Tierra Firme and New Granada during Pablo Morillo's counter-insurgency in the early nineteenth century. This "loyalist overkill," meant to cement Spanish control in the confrontation with the separatist revolt, multiplied the cost of colonialism by greatly adding to the fiscal burdens that Santo Domingo and Mexico had already placed on the Cuban budget. Rather than the stripped-down colonial regime that Bona and other liberals had imagined spreading from Santo Domingo to Cuba and Puerto Rico, the outcome of intervention and annexation was an even more cumbersome and repressive state in the core colonies. Who would pay for counterinsurgency, and how, became vexing problems that would preoccupy Madrid's politicians and bureaucrats for years to come. It threw into question for the first time the economic value of Spain's richest colony.[33]

AS MATT D. CHILDS shows in his essay, one of the unintended consequences of Cuba's Grito de Yara was the undermining of slavery, as slaves

flocked to the insurgent camp in quest of liberation. Planters and the colonial state proved adept at holding off the collapse of slavery, it was not fully
abolished in the island until 1886, but the revolt and its challenge to slavery
and to Spanish sovereignty demanded a response from the metropole.
However, the response was multivalent and sometimes equally threatening
to colonial and slaveholding interests because another consequence of
the U.S. Civil War, besides altering the geopolitics of colonialism and slavery, was to spark widespread interest and commitment to abolition in Spain.

Not that antislavery was always absent from the metropole, as a quick
survey of the decades prior to 1868 show. A spate of recent works has demonstrated that through the early to mid-nineteenth century, there were frequent
expressions of antislavery made in literary works, the theater, pamphlets, the
political press, and in the Cortes, especially during the Cortes of Cadiz
(1810–14), the government of resistance to the French occupation during
the Peninsular War.[34] However, these diverse displays of antipathy toward
slavery and the slave trade, especially as manifested in the dramatic rise of
the Cuban plantation system, never coalesced into an active abolitionist
movement. The U.S. Civil War helped to change that.

Before examining the roots of Spanish abolitionism and how the U.S.
Civil War allowed them to sprout, it will be useful to consider the connections and parallels between Cuban and U.S. slavery over the course of the
nineteenth century. As we have seen, western Cuba and the southern United
States, as well as southeastern Brazil (as Rafael Marquese's essay in this volume demonstrates), were dramatic manifestations of the "second slavery" in
the nineteenth-century global economy. Even though there were significant
differences between North American and Spanish colonial slavery in this
era (the slave trade, jurisprudence, social structure, religious institutions),
there was also a convergence of interests. This was particularly evident in
the defense of slavery against domestic foes and in the resistance to British
abolitionism internationally. Cuban and Southern slaveholders experienced
a similar insatiable thirst for opening vast hinterlands to slave-based production, for Cubans in the central portions of the island and for Southerners in the
West (and perhaps beyond if the South's filibusters got their way). That convergence of nineteenth-century slave societies helps to explain why the U.S. Civil
War could spark abolitionist mobilization in Spain, as the battle over slavery
and territorial integrity in North America became a sounding board, a "broken
image," for Spanish reformers confronted by similar challenges.[35]

The tremendous growth of the Cuban plantation system made Spanish
observers more interested in American antislavery by the mid-nineteenth

century. Receptions, glosses, and reworkings of Harriet Beecher Stowe's *Uncle Tom's Cabin*, as well as her *Key to Uncle Tom's Cabin*, show that many Spaniards found Anglo-American abolitionism directly relevant to understanding and debating colonial slavery, territorial control of Cuba, and the slave traffic. As Lisa Surwillo has demonstrated, the novel exploded onto the Spanish scene shortly after its publication in the United States in 1852, translated in various editions, serialized in the major newspapers of the day, and rewritten for theatrical productions.[36] One version staged in the port city of Cádiz in 1853, a play called *Haley, o, el traficante de negros*, picked up on the theme of the slave trade in Stowe's novel and adapted it to the Spanish setting to explore how defense of the traffic imperiled Spanish sovereignty in Cuba by inciting possible interventions by the United States and Britain. The implicit message of the work was that to preserve Cuba, and its plantation economy, Spain must abolish the slave trade, if not slavery.[37]

Other versions of the novel spelled out different lessons. The most unequivocally abolitionist reading came from the well-known novelist, translator, and publisher Wenceslao Ayguals de Izco (later a member of the Spanish Abolitionist Society), who introduced his translation by reminding the readers of his long-standing views in favor of abolishing slavery. He called attention to his play *Los Negros* (set in Jamaica, not Cuba or Puerto Rico), staged in Valencia in 1836, in which he attacked the cruelty and injustice of colonial slavery to much fanfare and support: "I will say that I was grateful for the public's applause for the morality of my work, its humanitarian tendencies, its faithful rendering of the horrors of slavery, and the condemnations that rang from all of its lines against the abominable traffic in blacks."[38]

The emphasis on the horrors of slavery, such as separation from family and extreme physical punishment, were important themes in Stowe's follow-up work, *A Key to Uncle Tom's Cabin* (1853), in which the author sought to demonstrate the veracity of her novel by recounting the real episodes upon which she based it. As with the novel, a translation soon followed, *La llave de la cabaña del tío Tom* in 1855, though with an important addition: the Spanish edition was vividly illustrated by Vicente Urrabieta y Ortiz to dramatize several of the anecdotes. Among them was a punishment scene in which a black man was tied to a whipping post and beaten with a rod by a white man who would fit the visual description of an overseer that later appeared in Spanish abolitionist publications (broad-brimmed hat and glowering expression). In the background, slaves labored in a field, while a fat, well-dressed white man, presumably the planter, shaded himself with a parasol as he watched the punishment being meted out.[39] Other illustrations depicted shackled women street-cleaning in a city, a black man hanged by a mob, another beheaded aboard a ship, and a proslavery mob in St. Louis attacking and burning the offices of a newspaper that had defied public opinion. The Spanish version of the *Key* thus not only related the events that Stowe transmuted into her fictional account of slavery and trafficking but also provided striking images of slavery, slave-owning, corporal punishment, and mob violence in defense of slavery that might provide relevant parallels to the situation in Spain and its colonies.

Though abolitionist works and images circulated through Spain before the outbreak of the American Civil War, an abolitionist movement did not take shape until the abolition of slavery and the end of the war in the United States, events much commented upon in the press and actively discussed in official and private circles.[40] The U.S. Civil War became a rallying point for domestic opposition to the monarchy of Isabella II and its increasingly dictatorial political allies. Among those liberals and republicans in opposition, there was widespread admiration for the republican Lincoln and sympathy for the goal of abolishing slavery. Indeed, from the beginning, Spanish advocates believed the North would triumph sooner by immediately abolishing slavery. A recent study of the image of Lincoln in Spain has found that Lincoln the emancipator was more revered than Lincoln the savior of the Union.[41]

Abolitionism soon emerged from this crucible, encouraged by the government's realization that it needed to take action in the Caribbean colonies. Together with U.S. and British agreement to stamp out the slave trade to Cuba, the profound changes in the United States compelled Cuban planters and the Spanish government to consider transitions toward new kinds of labor, however hesitant they were to give up on slavery. Since the late 1850s, the global price of sugar had spiked; in response, so did the price of slaves imported to Cuba. Planters were also modernizing production by investing heavily in railroads and industrial sugar-processing technology. The crisis of the second slavery occasioned by war and abolition in the United States thus coincided with a new phase of expansion and investment in Cuba's slave-worked plantations.[42]

Nonetheless, the emerging geopolitical realities were undeniable, so the Spanish government sought to open discussion of a controlled and protracted abolition process that included the definitive suppression of the slave trade in 1867. Among the changes wrought by the altered political conditions was greater public debate in Spain and, to a lesser degree, in the colonies concerning the ways to abolish slavery and reform the colonial order. In this atmosphere, Spanish and Antillean (chiefly Puerto Rican) reformers founded in 1865 the Spanish Abolitionist Society in Madrid. It consciously adopted Anglo-American forms of organization and agitation including public meetings (called "mitins" in Spanish), petition campaigns, regional chapters, and an ample presence in print through a periodical, *El Abolicionista*, and numerous pamphlets and collections of essays and poems about slavery. From its founding until the abolition of Cuban slavery in 1886, the antislavery movement played a significant role in pressing the Spanish colonial state to end Antillean slavery, though its influence ebbed and flowed considerably during those two decades, reaching its high water mark during the September Revolution.

At first, the proposals of Spanish and Antillean abolitionists active in the imperial capital were moderate: abolition of the slave trade and a gradual, controlled, and compensated abolition of slavery, which were in line with the aims of the Spanish government. However, tensions soon emerged because of the distinctive nature of slavery and the plantation economy in Puerto Rico and Cuba. Among the founders of the Spanish Abolitionist Society were the Puerto Rican Julio de Vizcarrondo and his wife, Harriet Brewster de Vizcarrondo. They came to the capital from a colony where the slave trade had come to an effective end by 1850, the slave population had been in decline, and the main export crop was transitioning from sugar to coffee, a crop less dependent on slave labor. Puerto Rican goals and interests, while far from being uniform as proslavery advocates remained alive and well, were more far-reaching than were those of their Spanish and Cuban counterparts.[43] Vizcarrondo and others were in favor of the immediate abolition of slavery in the island, and while they insisted that they did not speak for Cuba, Cubans perceived their demands as an immediate threat to the larger island's security and prosperity.

The events of 1868 radicalized abolitionism, giving Vizcarrondo and other advocates of immediate action a broader scope for publicity and debate. The Puerto Rican uprising was short lived; however, the resilience of the rebellion in Cuba forced the question of abolition to the front and center. Rebel leaders had to respond to the reality of slaves fleeing from slavery as Matt D. Childs shows, while in the metropole, abolitionists came to argue that only immediate abolition would quell the rebellion by ensuring the gratitude and loyalty of slaves emancipated by Spain.[44] The new regime in the metropole was democratic and introduced broad freedoms of the press and association, greatly increasing the space for abolitionist agitation and propaganda. Demands for abolition were no longer allusive but direct and persistent. Abolitionists marched through cities such as Madrid and Seville, forming organized campaigns to petition the government that mobilized numerous associations, parties, and municipalities from throughout the peninsula requesting action against slavery. For the first time since the Cortes of Cádiz (1810–14), slavery and abolition were subject to open parliamentary debate as abolitionists rose to positions of power in both the legislative and executive branches of government. Moreover, in Puerto Rico, where conservative opinion was less robust and militant than in Cuba, abolitionists not only represented the colony in the metropolitan Cortes but also assumed important local offices. They used their authority to intervene directly on behalf of slaves against masters as they sought to exercise the new freedoms created by legislation, including the gradualist Moret Law (1870) and the abolition of slavery in the island (1873).[45]

In response to the unprecedented push for abolition, the powerful vested interests in Spain and Cuba that sought to defend slavery, or at least delay its suppression, organized their own associations, periodicals, demonstrations, and petition campaigns as the politics of the second slavery played out in the streets, theaters, political forums, and meeting rooms of the metropole.[46] In the short run, they achieved their goals, as immediate abolition in Cuba, and to a certain degree in Puerto Rico, failed to transpire despite widespread antislavery sentiment and the willingness of some of the revolutionary parties to tackle slavery head on. Nonetheless, planters, merchants, bankers, and high military and political officials had to fight tooth and nail in Madrid and Havana to get their way. In the long run, the type of colonial regime built around slavery, which the militarist foreign policy of the 1860s had sought to reinforce, was transformed in spite of the counterrevolutionary resistance, as slavery gradually diminished and Spanish control of Cuba faced armed opposition in the colony and anxiety about its costs in the metropole.

The outbreak of the U.S. Civil War coincided with a period of aggression and optimism in Spanish foreign and colonial policy. Taking advantage of the North American republic's crisis, officials sought to reinforce sovereignty and slavery in Cuba and Puerto Rico by annexing Santo Domingo, a move they believed would neutralize perceived threats to Antillean security and prosperity from Hispañola and the United States. By the end of the U.S. Civil War and the end of the decade, however, Spain found itself immersed in its own fratricidal conflict that would also undermine slavery and reshape sovereignty in the colonial empire. What had seemed like an opportunity in 1861 proved to be a broken image of Spain's own impending, and connected, political, military, and economic crises. Slavery was under siege in the Antilles and in the metropole, even though Cuban planters proved adept at keeping their haciendas working profitably through the 1870s and until the final abolition of slavery in 1886.[47] Moreover, the costs of colonialism were becoming more equivocal. If property and sovereignty were insecure and the Cuban treasury in disarray, then investors, producers, and the state might look elsewhere in the colonial empire for opportunities. By the end of the 1860s, leading sectors of the metropolitan economy were assessing the Philippines as an alternative and lobbying the government for reforms that would promote their interests. The instability in Cuba motivated them, but so did the opening of the Suez Canal in 1869, which provided a more direct oceanic route to the archipelago from busy peninsular port cities with a strong colonial vocation like Barcelona. Thus, from the 1860s onwards, dramatic changes came not only to the Antilles but also to the Philippines as the metropolitan government slowly but surely enacted measures that favored Spanish shipping and goods in the distant colonial market.[48] However, one should not exaggerate the decline of Antillean prosperity, for it was neither total nor rapid. Spanish immigrants came in droves to Cuba after the abolition of slavery, some to work as laborers and farmers in the restructured agrarian economy, others as professionals and soldiers, some as investors who came to dominate the sugar industry and to eclipse the Creole landowning elite, whose fortunes were tied so closely to slavery.[49] Spanish interests and connections to Cuba thus remained vital and defiant in spite of the radically changed conditions of colonialism, as the violent, deadly, and destructive response to the outbreak of revolution in 1895 would demonstrate.

Suggested Readings

Bona, Félix de. *Cuba, Santo Domingo y Puerto Rico*. Madrid: Imprenta de Manuel Galiano, 1861.

Cubano-Iguina, Astrid. "Freedom in the Making: The Slaves of Hacienda La Esperanza, Manatí, Puerto Rico, on the Eve of Abolition, 1868–1876." *Social History* 36 (August 2011): 280–93.

de Labra, Rafael María. *La cuestión colonial*. Madrid: Gregorio Estrada, 1869.

de Reus, El Conde. "Mi viaje a los Estados Unidos," *La Iberia* (Madrid), February 17, 1864, translated into English as *General McClellan, and the Army of the Potomac*. New York: J. Bradburn, 1864.

Fradera, Josep M. and Christopher Schmidt-Nowara, eds. *Slavery and Antislavery in Spain's Atlantic Empire*. New York: Berghahn Books, 2013.

Marquese, Rafael and Tâmis Parron, "Internacional escravista: a política da Segunda Escravidão." *Topoi* 23 (2011): 97–117.

Martinez-Fernandez, Luís. *The Hispanic Caribbean between Empires: Economy, Society, and Patterns of Political Thought in the Hispanic Caribbean, 1840–1868.* Athens: University of Georgia Press, 1994.

Tomich, Dale. *Through the Prism of Slavery: Labor, Capital, and World Economy.* Lanham: Rowman and Littlefield, 2004.

Torrente, Mariano. *Política ultramarina: Que abraza todos los puntos referents a las relaciones de España con los Estados Unidos, con la Inglaterra y las Antillas, y señaladamente con la isla de Santo Domingo.* Madrid: Compañía general de Impresores y Libreros del Reino, 1854.

Notes

1. Iván Jaksic, *The Hispanic World and American Intellectual Life, 1820–1880* (New York: Palgrave Macmillan, 2007); and Christopher Schmidt-Nowara, "The Broken Image: The Spanish Empire in the United States after 1898," in *Endless Empire: Spain's Retreat, Europe's Eclipse, America's Decline,* ed. Alfred McCoy, Josep M. Fradera, and Stephen Jacobson (Madison: University of Wisconsin Press, 2012), 160–66.

2. Most recently treated in Robert E. May, *Slavery, Race, and Conquest in the Tropics: Lincoln, Douglas, and the Future of Latin America* (New York: Cambridge University Press, 2013).

3. Quoted in Javier Morillo-Alicea, "Uncharted Landscapes of 'Latin America': The Philippines in the Spanish Imperial Archipelago," in *Interpreting Spanish Colonialism: Empires, Nations, and Legends,* ed. Christopher Schmidt-Nowara and John Nieto-Phillips (Albuquerque: University of New Mexico Press, 2005), 32. Balaguer was especially interested in the Philippines.

4. See Dale Tomich, "The 'Second Slavery': Bonded Labor and the Transformation of the Nineteenth-Century World Economy," in *Through the Prism of Slavery: Labor, Capital, and World Economy* (Lanham: Rowman and Littlefield, 2004), 56–71; Márcia Berbel, Rafael Marquese, and Tâmis Parron, *Escravidão e política: Brasil e Cuba c. 1790–1850* (São Paulo: Editora Hucitec: FAPSEP, 2010); and Josep M. Fradera and Christopher Schmidt-Nowara, eds., *Slavery and Antislavery in Spain's Atlantic Empire* (New York: Berghahn Books, 2013).

5. Nicolás Sánchez-Albornoz, "El trasfondo económico de la Revolución," and Gabriel Tortella, "Ferrocarriles, economía y Revolución," in *La revolución de 1868: Historia, pensamiento, literatura,* ed. Clara E. Lida and Iris M. Zavala (New York: Las Americas Publishing Company, 1970), 64–79, 126–37; and Raymond Carr, *Spain, 1808–1975,* 2nd ed. (Oxford: Oxford University Press, 1982), 257–304.

6. Tortella, "Ferrocarriles"; and Wayne Bowen, *Spain and the American Civil War* (Columbia: University of Missouri Press, 2011), ch. 2.

7. Treated in Agustín Sánchez Andrés, *El Ministerio de Ultramar: Una institución liberal para el gobierno de las colonias, 1863–1899* (La Laguna/Michoacán: Centro de la Cultura Popular Canaria/Universidad Michoacana de San Nicolás de Hidalgo, 2007).

8. Recent overviews are Stephen Jacobson, "Imperial Ambitions in an Era of Decline: Micromilitarism and the Eclipse of the Spanish Empire, 1858–1923," *Endless Empire*, 74–91; and Bowen, *Spain and the American Civil War.*

9. See Carlos Serrano, *El nacimiento de Carmen: Símbolos, mitos, nación* (Madrid: Taurus, 1999); Albert Garcia Balañà, "Patria, plebe y política en la España isabelina: la Guerra de África en Cataluña (1859–1860)," in *Marruecos y el colonialismo español: De la Guerra de África a la "penetración pacífica,"* ed. Eloy Martín Corrales (Barcelona: Ediciones Bellaterra, 2002), 13–77; and Susan Martin-Marquéz, *Disorientations: Spanish Colonialism in Africa and the Performance of Identity* (New Haven, CT: Yale University Press, 2008), 101–60.

10. See Juan Antonio Inarejos Muñoz, *Intervenciones coloniales y nacionalismo español: La política exterior de la Unión Liberal y sus vínculos con la Francia de Napoléon III (1856–1868)* (Madrid: Sílex, 2010).

11. Tortella, "Ferrocarriles."

12. On Prim, another major proconsul of the era, see Josep M. Fradera, "Prim conspirador o la pedagogía del sable," in *Liberales, agitadores y conspiradores: Biografías heterodoxas del siglo XIX,* ed. Isabel Burdiel and Manuel Pérez Ledesma (Madrid: Espasa Calpe, 2000), 241–66.

13. The hypothesis sketched in Albert Garcia Balañà in "'El comercio de España en África' en la Barcelona de 1858, entre el Caribe y Mar de China, entre Londres y París," *Illes i Imperis,* nos. 10 and 11 (2008): 167–86.

14. Recent treatments of political and social conflict at mid-century include Manuel Barcia, *Seeds of Insurrection: Domination and Resistance on Western Cuban Plantations, 1808–1848* (Baton Rouge: Louisiana State University Press, 2008); and Michele Reid-Vazquez, *Year of the Lash: Free People of Color in Cuba and the Nineteenth-Century Atlantic World* (Athens: University of Georgia Press, 2011).

15. Robert L. Paquette, *Sugar Is Made with Blood: The Conspiracy of La Escalera and Conflict between Empires over Slavery in Cuba* (Middletown, CT: Wesleyan University Press, 1988).

16. Francisco Scarano, *Sugar and Slavery in Puerto Rico: The Plantation Economy of Ponce, 1800–1850* (Madison: University of Wisconsin Press, 1984); and Rebecca J. Scott, *Slave Emancipation in Cuba: The Transition to Free Labor, 1860–1899* (Princeton, NJ: Princeton University Press, 1985), ch. 1. However, in Puerto Rico coffee would surpass sugar as the major export crop in the later nineteenth century, and coffee always relied largely on proletarian labor. See Fernando Picó, *Libertad y servidumbre en el Puerto Rico del siglo XIX* (Río Piedras: Ediciones Huracán, 1979); Laird Bergad, *Coffee and the Growth of Agrarian Capitalism in Nineteenth-Century Puerto Rico* (Princeton, NJ: Princeton University Press, 1983); and Astrid Cubano Iguina, *El hilo en el laberinto: claves de la lucha política en Puerto Rico (siglo XIX)* (Río Piedras: Ediciones Huracán, 1990). On responses to the perceived crisis of slavery in Puerto Rico, see Jorge Chinea, "Confronting the Crisis of the Slave-Based Plantation System in Puerto Rico: Bureaucratic Proposals for Agricultural Modernisation, Diversification and Free Labor, c. 1846–1852," *Journal of Latin American Studies* 42 (February 2010): 121–54.

17. On this topic, see Cristóbal Robles Muñoz, *Paz en Santo Domingo, 1854–1865: El fracaso de la anexión a España* (Madrid: CSIC, 1987); Luis Martínez-Fernández, *Torn between Empires: Economy, Society, and Patterns of Political Thought in the Hispanic Caribbean, 1840–1878* (Athens: University of Georgia Press, 1994); Anne Eller, "Let's Show the World We Are Brothers: The Dominican *Guerra de Restauración* and the Nineteenth-Century Caribbean" (PhD dissertation, New York University, 2011); Inarejos Muñoz, *Intervenciones coloniales*, ch. 3; and Bowen, *Spain and the American Civil War*, ch. 3.

18. See Torrente's report of his mission to both countries in, *Política ultramarina: Que abraza todos los puntos referents a las relaciones de España con los Estados Unidos, con la Inglaterra y las Antillas, y señaladamente con la isla de Santo Domingo* (Madrid: Compañía general de Impresores y Libreros del Reino, 1854).

19. Christopher Schmidt-Nowara, *The Conquest of History: Spanish Colonialism and National Histories in the Nineteenth Century* (Pittsburgh: University of Pittsburgh Press, 2006), ch. 2. Spanish officials had supposedly evacuated Columbus' remains to Havana in 1795 after the Treaty of Basel transferred control of Santo Domingo to revolutionary France.

20. Félix de Bona expressed this liberal perspective in *Cuba, Santo Domingo y Puerto Rico* (Madrid: Imprenta de Manuel Galiano, 1861). This current of opinion would turn abolitionist after the U.S. Civil War and the evacuation of Santo Domingo. On this liberal milieu, see Christopher Schmidt-Nowara, *Empire and Antislavery: Spain, Cuba, and Puerto Rico, 1833–1874* (Pittsburgh: University of Pittsburgh Press, 1999), chs. 3 and 4.

21. Eller, "Let's Show the World," 165.

22. El Conde de Reus, "Mi viaje a los Estados Unidos," *La Iberia* (Madrid), 17 February 1864. Quote taken from English translation, Prim, *General McClellan and the Army of the Potomac* (New York: John Bradburn, 1864), 23. On Prim's political peregrinations during this period, see Fradera, "Prim conspirador." By this time, he was the leading figure of the Progressive Party and would take an active role in the plotting to overthrow the monarchy of Isabella II.

23. Inarejos Muñoz, *Intervenciones coloniales*, 73; Jacobson, "Imperial Ambitions," 80–81.

24. The uprising took place on September 18th, 1868. On September 30th, Isabella II went into exile from which she would never return. General Francisco Serrano y Domínguez headed the revolutionary regime as regent until Amadeus of Savoy, selected by the Cortes, took the throne at the beginning of 1871 as Amadeus I. When he abdicated two years later, Spain's First Republic (February 1873–January 1874), an unstable federal regime, was declared. It was overthrown and replaced by a unitary republic under Serrano, who in turn was deposed at the end of 1874 in favor of the restored Bourbon monarchy in the person of Alphonse XII, Isabella II's son.

25. Jordi Maluquer de Motes, "Abolicionismo y resistencia a la abolición de la esclavitud en la España del siglo XIX," *Anuario de Estudios Americanos* 43 (1986):

311–31; and Josep M. Fradera, *Colonias para después de un imperio* (Barcelona: Ediciones Bellaterra, 2005).

26. See the cogent summary in Sánchez-Albornoz, "El trasfondo económico." See also Tortella, "Ferrocarriles." On the cotton famine and the global restructuring of the industry, see Sven Beckert, "Emancipation and Empire: Reconstructing the Worldwide Web of Cotton Production in the Age of the American Civil War," *American Historical Review* 109 (December 2004): 1405–38. On French finance and Spanish politics, see Niall Ferguson, *The House of Rothschild, Volume 2: The World's Banker, 1849–1999* (New York: Penguin, 1999).

27. See Arthur Corwin, *Spain and the Abolition of Slavery in Cuba, 1817–1886* (Austin: University of Texas Press, 1967), ch. 11; David Murray, *Odious Commerce: Britain, Spain and the Abolition of the Cuban Slave Trade* (Cambridge: Cambridge University Press, 1980), ch. 14; and Schmidt-Nowara, *Empire and Antislavery*, ch. 5.

28. On the colonial dimension of the September Revolution, and its overthrow, see Manuel Espadas Burgos, *Alfonso XII y los orígenes de la Restauración*, 2nd ed. (Madrid: CSIC, 1990); José A. Piqueras, *La revolución democrática (1868–1874): Cuestión social, colonialismo y grupos de presión* (Madrid: Ministerio de Trabajo y Seguridad Social, 1992); and Inés Roldán de Montaud, *La Restauración en Cuba: fracaso de un proceso reformista* (Madrid: CSIC, 2000).

29. A cogent contemporary attack on the inertia and dissimulation of Cánovas, López de Ayala and their Liberal Union circle of politicians was made by the abolitionist Rafael María de Labra in his *La cuestión colonial* (Madrid: Gregorio Estrada, 1869).

30. See Astrid Cubano-Iguina, "Freedom in the Making: The Slaves of Hacienda La Esperanza, Manatí, Puerto Rico, on the Eve of Abolition, 1868–1876," *Social History* 36 (August 2011): 280–93.

31. May, *Slavery, Race, and Conquest in the Tropics*, chs. 1 and 2.

32. Sociedad Abolicionista Española, *Al excelentísimo señor D. Manuel Ruiz Zorrilla, Presidente del Consejo de Ministros sobre el cumplimiento de la Ley Prepatoria (de Julio de 1870) para la abolición de la esclavitud en las Antillas españolas* (Madrid: Secretaría de la Sociedad Abolicionista Española, 1872). The abolitionists detailed how through the policy of confiscation the state was becoming a large slave owner, even though according to Article 5 of the Moret Law of 1870, a gradual abolition law, it was supposed to dispossess itself of slave ownership.

33. Alfonso Quiroz, "Loyalist Overkill: The Socioeconomic Costs of 'Repressing' the Separatist Insurrection in Cuba, 1868–1878," *Hispanic American Historical Review* 78 (May 1998): 261–305. The politics around the colonial debt in the second half of the nineteenth century are treated at length in Roldán, *La Restauración en Cuba*. On these issues at the end of the nineteenth century, see Jordi Maluquer de Motes, *España en la crisis de 1898: de la Gran Depresión a la modernización económica del siglo XX* (Barcelona: Ediciones Península, 1999). See also Joan Casanovas, *Bread, or Bullets! Urban Labor and Spanish Colonialism in Cuba, 1850–1898* (Pittsburgh: University of Pittsburgh Press, 1998) on the Volunteers and Spanish reaction in the colony.

34. See Christopher Schmidt-Nowara, "Wilberforce Spanished: Joseph Blanco White and Spanish Antislavery, 1808–1814" and Albert Garcia Balañà, "Antislavery before Abolitionism: Networks and Motives in Early Liberal Barcelona, 1833–1844," in *Slavery and Antislavery in Spain's Atlantic Empire*, 158–75, 229–55; Joselyn M. Almeida, *Reimagining the Transatlantic, 1780–1890* (Burlington, VT: Ashgate, 2011), ch. 3; Camillia Cowling, *Conceiving Freedom: Women of Color, Gender, and the Abolition of Slavery in Havana and Rio de Janeiro* (Chapel Hill: University of North Carolina Press, 2013), ch. 4; Lisa Surwillo, "Representing the Slave Trader: *Haley* and the Slave Ship; or, Spain's *Uncle Tom's Cabin*," *PMLA* 120 (May 2005): 768–82; idem., *Monsters by Trade: Slave Traffickers in Modern Spanish Literature and Culture* (Stanford, CA: Stanford University Press, 2014); Catherine Davies, "The Poet(isa) and the Queen: The Paradoxes of Royal Patronage in 1840s Spain," *Hispanic Research Journal* 8 (September 2007): 319–32; and Henriette Partzsch, "Violets and Abolition: The Discourse on Slavery in Faustina Sáez de Melgar's Magazine *La Violeta* (Madrid, 1862–1866)," *Bulletin of Spanish Studies* 89 (2012): 859–75.

35. See Tomich, "The 'Second Slavery' "; Rafael Marquese and Tâmis Parron, "Internacional escravista: a política da Segunda Escravidão," *Topoi* no. 23 (2011): 97–117; and Christopher Schmidt-Nowara, "Spain and the Politics of the Second Slavery, 1808–1868," *Review: Journal of the Fernand Braudel Center*, forthcoming.

36. Surwillo, "Representing the Slave Trader."

37. Ángel de Luna and Rafael Leopoldo de Palomino, *Haley, o el traficante de negros: drama en cuatro actos, en prosa* (Cadiz: F. Pantoja, 1853).

38. An edition of *Los Negros* can be found in *El cancionero del pueblo, colección de novelas, comedias, leyendas, canciones, cuentos y dramas originales: Escritos y dedicados al pueblo español por Villegas y Ayguals de Izco*, 2nd ed. (Madrid: Imprenta de Ayguals de Izco, 1847), 97–207. "Advertencia preliminar," *La choza de Tom, o sea vida de los negros en el sur de los Estados Unidos, novela escrita en ingles por Enriqueta Beecher Stowe, traducida por Don Wenceslao Ayguals de Izco* (Madrid: Imprenta de Ayguals de Izco Hermanos, 1853), 3.

39. Harriet Beecher Stowe, *La llave de la cabaña del tío Tom: Segunda parte de la celebre novela de Mistress Enriqueta Beecher Stowe, la cabaña del tío Tom, que contiene los hechos y documentos originales en que se funda la novella, con las piezas justificativas, traducida de la última edición por G. A. Larrosa* (Barcelona: Imprenta Hispana de V. Castaños, 1855), 14.

40. Bowen, *Spain and the American Civil War*; James W. Cortada, *Spain and the American Civil War: Relations at Mid-Century, 1855–1868* (Philadelphia: Transactions of the American Philosophical Society, 1980); and Lisa Surwillo, "Poetic Diplomacy: Carolina Coronado and the American Civil War," *Comparative American Studies* 5 (2007): 409–22.

41. Carolyn Boyd, "A Man for All Seasons: Lincoln in Spain," in *The Global Lincoln*, ed. Richard Carwardine and Jay Sexton (Oxford: Oxford University Press, 2011), 189–205.

42. Laird Bergad, Fe Iglesias García, and María del Carmen Barcia, *The Cuban Slave Market, 1790–1880* (New York: Cambridge University Press, 1995).

43. Cubano-Iguina, "Freedom in the Making."

44. See the analysis of the situation made by the abolitionist Rafael María de Labra in *Carta que a varios electores del distrito de Infiesto (Oviedo) dirige su ex-diputado a Cortes* (Madrid: Imprenta de José Norguera, 1872). See also "Los negros de la insurrection cubana," *El Abolicionista* (Madrid), November 1, 1872.

45. See especially Cubano-Iguina, "Freedom in the Making." Also on Puerto Rican emancipation, see Luis A. Figueroa, *Sugar, Slavery, and Freedom in Nineteenth-Century Puerto Rico* (Chapel Hill: University of North Carolina Press, 2005); and Ileana M. Rodríguez-Silva, "Abolition, Race, and the Politics of Gratitude in Late Nineteenth-Century Puerto Rico," *Hispanic American Historical Review* 93 (November 2013): 621–57.

46. Jordi Maluquer de Motes, "La burgesia catalane i l'esclavitud colonial: modes de producció I pràctica política," *Recerques* 3 (1974): 83–136; and Martin Rodrigo y Alharilla, "Spanish Merchants and the Slave Trade: From Legality to Illegality, 1814–1870," in *Slavery and Antislavery in Spain's Atlantic Empire*, 176–99.

47. Laird Bergad, *Cuban Rural Society in the Nineteenth Century: The Social and Economic History of Monoculture in Matanzas* (Princeton, NJ: Princeton University Press, 1990), ch. 11.

48. Josep M. Delgado Ribas, " 'Menos se perdió en Cuba': La dimension asiática del 98," *Illes i Imperis* 2 (1999): 49–62; Martin Rodrigo y Alharilla, "Intereses empresariales españoles en Filipinas: La reconquista económica del archipelago durante la Restauración," in *Las relaciones entre España y Filipinas, siglos XVI–XX*, ed. María Dolores Elizalde Pérez-Grueso (Madrid: CSIC, 2002), 207–20; and Morillo-Alicea, "Uncharted Landscapes of 'Latin America.' "

49. On immigration, see Jordi Maluquer de Motes, *Nación e inmigración: Los españoles a Cuba (ss. XIX y XX)* (Oviedo: Ediciones Júcar, 1992). On changes in the agrarian economy and society, see Bergad, *Cuban Rural Society*, chs. 11–16.

CHAPTER SEVEN

Dominican Civil War, Slavery, and Spanish Annexation, 1844–1865

Anne Eller

On March 18, 1861, a small group of Spanish officials observed as Dominican authorities lowered the flag of the Dominican Republic and announced the territory's reintegration as a colony of Spain. Spain promised to maintain Santo Domingo as a free colony, even though it was flanked by the Spanish plantation regimes of Cuba and Puerto Rico. In fact, the annexation had been a voluntary act. Dominican president, Pedro Santana, worked with the Cuban governor to bring about reincorporation. Like the Conservative authors of Maximilian's arrival in Mexico, the Dominican leader hoped to silence partisan struggles and forestall the United States with the aid of a European power. That it was also the territory's former colonial power and a Catholic nation made it so much the better. The timing was auspicious for this reshuffling of regional control. Less than a month after Spanish authorities and troops began to trickle into Dominican territory, Confederate forces attacked Fort Sumter. With the beginning of the U.S. Civil War, one of the largest potential opponents to Spanish annexation was suddenly preoccupied. By late spring 1861, a new moment dawned for Spanish colonialism in the Caribbean.

Annexation was a surprising event for all of its witnesses. Madrid authorities had not authorized the Cuban governor to make such a move, and peninsular newspapers debated the project for several months after news arrived to Madrid. After initial recalcitrance, even surprise and indignation, many Spanish observers embraced the project, however. They began to see the Dominican occupation as a potential model of a post-slavery future for the empire and an impetus for legislative reform in Cuba and Puerto Rico as well. A number of observers in Madrid and Havana were even more ambitious. Sometimes under the guise of cultural fraternity with former Spanish republics, sometimes with more nakedly expansionist ambitions, commentators imagined Spain might swallow up more territory in the Americas. "The *Times* says Haiti will soon be annexed [too], we say 'let it be so,'" one author announced. "With all of the la Española, discovered by Isabel I and regained by Isabel II, the strength of the Spanish in the Antilles is unmatched," the narrator bragged.[1] Other regional powers were surprised at the new gain but largely quiescent. Britain and France, on the precipice of their own intrigue in Mexico, acknowledged Spanish plans with relative equanimity. Given the powerful distraction of war in the north and a decidedly imperial climate in the greater Gulf region, Dominican annexation proceeded with very little international opposition at all. Haiti and the Dominican Republic had been the only two independent island states in the region, anyway. After years of outside aspersion, cession of the latter back to a European power did not offend the sensibilities of other European states.

Attentive observers might have predicted the conflict that was to come. Responding as they were to Pedro Santana's annexationist appeals, Spanish authorities cast the annexation as an act of *noblesse oblige* toward the troubled territory, claiming Dominicans had shown "the keenest desire to return to the breast of the Mother Country."[2] In the larger towns of the former republic, like Santo Domingo and Santiago de los Caballeros, some merchants, would-be industrialists, and a rotating cast of political aspirants were in favor of annexation. They hoped that more political security would bring prosperity, at last. Residents of the Dominican countryside were nearly unequivocal in their opposition, however. The would-be modernizers of the returning Spanish administration implemented a number of measures meant to groom a more orderly populace, and many of these stood to infringe on the considerable autonomy of most Dominicans. Furthermore, Spanish officials clashed with Dominican residents and officials alike. The result was disastrous. Despite the best of imperial intentions, Spain would evacuate its last troops just over four years after they arrived.

Spanish annexation punctuated unsteadily increasing U.S. involvement in Dominican affairs. The territory's economy was feeble and its people, to northern white observers, racially suspect. Beginning in the 1840s, U.S. agents traveled to the Republic, intending to assess its resources, government, and population. In the following decade, a handful of speculators began to arrive, forwarding a number of colonization and exploitation schemes. Small filibuster groups from the United States also arrived, their eyes trained primarily on Cuba. Dominican politicians vacillated, their pro-annexation sentiments muted by wariness toward these schemes. Popular opposition, too, forestalled other concessions. Members of a community of U.S. freed people and their children marched all the way from the northern Samaná peninsula down to the Dominican capital to oppose a U.S. treaty in 1854, for example.[3] Over the next decade, as slavery ended in the United States, and anti-occupation fighting ravaged the Caribbean, territorial negotiations would begin anew.

ESTABLISHED IN 1844, the Dominican Republic was a fragile and fractious political entity with a complicated past. The first Spanish colonial era had ended quietly when a small group in the capital city proclaimed the territory to be the "Independent State of Spanish Haiti" in late 1821. Just a few months later, Haitian president Jean-Pierre Boyer united the whole island under Haitian rule, which lasted from 1822 to 1844. With time, political complaints arose on both sides of the island, and a coalition of factions toppled Boyer from power in 1843. East-West unification quickly crumbled, and a small group of nationalists proclaimed the east, the former Spanish territory, to be the independent Dominican Republic in the early spring of 1844. Political intrigue and economic problems beset the new eastern state, however. Presidential candidates relied on military mobilizations to hold onto the government as much as they did any electoral process. Geographical divisions, rampant inflation, and the instability of political bonds exacerbated public tensions. Two southern caudillos, Pedro Santana and Buenaventura Báez, dominated the presidency for much of the first decades, bolstered by bonds of party patronage and, in Santana's case, military renown. Liberal reformers and any aspirants from outside the capital city found themselves excluded from the government except as party affiliates or auxiliaries. Both caudillo leaders preferred executive mandates to constitutional rule. Still, neither Santana nor Báez could wrangle a stable period of power. They competed with each other, and with more powerful economic interests in the Cibao Valley to the north.

In this climate, annexation by Spain was an omnipresent political recourse for competing Dominican elites. The roots of pro-annexation partisanship were deep. Even before separation from Haiti in 1844, future Dominican president Buenaventura Báez angled for a French protectorate. Ambitious French diplomats, for their part, supported any scheme (including Dominican reunification with Haiti) that might hasten repayment of Haiti's so-called indemnity, a sum France demanded for Haiti's recognition. The French consul in Haiti openly entertained Dominican overtures.[4] Spain, meanwhile, largely rebuffed Dominican entreaties in the 1840s and 1850s. Britain showed no interest beyond commerce and mediation between the Dominican Republic and Haiti. Dominican relations with the United States foundered gravely over the question of slavery, as diplomats could not promise protection for Dominican travelers to U.S. southern ports.[5] All the while, the tobacco merchants and others in the Cibao Valley grew ever more restive. As the southern politicians continued to frustrate democratic reforms and to print more and more paper money to fund their administrations, a group in the central valley decided to mount a coup d'état. They drafted their own liberal constitution—similar to the 1857 Liberal constitution reformers drafted at the same moment in Mexico—and demanded a voice in the capital, Santo Domingo. Without armed forces of their own, the center-valley reformers called on Santana to defeat Báez. He did so, after a protracted siege of the capital in 1858, and then marginalized the reformers and ascended to dictatorial power once more. The liberal revolution had failed.

For the next several years, instability intensified. Annexation appeals, which had never ceased, gained traction. Soon after his return to power, Santana found a willing ear in the governor of Cuba, Francisco Serrano. Serrano was eager to preserve Spain's influence in the Caribbean, which was threatened both by unrest in Cuba and by the expansionist ambitions of the United States. Like other administrators before him, Serrano imagined abolitionist conspiracies at every turn. Their authors were, in different iterations, activist British consuls, Haitian rulers and their allies, or simply the omnipresent fear of domestic insurrection. Adding to the tension were the actions of U.S. filibusters throughout the greater Caribbean. Serrano imagined that a re-annexed Dominican Republic might forestall a rising tide of U.S. intrusion in the Caribbean. Finally, Santana invoked as a pretext for annexation the military threat of invasion from Haiti, a claim that found perpetually eager ears, despite all evidence that Haiti's President Geffrard desired only peace. There were also proponents of annexation in Spain who argued Dominicans were part of a "Spanish family" that embraced current and former colonies, a *raza hispánica* threatened by British and U.S. encroachment. Their claims echoed annexationists among Mexico's conservative elite. Santana, politically threatened, offered ostentatious narratives of Dominican fidelity to Spain: "Religion, language, beliefs, and customs, all we preserve with purity."[6]

The Cuban governor, eager to increase Spain's regional advantage, proceeded forth without the permission or even knowledge of the Spanish crown. News of the Spanish occupation of Santo Domingo in March 1861 reached Puerto Rico first and then crossed the Atlantic. As the spring of 1861 faded into summer, Madrid's public warmed to the annexation, now a *fait accompli*. Observers of various political inclinations began to imagine a new day for Spanish empire. "Columbus' island should not be abandoned again by Spain," one Madrid journalist urged.[7]

With Haitian rule, Dominicans had abolished slavery in 1822, and by prior agreement with Spanish officials, there was to be no slavery in this "new" Caribbean colony. Spanish authorities promised a delicate entente with the island's residents, that metropolitan civil codes would rule the island. Both Cuba and Puerto Rico had separate legal codes, and both were under a tight grip from Madrid. The Cuban governor openly hoped that Santo Domingo's more autonomous legal status might spur reform in the governance of Cuba and Puerto Rico, including colonial representation in parliament in Madrid. Annexation gave Santana a way to bargain for continued power; Spanish officials appointed him colonial governor. Governor Serrano dreamed that the annexation might portend something bigger still: the expansion of Spanish power into the Gulf of Mexico, with the Dominican Samaná peninsula serving as a strategic coaling station and a bulwark against U.S. aggression.

ON THE DAY OF annexation, March 18, 1861, small groups of Dominican officials lowered the Dominican flag and raised the Spanish one in a number of towns across the country. In the capital, the ceremony seemed to proceed without complication. Over the following months, Governor Serrano and a handful of other high-ranking Spanish officials stationed in Cuba made trips to the island, hastily crafting reports to the crown. Mostly, they were aghast at the informal nature of the government they were taking over. "There are no statistics, not even approximated ones," one frustrated Spanish official wrote.[8] They lamented the lack of economic development in their new colony. "Virgin forests . . . sparse population, barely any production, industry dead, commerce almost unknown," the Cuban governor claimed.[9] Meanwhile, divisions of Spanish troops arrived during the late spring and summer of 1861, totaling 10,000. Some of them came from the Spanish peninsula, some even from the brigade that had recently won victories at Ceuta, in northern Africa. The majority of Spain's soldiers, however, arrived from the neighboring Spanish possessions, particularly Cuba. Cuba's treasury funded the whole endeavor, and the cost soon ballooned to hundreds of thousands of pesos.

The first goal of the Spanish occupation, therefore, was to find a means to make the Dominican territory less of a drain on Cuban coffers, and to make it profitable. The Samaná peninsula was a promising harbor and coaling station, and Spanish authorities sent engineers to survey its prospects. By early fall, officials linked it into a mail route that connected it to the neighboring islands and began a series of reports on potential coal mining sites in its vicinity. To foment cash-crop agriculture, especially cotton, schemes for bringing immigrants to the colony abounded. Both Spanish officials and citizens proposed numerous plans to boost Dominican production, many based on the contract-labor models from neighboring islands, in which they called for the importation of men and women from South and East Asia, Africa, and Cuba as contract laborers.

Some explicitly called for white workers, and the Spanish consul to Haiti suggested they might come from the "Spanish" communities of the U.S. South, including Florida and Louisiana.[10] Small groups of migrants from the Spanish peninsula arrived in Santo Domingo, pleasing authorities and pro-Spanish observers. "*Españolismo* lives," one Spanish diplomat gushed.[11] 1861 may have felt like something of the apogee of Spanish resurgence in the Western Hemisphere. Later that year, Spain joined Britain and France in the allied invasion of Mexico.

Spanish authorities imagined themselves to be modernizers of the Dominican populace as well. Their approach immediately rankled many Dominicans, however. The new Spanish rulers imposed Cuba's oppressive civil codes on the island. These ranged from anti-gaming initiatives and vagrancy laws to edicts regulating house painting and individual dress. These regulations were not only intrusive and rigid, many were simply impractical in the Dominican setting, and town residents bristled at the fines inflicted upon them. Where Maximilian sought separation of church and state in Mexico, Spanish authorities sought to revive and fortify Catholic Church authority in Santo Domingo. An incoming archbishop, Bienvenido Monzón, issued a plethora of decrees intended to reform the Dominican populace and restore proper Catholic religious practices. He commanded a salary of more than 14,000 pesos for his new post.[12] Some priests embraced the new institutional oversight, but more resented their role as fee collectors for new fines. A few openly denounced Spanish presence entirely, earning them exile. Meanwhile, one population, the Protestant communities on the northern coast, divided the zealous archbishop even from Spanish secular authorities. These families and towns were comprised of African American migrants, émigrés from the British islands, and other Methodist and Anabaptist faithful. The archbishop was scandalized by their open practice, by this time long established on the island. Despite laws in Cuba and Puerto Rico that mandated Catholicism as the state religion, authorities were circumspect about how to proceed in the new colony. The British consul interceded on the behalf of the Protestant communities, and Spanish authorities decided it best to avoid international incident. The archbishop, unmoved, continued to urge for the suppression of Protestant practices.

Optimism floundered somewhat by 1862. In the fall of 1861, Spanish authorities moved to reform the military, another measure that earned widespread resentment. They separated Dominican soldiers from the Crown's forces, assigning them to reserve regiments, even after having served in combined forces during the first summer of occupation. Pay for the reserves was significantly less than that for the Spanish. Furthermore, a classification committee subdivided the reserves into active and passive groups. A number of Dominican officers were demoted to "passive" status—effectively, they were decommissioned—on a number of pretexts. For men who had served much of their adult lives in periodic mobilizations, this demotion was an acerbic blow. Changes occurred at the top of the administration as well. Santana resigned his post as Captain-General in mid-1862, succeeded by a Spanish official. The Cuban governor, Serrano, had come to be deeply disappointed in Santana, calling the intractable Dominican general "an almost insuperable obstacle" to Spanish rule.[13] Replacements continued. Spanish men successively replaced a number of loyal, prominent Dominicans who had accepted posts in the transition administration. Others offered their resignation. With the arrival of Brigadier Manuel Buceta, a particularly condescending and difficult commander, professional conflicts proliferated. Even his peninsular contemporaries condemned his conduct. Meanwhile, a number of Dominican loyalists chose to leave their posts, even leaving the city of Santiago de los Caballeros, in protest.

Furthermore, there were ongoing logistical problems. Many of the Spanish colonization projects collapsed immediately, due to a lack of provisions, disagreements on land allotments, and high mortality that felled arriving settlers. There is no evidence of any revival of these efforts after early failures. Low-level administrative posts went unfilled by local candidates, even in ostensibly prime locations, such as the new Spanish outpost on the Samaná peninsula.[14] Officials in the capital city repeatedly pleaded for Madrid to requisition more funds from Cuba's treasury, but stipends were slow to reach the territory. Public works, a potential boon for popular support, floundered because the funds from Havana were far from sufficient to build the projected roads and railroads, or dredge ports. Although Spanish authorities had promised to redeem Dominican paper money with hard specie, redemptions were slow and frequently disputed. Everywhere, money was "a delicate subject," and there existed a "total lack of capital . . . to make large-scale industry," the incoming governor lamented. No financial support of any kind arrived from Cuba during several months in the summer of 1862, and government projects stalled further. The overseas minister in Madrid warned the new Spanish governor that he would simply have to take a pay cut for the following year.[15]

Most detrimental to the new project, the behavior of Spanish military and civil authorities towards residents of the former republic ranged from occasionally high-handed and insensitive to vitriolic and overtly racist. Many of the arriving officials and troops disembarked in Santo Domingo after years of being stationed in the neighboring plantation juggernaut of Cuba. Their attitudes reflected the hierarchies that reigned there. Some conflicts, like Brigadier Buceta's haughty treatment of a number of prominent Dominicans in Santiago, centered on the material poverty of the new colony. Buceta refused to meet in the meeting hall that the group had prepared for him, deeming it "not even fit for troops to sleep in." The council members were humiliated.[16] Other incidents were openly racist. Spanish authorities had acknowledged that Dominicans of color were in prominent positions of military and civil authority; the Crown had explicitly called for incoming Spanish officials to avoid demonstrations of racial prejudice.[17] However, numerous incidents of Spanish soldiers lobbing racist insults at their Dominican military contemporaries dot the record. Troop comportment towards civilians in towns across the island also dipped into hostility. In one court case about the assault of some drunken soldiers against several townswomen in their home, the accused soldiers tried to dismiss the complaints against them by explaining it as "a dispute with some blacks in the street."[18] As such incidents repeated in towns across the island, distrust and hostility bloomed.

A MIXED INTERNATIONAL discourse prevailed regarding the Spanish project in Santo Domingo. The U.S. Secretary of State William Seward condemned Spain's annexation, but his protests were totally in vain. Politicians in several Latin American nations expressed opposition to annexation from its earliest days. The government of Peru, on the brink of its own conflict with Spain over the guano-rich islands of Chincha, strongly condemned Spain. Colonial assembly members in the British colony of Jamaica collected more than 3,700 signatures opposing Spain's occupation of Santo Domingo, a petition they sent to London. Nothing further came of the protests, however. In St. Thomas and Grand Turk, supportive private newspapers republished Dominican antiannexation screeds.[19] The Dutch island of

Curaçao, ever an entrepôt for arms and opportunistic funding, harbored many Dominican exiles. Many openly plotted against Spain and sought financial backers for their exploits. Finally, quieter support came from a number of sources in the neighboring Spanish colonies of Cuba and Puerto Rico. The western city of Mayagüez, Puerto Rico, became a refuge, for example. Despite the treacherous Mona Passage, the town was at reasonable reach by humble vessel from the easternmost province of Dominican territory, Higüey. A number of early Dominican exiles found welcome shelter in the neighboring colony. As months passed, anti-Spanish organizing increased.

More pivotal than the actions of any of these regional neighbors was the response of neighboring officials in Haiti, immediately bordering Dominican territory. The western island nation was enjoying a moment of political and economic renaissance. After a decade of monarchical despotism, republican revolution swept President Fabré Nicholas Geffrard into power in 1859, and many urban reformers were optimistic about the country's immediate political future. U.S. President Lincoln finally extended recognition to the state in 1862, and formal recognition by the Catholic Church, after decades of ostracism, came at last. Furthermore, the onset of the U.S. Civil War to the north had rendered the international cotton market especially auspicious for Haitian producers. Geffrard offered bounties for its production, and national output more than doubled during the very first year of U.S. conflict.[20] The country was easily wealthier than its Dominican neighbor. Despite these upswings, however, the president had good reason to be troubled with Spanish return. An aggressive imperial power that kept hundreds of thousands enslaved in neighboring islands promised to be a dangerous colonial neighbor. Furthermore, the precedent of forfeiture of national sovereignty cast a hostile shadow over the whole island.

For a few months in the spring of 1861, Haitian opposition to Dominican annexation was overt. President Geffrard issued an immediate and ringing condemnation of Spanish aggression and Dominican betrayal. Writing in French and Spanish in the government paper, *Le Moniteur Haïtien*, he urged that the destinies of both states on the island were inextricably linked.[21] To the "brothers of the east," he warned that Spain, a slave power, could not be trusted. He condemned former president Santana as greedy, corrupt, and criminal. Furthermore, he called on the Haitian public to lend their support to resist the occupation, announcing that a military mobilization would follow. Before any mobilization could occur, however, Spain launched a convincing counteroffensive. On July 5, 1861, six Spanish steamships from Havana appeared in the harbor of Port-au-Prince, provoking "great sensation" in the capital.[22] Haiti's army was no match for Spanish naval power. For five days, a tense standoff ensued, with martial law in the capital. Finally, with the mediation of British and French diplomats, President Geffrard acquiesced and saluted the Spanish ships. With an omnipresent military threat overshadowing the west of the island for the immediate future, the president was forced into silence and a position of public neutrality.[23]

Despite Spanish repression, all evidence suggests that Dominican and Haitian collaboration against annexation slowly grew. Famous Dominican opponents included two "Founding Fathers" from separation in 1844, generals Ramón Mella and Francisco del Rosario Sánchez. Both of them were in secret communication with Haitian officials and took refuge in Cap Haïtien, Port-au-Prince, and border towns at the center of the island. Haitian military officials along the border were so sympathetic to the cause of Dominican independence that President Geffrard had to transfer some of them to new posts, in order to keep up appearances.[24] Sánchez was killed in the summer of 1861, executed at the orders of Santana himself. For having participated in a small insurrection near the border, nineteen other men were killed along with him, with no trial. Despite all evidence that the rebellion was primarily led by Dominicans—in fact, another skirmish had taken place in the central-valley town of Moca, far from the border—Spanish officials firmly placed the blame for the unrest on Haiti. Military authorities demanded that the western government pay an indemnity of 25,000 pesos for the disturbances.[25] In the Dominican capital city, meanwhile, the government press blamed the whole affair on Haitian agitators. Clearly, Spanish authorities heeded Santana's vociferous proclamations about Dominican loyalty to Spain. One probably apocryphal newspaper account told the story of a young, unnamed Dominican man who had saved the Spanish flag from so-called "Haitian hordes" on the border. Madrid papers eagerly republished the tale.[26]

IN THE WAKE of the summer unrest in 1861, Santana urged his audience, "We are children of the same August Mother of all Spaniards . . . of all Spaniards born in Europe, America, Asia, and Africa!"[27] It is impossible to estimate how widely his proclamation would have reached, although it was doubtless printed, posted, and discussed at the behest of Spanish officials in towns throughout the colony. Santana's influence had not diminished. Even after he retired in 1862, he would return the following year to lend a hand to the Spanish forces. For a time, in the summer and fall of 1862, calm returned to the Spanish province. Financial worries and low-grade conflicts persisted. Dominicans who had left their communities during the unrest of 1861 slowly returned to their homes, taking advantage of an amnesty promised by the Spanish governor. Many had been away for almost a year. Tension bubbled just below the surface of day-to-day operations, however. Political signs cropped up to proclaim "Long Live the Republic" and "Brave Dominicans!" The governor reported that the mood in the Cibao Valley was "alarming and hostile to the highest degree." He asked for more troops, fearing the worst.[28]

Barely three months after the governor's plea, in the early spring of 1863, open armed conflict began again. In the town of Neiba in mid-February, about forty men held the town's military commander hostage for a whole morning before they were captured and arrested. A few weeks later fighting broke out in a handful of small towns, thirty and forty kilometers distant. Before the end of February, the most important financial center of the Cibao Valley, Santiago de los Caballeros, was embroiled in revolt. The Spanish governor acted quickly. He declared the whole island to be in a state of siege, and the suspected conspirators were to be tried by military tribunal. In the valley, martial law dictated that no one could walk around in groups larger than three after dusk, on the threat of being summarily shot.[29] A new round of amnesty aimed to convince rebels to return to their homes. The governor emphasized clemency, including pardons that Queen Isabel II had personally dictated for a handful of condemned men. "Dominicans, love her as a mother," the governor urged.[30] Once again, a tentative peace was re-established. Loyalist newspapers criticized those who had participated in the rebellions as opportunists and partisans; they lauded townspeople who, for a few short weeks, collaborated in reasserting Spanish order.

Historians mark the solid fighting that began after mid-August, 1863, as the beginning of the Dominican War of Restoration. Fighting would continue constantly for the next two years. Famed Spanish major general José de la Gándara, distinguished veteran of more than twenty years of service, later pinpointed August 1863 in his memoirs as the moment the fate of Spanish annexation was sealed. "The vacuum was complete," he lamented, "the misfortune, without remedy."[31] In Santiago de los Caballeros, nationalist rebels convened to form the Dominican Provisional Government. For the first time since the failed revolution of 1857–58, leaders in the valley were poised to contest the domination of the southern capital. The most pressing order of business, however, was to reject Spanish rule. They easily rallied popular support. Brigadier Buceta's dictatorial mandate in the valley was massively unpopular. "Before God, the entire world, and the throne of

Spain, just and legal reasons have obliged us to take arms to restore the Dominican Republic and reconquer our liberty," the provisional government's declaration of independence read.[32]

GUERRILLA FIGHTING CHARACTERIZED the majority of Restoration battles. Small groups, taking advantage of their superior knowledge of the rural terrain, outmaneuvered and ambushed Spanish troops. Cut off from water sources, each other, or high ground, Spanish regiments could not best the poorly armed rebels. Women often spread news about the fighting from house to house and town to town, hiding in key locations at the town's edge.[33] Meanwhile, daily life in Spanish-controlled areas was greatly interrupted. A four-month debt reprieve could not make coastal merchants solvent, public works everywhere came to a standstill, some towns were virtually emptied, and other towns burned.[34] Repeatedly, the Spanish governor called for a large force, large enough to crush a resistance that was multiplying and spreading rapidly across the countryside. A new governor replaced him mid-fighting, but he lasted barely a year. General de la Gándara, the third Spanish governor in as many years, took the reins in 1864. For all of his military and political aptitude, administration around the territory remained paralyzed. Rebels targeted the municipal buildings from town to town, destroying court proceedings and other Spanish documents. Spanish authorities shuffled some prisoners from one area to another, but they could not control beyond prison walls.

A loyalist propaganda offensive sought to preserve Spanish foothold in the Dominican territory. Dominicans were divided. Some fought for the Reserve forces alongside Spanish troops. Santana returned to lead them. He urged, "Soldiers, sons of Dominican soil, you who have always heard my voice . . . you will not waver in following me!"[35] Loyalist papers like the capital city's *La Razón* heaped praise on Dominican collaborators and meticulously reported the names of those who were accorded Spanish laurels for their efforts. Some towns, like the southern port town of Azua, remained firmly in support of Spanish presence. Their town councils issued statements in support of authorities and the immediate reestablishment of order. Meanwhile, these outlets condemned the insurrection as the work of partisans, ignorant men, bandits, and agitators. They urged the majority of the population to return to their homes. "Come, come without fear, because no one is impeding your entry or exit," one decree urged.[36] After Santana's death from rheumatic fever in 1864, fissures between loyalists and rebels probably deepened. "In all of the Cibao, the Dominican flag is flying," one rebel wrote encouragingly to a friend, trying to get him to join.[37] The fighting spread.

Despite overwhelmingly difficult conditions and tremendous sacrifice, few Dominican families caught up in the fighting returned to their homes. A consistent fear underpinned this reluctance: fear of enslavement by the Spanish. Although the institution was forty years gone from the territory, residents of the east continued to grapple with the institution long after abolition. In 1844 and early 1845, a number of Dominicans near the capital city distrusted the transition to Dominican rule precisely on the fear of re-enslavement, and they refused to join the militia campaign against Haiti.[38] The U.S. treaty of 1854 had collapsed precisely on issues of prejudice and U.S. slaveholding. Every single Dominican constitution had re-announced slavery's prohibition as its first article. The arriving Spanish authorities, despite presiding over slave regimes in Cuba and Puerto Rico, had agreed to make the same proclamation. Several years in to the occupation, however, Spanish actions embodied all of the hostility that was being leveled at emancipated peoples in surrounding Caribbean islands. As the fighting continued, racist incidents became more acute. Spanish soldiers were openly hostile to Dominicans of color, and incidents of unprovoked violence against black Dominicans and migrants in the towns proliferated.[39] In this atmosphere, whole families made the pragmatic assessment that it was best to remain in the countryside. Decrees urged calm and promised amnesty, to no avail. More urgently still, they assured the townspeople that slavery would never be reestablished. However, few found reason to trust the sincerity of the authorities or the troops.

The provisional government, meanwhile, launched a multipart offensive in search of allies. Dominican exiles in Curaçao, St. Thomas, and elsewhere sought funding and arms, although both were often lacking. More profitably, a growing market of foodstuffs, weapons, and other essentials connected Haitian vendors with the Cibao Valley. Along the central border and in the northern coast, open collaboration with Haitian military figures flourished.[40] The Dominican rebel government sought to formalize this connection. In the summer of 1864, they made a number of overtures to President Geffrard's ministers in Haiti. Missives urged solidarity, imploring to the west: "How can two peoples composed of the same race, the same political interests, ruled by republican institutions, and who have lived together as good friends, look at each other with indifference when one of them is in danger?"[41] Three years after Geffrard's bold condemnations, however, the president found himself in too much of a political bind to reciprocate.

Spanish pressure and internal political divisions weighed on the west heavily. At any rate, informal collaboration between Haitian and Dominican citizens continued positively unabated. The eastern rebel spokespeople turned their overtures to Spain, condemning the hostilities and making the case for restored Dominican independence. Authors compared the Dominican plight with nationalist movements in Italy and Poland, and they praised the heroism of the struggle.[42]

Meanwhile, regional attention to the war grew. Contact between Dominican rebels and prominent pro-independence and pro-abolition figures in Puerto Rico like Ramón Emeterio Betances increased. Exiles brought news to communities all over Puerto Rico, but so did political prisoners. The Puerto Rican captain-general was so eager to prevent communication between these groups and colonists of his territory that he ordered Dominican captives to be kept in the basement of the royal prison.[43] News of Dominican victories loomed over Spain's other Caribbean possession, as well. Documentation is difficult, but it seems that a number of Cuban residents sent aid to the Dominican resistance by ship. Furthermore, individuals read news of the Spanish defeats to large groups. One man stood trial near Santiago de Cuba for spreading news about the insurrection to meetings of free and enslaved people of color in the area.[44] Individuals in Curaçao, St. Thomas, Turks and Caicos, and Venezuela lent refuge, sold weapons, and ferried contraband supplies. They also continued to republish Dominican rebel missives and praise their efforts.[45] Other republics chimed in. Nicaragua, Bolivia, Colombia, and Argentina all echoed their support. Peru, in steady opposition to Spanish annexation from its first days, continued to issue condemnations. Annexation was "neither free, nor legal, nor in accordance with the Rights of Peoples, nor the practice of Nations, nor the spirit of the century," the Peruvian chancellor proclaimed.[46] The U.S. consul in Santo Domingo wrote Washington repeatedly excoriating Spanish comportment, and sympathizers in Boston sent secret aid to the Dominican rebels.[47]

As 1864 wore on, Spanish troops were ravaged by yellow fever, extraordinarily difficult campaign conditions, and widespread popular opposition. Despite several offensives, La Gándara and his forces could not make territorial gains. Dominican rebels frequently managed to cut off Spanish supply lines, even in loyalist pockets of the south. Supplies were spare, and medical care was in an absolutely abysmal state. Triage care was often conducted in little more than a makeshift hut. "Hospital is a magic and terrible word that the soldiers instinctively reject," one Spanish official lamented.[48] Steady rains in the fall of 1864 dampened conditions and morale even further. Not surprisingly in the face of these adversities, discipline faltered. Soldiers committed a wide variety of infractions, from fighting to outright desertion. The dwindling ranks of Dominican Reserves left their post, sometimes simply to seek provisions in the surrounding countryside. Some Spanish deserters defended the Reserves and the Dominican resistance as a whole, sending anonymous letters back to their regiments. "Dominicans are just and virtuous," one letter writer attested. He criticized Buceta and the other commanders, and urged his fellow soldiers to empathize with the Dominican cause and abandon their lines. Spanish officials took pity on some deserters, but other returning or captured soldiers faced as much as a decade in prison, even execution for flight during wartime.[49]

By 1865, Santana was dead, a new prime minister had come to power in Spain, and Serrano had moved on from his post in Cuba. Cuba's new governor, Domingo Dulce, heartily opposed the drain on his coffers that the Dominican campaign caused, and he was pessimistic about its prospects. He proposed a dramatic campaign to crush the insurgency—an example for neighboring Cuba and Puerto Rico—and the offer, after submission had been achieved, of a simple protectorate.[50] In Madrid, recalcitrant narratives bubbled. "The island of Santo Domingo is ours . . . it has been ever since it opened its eyes to civilization," one author insisted.[51] By January of 1865, however, the Spanish legislature recommended evacuation. In a tempered missive to the queen, lawmakers reiterated what they had seen as the fundament of the project: the voluntary cession of power by the Dominican Republic to Spain. When the occupation had taken the nature of reconquest, they argued, the nature of the project had changed. Like the new Cuban governor, the ministers observed that a dramatic show of repression might be in Spanish interests. Ongoing occupation, however, they judged to be impossible.[52] Dominican emissaries to Spain echoed this civility and emphasized Santana's duplicity to the Spanish legislature and the Crown. "Think, Queen, where there were flourishing cities, now there are just piles of ruins and ashes," they entreated.[53] Annexation had failed.

In the wake of Spanish withdrawal, much was transformed in the Dominican landscape. President Geffrard helped negotiate the exchange of prisoners between the two sides, which proceeded peacefully. The last of the Spanish administrators and troops disembarked without incident in July. Elsewhere, there was more disruption. Towns across the island had burned, agriculture had countenanced two years of disruption, and communities suffered thousands of casualties. The Cibao Valley's tenuous hold on political influence faltered by the fall, when Santo Domingo authorities reclaimed power from the provisional government. Santana's old rival, Buenaventura Báez, took advantage of the divided political scene and ascended to power not long thereafter. Báez was as eager as Santana had been to solidify his tenure, and he was willing, once again, to barter sovereignty in exchange. Annexation intrigues began anew.

DOMINICAN AUTHORITIES CONTINUED to toy with proposals for territorial cessions, protectorates, and outright annexation. Báez returned to power politically unscathed; he had weathered most of the Restoration War in Europe. Unfazed by the overwhelming popularity of the Restoration fight, Báez entered into negotiations with a U.S. commission in 1869, albeit in secret. He offered a tidy trade: sovereignty for a small sum, debt financing, and arms. Authorities orchestrated a farcical referendum in approbation of his proposal. U.S. officials were as interested in the Samaná Peninsula as Spanish, French, and British officials had been, and President Grant led other Republicans in supporting the plan. That Báez promised the voluntary adhesion of the Dominican people only rendered the proposition more attractive. Frederick Douglass imagined that the cession might soon grow to admit Haiti to U.S. statehood, with Cuba not far behind.[54] Senator Charles Sumner led opposition to the proposal. Others opponents argued for the supposed danger of admitting a territory whose residents, they emphasized, were mostly of color. The measure tied in the Senate, and, despite a commission sent to the Dominican Republic the following year, the scheme proceeded no further. Despite eager lobbying on the part of a handful of commercial agents and their allies, U.S. presence in the Dominican Republic did not grow appreciably until sugar investments of following decades.[55]

Despite devastation and political division, democratic and idealistic forces thrived, too, in and beyond Dominican shores. On the island itself, Dominican ties of politics, trade, travel, and exile to Cap-Haïtien, Port-au-Prince, and Jacmel continued. As political instability troubled both sides of the island, networks across the island threw their alliances in support of each other's candidates, sometimes idealistically, sometimes pragmatically. In the town of Puerto Plata, on the northern coast of the Dominican Republic, a newspaper called for the two nations to formalize their collaboration, and urged for a move to dual citizenship across the island.[56] Although it did not come to fruition, the proposal reflected a long tradition of creative federation plans, on the island and in the region. Accordingly, Puerto Rican and Cuban independence fighters drew their inspiration directly from the

War of Restoration struggle. Within three years after fighting ended in Santo Domingo, uprisings began in both remaining Spanish colonies. In both islands, Dominican veterans joined the independence fight. Within the decade, Spanish colonialism began to crumble, and rebels won emancipation.

Suggested Readings

Álvarez, Luis. *Dominacion colonial y guerra popular 1861–1865.* Santo Domingo: Universidad Autonoma de Santo Domingo, 1986.

de Lespinasse, Pierre Eugène, Jean Price-Mars, and Augustín Ferrer Gutierrez. *Haïti et la restauration de l'indépendance dominicaine.* Port-au-Prince: Bibliotèque Nationale d'Haïti, 2013.

Hernández Flores, Ismael. *Luperón, héroe y alma de la Restauración: Haití y la Revolución Restauradora.* Santo Domingo: Lotería Nacional, 1983.

Martínez-Fernández, Luis. *Torn between Empires: Economy, Society, and Patterns of Political Thought in the Hispanic Caribbean, 1840–1878.* Athens: University of Georgia Press, 1994.

May, Robert E. "Lobbyists for Commercial Empire: Jane Cazneau, William Cazneau, and U.S. Caribbean Policy, 1846–1878." *Pacific Historical Review* 48 (August 1979): 383–412.

Schmidt-Nowara, Christopher. *Empire and Anti-Slavery: Spain, Cuba, and Puerto Rico, 1833–1874.* Pittsburgh: University of Pittsburgh Press, 1999.

Notes

1. Quoted in Emilio Rodríguez Demorizi, *Antecedentes de la Anexion a España* (Ciudad Trujillo [Santo Domingo]: Editora Montalvo, 1955), 155.

2. Mariano Torrente, *Política ultramarina, que abraza todos los puntos referentes á las relaciones de España con los Estados Unidos, con la Inglaterra y las Antillas, y señaladamente con la isla de Santo Domingo* (Madrid: Imp. de la Cia. Gral. de Impresores, 1854), 342.

3. Alfonso Lockward, *Documentos para la historia de las relaciones dominico-americanas, Tomo 1: 1837–1860* (Santo Domingo: Editora Corripio, 1987), 233.

4. Jean-François Brière, *Haïti et la France, 1804–48: Le rêve brisé* (Paris: Editions Karthala, 2008).

5. Juan Abril to Don Leopoldo Augusto de Cueto, Ministro de SMC en Washington, July 23, 1854, AMRREE 2374, Expte. s/n.

6. Pedro Santana. March 18, 1861. Quoted in Gaspar Núñez de Arce, *Santo Domingo* (Madrid: Imprenta de Manuel Minuesa, 1865), 67.

7. Quoted in Antonio Fontecha Pedraza y Eduardo González Calleja, *Una cuestión de honor: La polémica sobre la anexión de Santo Domingo vista desde España (1861–1865)* (Santo Domingo: Fundación García Arévalo, 2005), 57.

8. Malo de Molina to Serrano, July 15, 1861, Archivo Histórico Nacional (hereafter AHN), Ultramar 3532, Expte. 1, Doc. 2.

9. Serrano, *Informe de la visita a Santo Domingo*, September 5, 1861, in Rodríguez Demorizi, *Antecedentes*, 245.

10. Manuel de Cruzat to Felipe Ribero, August 15, 1862, Archivo Nacional de Cuba (hereafter ANC): Audiencia de la Habana, 245, 1.

11. Ibid., Expte. 2.

12. *Colección de leyes, decretos y resoluciones emanadas de los poderes legislativo y ejecutivo de la República Dominicana*, Tomo 4 (Santo Domingo: Imprenta de García Hermanos, 1883), 134–46.

13. Quoted in Demorizi, *Antecedentes*, 258.

14. Colmenares to Min. de Guerra, September 9, 1862, AHN, Ultramar 3533, Expte. 2.

15. Felipe Rivero to Superintendencia de Cuba, August 18, 1862, AHN, Ultramar 3528.18; Real Orden de 5 de Octubre de 1861. Min. de la Guerra y Ultramar, AHN, Ultramar 3531, Expte. 27.

16. Alejandro Ángulo Guridi to Cap. Gen. Santiago, July 17, 1863, Archivo General de la Nación, República Dominicana (hereafter AGN-RD), Colección Herrera, Tomo 15, 69.

17. Minuta de Real Orden (reservada), from Min. de la Guerra y Ultramar to Teniente Gral D. Felipe Rivero, June 19, 1862, AHN, Ultramar 3525, Expte. 14.

18. "Copía testimoniada del Testimonio de la Causa instruida contra los Subtenientes D. Pedro Obanos y Alcalde, y D. Pedro García Maquina y varios individuos de la clan de tropa y carabineros de Hacienda pública . . . 18 de Agosto de 1862," Plaza de la Habana, 1867, Archivo General de Indias (hereafter AGI), Cuba, 1015A, doc s/n.

19. "Santo Domingo," *The Royal Standard and Gazette of the Turks and Caicos Islands*, November 7, 1863, 2.

20. Spenser St. John, *Hayti: Or, the Black Republic* (Pittsburgh: Ballantyne Press, 1884), 367.

21. *Moniteur Haïtien* 18 (April 6, 1861), 5.

22. Demorizi, *Antecedentes*, 215.

23. Francisco Febres-Cordero Carrillo, "La anexión y la Guerra de Restauración dominicana desde las filas españolas (1861–65)" (PhD dissertation, Universidad de Puerto Rico, 2008), 220.

24. Ismael Hernández Flores, *Luperón, héroe y alma de la Restauración; Haití y la Revolución Restauradora* (Santo Domingo: Lotería Nacional, 1983), 106.

25. Real Orden de 12 Sep 1861, AHN, Ultramar 5485, Expte 15.

26. *La Razón*, July 1, 1861, 2; Demorizi, *Antecedentes*, 221.

27. Santana, "DOMINICANOS," *La Razón*, June 20, 1861, 4; and *La Razón*, June 27, 1861, 1.

28. Felipe Ribero to Min. de Guerra y Ultramar, December 14, 1862, AGI, Cuba 1018 (libro).

29. Bando, Achilles Michel, February 25, 1863, AGN-RD, Colección Herrera, Tomo 19, AGI, Cuba, 1004B, 27.

30. "Dominicanos" (Felipe Ribero). SD May 29, 1863, AHN, Ultramar 3525, Expte. 91.

31. José de la Gándara y Navarro, *Anexión y guerra de Santo Domingo*, Tomo 1 (Madrid: Impresora de "el correo militar," 1884), 382, 299.

32. Acta de Independencia. Santiago, September 14, 1863, in Comisión Permanent de Efemérides Patrias, *Proclamas de la Restauración* (Santo Domingo: CPEP, 2005), 13.

33. Declaración de D. Rafael Leandro García in Proceso Contra varios individuos de complicidad en la sublevación que tubo lugar en Puerto Plata en 27 de Agosto ultimo, AHN, Ultramar 881, 1 Pieza, 126.

34. [Sin firma] to Alejandro Guridi. Santiago, August 4, 1863, AGN-RD CH, Tomo 15, 49.

35. Pedro Santana, "SOLDADOS!" Monte Plata, September 17, 1863, AGI, Cuba, 947B, Expte. 332.

36. "Chismes," *La Razón*, September 19, 1863, 4.

37. "Proceso Instruido contra Lorenzo Munoz como complicado en la actual rebolucion por conductor de correspondencia enemiga." SD September 1863–January 1865, AGI, Cuba, 1012B.

38. Fradique Lizardo, *Cultura Africana en Santo Domingo* (Santo Domingo: Editora Taller, 1979), 68.

39. Jose de Villar to Gob. Superior Civil, December 10, 1864, AGN-RD, Anexión 27, Expte. 15; Gov. Eyre to Cap. Gen. de SD, May 18, 1864, AHN, Ultramar 3525, 124; Gov. Eyre to Cap. Gen de Cuba, ibid., ANC AP 225:4.

40. Juan Suero to Cap. Gen. de SD. PP, December 24, 1863, AGN-RD CH, Tomo 15, 240; Felipe Ribero to Min. de Ultramar, August 18, 1863, AHN, Ultramar 3525, Expte. 26, doc. 2.

41. "Una palabra a los dominicanos." Santiago June 8, 1864, quoted in Rodríguez Demorizi, *Actos y doctrina del Gobierno de la Restauración* (Santo Domingo, R.D.: Editora del Caribe, 1963), 125.

42. *Boletín Oficial*, 1864, quoted in Abelardo Vicioso, *El freno hatero en la literatura dominicana* (Santo Domingo: Editora de la UASD, 1983), 220.

43. Feliz Maria de Messina to Cap. Gen. de SD, September 27, 1863, AGI, Cuba, 953 B, 112 ("Deportados"), doc. s/n.

44. El General 2° en Gefe del Ejercito y Gob Sup Civil to Governor Eyre. SD, May 29, 1864, AHN, Ultramar 3525, 124, doc 3; Criminal de oficio contra Don Buenaventura Anglada, natural de Cataluña . . . para averiguar su modo de juzgar los sucesos políticos de StoDgo, November 17, 1863, ANC, AP 54, 5.

45. Min. de Estado to Min. de Ultramar, Madrid, August 9, 1864, AHN, Ultramar 3525, Expte. 121.

46. Fontecha Pedraza, *Cuestión de honor*, 62; Rodríguez Demorizi *Actos y doctrina*, 232.

47. Christopher Wilkins, "'They had heard of emancipation and the enfranchisement of their race': The African American Colonists of Samaná, Reconstruction, and the State of Santo Domingo," in *The Civil War as Global Conflict: Transnational Meanings of the American Civil War*, ed. David T. Gleeson and Simon Lewis (Charleston: University of South Carolina, 2014), 211–34, 217; Domingo Dulce to Min. de Ultramar, November 28, 1863, AHN 3525, Expte. 81.

48. Enrique Llansó y Oriol to [Cap. Gen.], Samaná November 4, 1864, AGN-RD CH, Leg. 24, Expte, 212, 32–33 (originally 42–43).

49. Roque Quintana to Soldiers of the Fort of Puerto Plata, January 14, 1864, AGN-RD CH 15, 198–99; "Instruido contra el soldado de la 1ª Compañía de 1er Batallón del Regimiento de la Habana Damián Soto Martínez . . ." December 1863. AGI, Cuba, 1011B.

50. Domingo Dulce to Min. de Ultramar, September 14, 1863, AHN, Ultramar 3525, Expte. 75.

51. Joaquín Muzquiz y Callejas, *Una idea sobre la cuestión de Santo Domingo* (Madrid: Imprenta Dubrull, 1864), 5.

52. Ministers to the Queen, January 1865, AHN, Ultramar 2775, Expte. 17.

53. "Exposición dirigida por el Gobierno Provisorio a SMC," January 3, 1865, in Demorizi, *Actos y doctrina*, 255–56.

54. Robert S. Levine, *Dislocating Race and Nation: Episodes in Nineteenth-Century American Literary Nationalism* (Chapel Hill: University of North Carolina Press, 2008), 201.

55. Martin F. Murphy, *Dominican Sugar Plantations: Production and Foreign Labor Integration* (New York: Praeger, 1991).

56. *La Regeneración*, September 10, 1865, 1–2.

CHAPTER EIGHT

Juárez vs. Maximiliano

Mexico's Experiment with Monarchy

Erika Pani

In 1863 Ignacio Aguilar y Marocho, a Mexican intellectual and political leader, observed that "in politics, as in morality, . . . nothing happens which is not related to the revolutions of the wondrous whole. . . . A moment of reflection is enough to convince us that Mexico's fate has been intimately linked to the fall of Louis Philippe, to the establishment of the French Republic of 1848, . . . to the creation of the French Empire, . . . to the division of the United States, who now devour each other without mercy, victims of their own resentments and vindictiveness, and finally, to the abuses and mistakes of all kinds that Mexican demagogy surrendered to."[1]

In the summer of 1863, as French troops occupied Mexico City, and a black coach headed north carrying what was left of the constitutional government—president Benito Juárez, his cabinet and the Republic's archives—an "Assembly of Notables," comprised of prominent Conservative politicians, met to discuss the nation's future. On July 10 they concluded, in the *Resolution* quoted at the start of this essay, that the "republican system" was "the fecund fountainhead of all the evils afflicting the Fatherland." Only monarchy, "which fused order and liberty," would allow the nation to overcome the "anarchy" that threatened to destroy it. They agreed that Mexico should become "a moderate, hereditary monarchy," ruled by a Catholic prince. The Mexican Crown should be offered to Ferdinand Maximilian von Hapsburg, heir to Spain's Catholic Kings and younger brother to Austria's emperor, Franz Joseph. If the young Archduke were to decline the honor, the Mexican nation would submit "to the benevolence of Napoleon III," who would designate another Catholic prince.

Documents setting down the basics of government until more permanent constitutional arrangements could be made were not uncommon in a young nation. Since independence from Spain in 1821 Mexico had labored—and failed—to establish the legal foundations for a stable, modern state.[2] But for all its flowery, hyperbolic language, its providentialist bent, and its sycophantic deference to the emperor of the French, the 1863 *Resolution* is

remarkable. It exalted monarchy as the natural choice for a country in which
it had previously proven to be disastrous political choice throughout the
first half of the nineteenth century. It was also remarkable in that it saw this
dramatic moment in Mexican history as part of a global struggle confronting order and anarchy in a world that was tightly wound up by common
"revolutions."

The *Resolution*'s authors drew attention to the transatlantic and hemispheric entanglements that characterized the turbulent decade of crisis
during the 1860s. For Mexico, that crisis began earlier. Between 1853
and 1867, Mexico was wracked by conflict and political experimentation.
In 1853, Conservative politicians thought a centralist, authoritarian regime
could impose law and order. Two years later, a young generation of Liberals
came to power through an armed revolt fueled by a thirst for regional autonomy and by the disaffection of a heterogeneous mix of malcontents: local
strongmen, frustrated financiers, and persecuted opposition politicians.
Casting rebellion as revolution, the Liberals drafted the constitution of 1857,
which they hoped would free the nation from "the ballast" of its colonial,
obscurantist past.[3] Instead, it sparked a fierce three-year-long civil war known
as the Reform War, as Conservatives and Catholics fought against a Liberal
constitution that, they argued, by curtailing church authority and restoring
federalism, destroyed the pillars of Mexican society—religion, authority,
property—and threatened to tear the country apart.

But, as the Conservatives were keenly aware, in a world turned upside
down by modernizing and nation-building efforts, by the assault against the
temporal authority of the Catholic Church, by the aggressive expansionist
policies of European empires, and by the American Civil War, theirs was
not just a Mexican story. As Stève Sainlaude shows, opportunity fashioned
the "old French fear" of U.S. expansion and Napoleon III's ambition into his
reign's "Grand Design"; the emperor of the French decided to intervene
militarily in the New World in order to set Mexico up as a dike against further U.S. encroachment in North America. In the wake of civil war, militarily defeated but not crushed, Mexican Conservatives played what they saw
as their last card: many lobbied for and most collaborated with a monarchical regime supported by French bayonets. This essay explores this dense,
complex, interconnected period in Mexican history; it traces the development of the Liberals' vision for a revitalized republic, of French ambitions in
America, and of Conservative experiments with dictatorship and monarchy. It outlines the hopes, fears, and political schemes that were spawned in
Mexico as war, political experimentation, and contending visions of free-

dom, nation, and empire transformed political structures, made over capitalism, and engendered new types of colonialism on a global scale.[4]

WHEN, IN 1848, Mexico signed over half of its territory to its northern neighbor, alarm bells sounded. In 1846, U.S. armies had not only swept through the distant northern territories of California and New Mexico, but they also had easily marched from the north and east and taken the capital, while most state militias stayed at home and local governors traded with American merchants. Defeat was proof that, as a young and brilliant politician from Jalisco argued, in Mexico, there were no shared affections, no common interests, in short, no nation.[5] Many were convinced that Mexico was on the verge of extinction; if they could not establish a government strong and stable enough to withstand internal rebellion and external aggression, it would soon disappear. With a growing sense of urgency, two increasingly intransigent political associations, the Liberals and the Conservatives, spent the next two decades trying out radical political schemes that they hoped would guarantee the nation's survival, and bring about peace, order, and prosperity.

In 1853, in the face of what they saw as the inefficiency of Mariano Arista's government (the first president who, since 1824, had taken office after a regular, generally recognized election), the Conservatives threw their weight behind military strongman Antonio López de Santa Anna and established a dictatorship. Following a slogan of "less politics, more administration," they hoped the regime would check political strife and provide the stability required to put together the instruments of governance that Mexico so sorely lacked. As they sought to impose the rule of law, they shut down representative bodies, restricted freedom of the press, and sent irritating Liberals into exile. They would ultimately fail in their efforts to rationalize public administration. It was difficult to reconcile the whims of General Santa Anna— who adopted the title of His Most Serene Highness and sold land to the United States—with the Conservatives' project, and the regime's heavy-handed authoritarianism alienated even its close collaborators.

The so-called Ayutla Revolution put an end to Santa Anna's seventh and last administration. A new generation of Liberals drafted a constitution that they hoped would abolish the colonial legacies that smothered the nation. Inspired by the democratic visions and the libertarian discourses of the 1848 revolutions, they sought to safeguard individual freedoms and equality before the law, to reform the church and reduce religion to the private sphere, and to release the market from outdated forms of taxation and property.

The 1857 constitution re-established federalism and—in the wake of an "essentially immoral and perverse dictatorship"—vested most authority in a single-chamber Congress that dominated a weak executive branch.[6] It established universal—if indirect—male suffrage, and drew up a long list of civil rights—which included, to the church's dismay, freedom of education and the right to publish on any topic, without previous censure—which it put under the protection of the Federal Judiciary.

Freedom of conscience was not among the fundamental rights declared, but, for the first time since independence, fundamental law did not warrant religious exclusivity. The constitution also eliminated special jurisdictions (*fueros*), except for those of the church and the army, whose courts would no longer try civil cases. In order to invigorate a sluggish economy, it eliminated internal taxes on the circulation of goods (*alcabalas*), and privatized the entailed land owned by the church, municipal governments, and Indian communities. A more dynamic land market, they assumed, would allow Mexican peasants to buy land, and thus transform masses of poor, landless sharecroppers and peons into small farmers. Energized by private ownership, these men would become productive, prosperous, and responsible citizens who would support liberalism. Beyond economic motivations and political hopes, many Liberals, committed Catholics convinced of the need to reform the church, believed that the compulsory sale of ecclesiastical lands would liberate the clergy from the worldly tasks of collecting rents and calculating interest, so that it could concentrate—like "the primitive Church of Our Lord"—on its pastoral mission.

The Liberals' efforts to unshackle and modernize the country elicited fierce resistance. The church reacted by reaffirming the justice of its prerogatives and, somewhat paradoxically, by insisting both on its independence from political authority and its responsibility in the definition of the norms of political community. As a perfect society founded by Jesus Christ well before the Mexican state, the church could not give up its property rights, restrict the reach of its courts, or allow Mexicans "the freedom to err"—and burn in hell—without the explicit authorization of the Pope. The Mexican bishops turned to Rome in order to bolster and legitimize their resistance at a time when Pope Pius IX, frustrated and besieged, was hardening his stance against the "chief errors of this most unhappy age," fostered by men who, "promising liberty whereas they are the slaves of corruption," promoted the separation of church and state, religious toleration and the precedence of civil over ecclesiastical authority.[7]

It was with the same sense of intransigence and righteous indignation that the Mexican hierarchy denied the government's authority to regulate the church's activities and vigorously condemned its unilateral actions. They affirmed that the constitution was "godless," "impious," and "atheistic," and was, as such, "unjust and immoral." It was not to be obeyed in any matters that touched upon religion or the church. Those who took an oath to respect and uphold the constitution—as the law required of all civil servants and elected officers—were guilty of a "very grave sin," and would be excommunicated.[8] This confrontation highlighted the failure of the Catholic Republic, one of the young nation's most relevant political projects. It no longer seemed like church and state could work together. Nevertheless, even those—politicians and clerics alike—who were more concerned with the nation's material well-being than with its spiritual salvation feared the consequences of a confrontation between civil and religious authorities. The chronic political instability and economic crisis that had followed independence had revealed the fractiousness of Mexican society. Putting an end to religious unity threatened to dissolve the bonds that precariously united a nation divided by geography, language, culture, and deep social inequalities.

On the ground, the conflict between church and state weakened the Liberal government's legitimacy, as was painfully brought to the fore by the controversies surrounding the constitutional oath. This, along with the uneven beginnings of the disentailment process and the disgruntlement of military officers, resentful of losing their privileges and wary of a constitution they thought would generate anarchy, unleashed widespread uneasiness and resistance. Throughout the central valley and the western Bajío region, towns, villages, and military detachments rose up to the cry of *"¡Religión y fueros!"* (Religion and privileges)—which had been the banner of the Spanish *Carlistas* who had opposed constitutional monarchy since the 1830s. In December of 1857, overwhelmed President Ignacio Comonfort abrogated the constitution, only to be unseated less than a month later by the capital's military commander, Félix Zuloaga. The president of the supreme court, Benito Juárez, a Zapotec lawyer and former governor of Oaxaca, assumed executive power and took up the defense of the constitution. Many state governors, fearing the return of centralism, stood behind him.

War divided the country in two. Rival governments—the Conservatives' military regime in Mexico City, the Liberals' constitutional government in Veracruz—battled each other, bankrupted their treasuries, entered leonine treaties with foreign powers—the Conservatives with Spain, the Liberals with the United States—and allowed no possibility for transaction or compromise. Their armies wrought destruction, relied on compulsory conscription, and repeatedly violated the principles they claimed to be fighting for: individual freedom and respect for life and property for the Liberals, and upholding the strict rule of law and the inviolability of church property for the Conservatives. Neither was able to break the military stalemate that had the Conservative army occupying the central region of the country and its most populous cities, while Liberal militias controlled the periphery, and Veracruz, the nation's main port.

In 1860, the Conservative armies began retreating. They were exhausted and destitute, while Liberal forces could count on the tariffs collected at the Veracruz customhouse. The Liberals were also invigorated by a more radical program. In July 1859, the Juárez government expropriated all church wealth as punishment for its inciting fratricidal war. The government secularized cemeteries, marriage, the civic calendar, and the registry of births and deaths, and declared independence between church and state. In December 1860, Liberal General Santos Degollado, known as "the hero of defeats," routed the troops commanded by the Conservatives' "young Maccabee," President Miguel Miramón. The constitutionalist government proclaimed religious freedom and returned to the nation's capital in January 1861. Many of the Conservative generals and all the bishops went into exile—where some of them would lobby for European intervention—while the Conservative army disbanded and resorted to guerrilla warfare. Armed conflict became less intense, more widespread territorially, and perhaps more uncompromising.

In July 1861, the Juárez government, riddled with internal divisions over the extent and meaning of reform, unable to quell Conservative resistance, its coffers depleted, declared a moratorium on its foreign debt payments. This unleashed a series of unexpected events that Mexican Conservatives would later describe as "admirable" and "providential."[9] As we have mentioned, the emperor of the French, Napoleon III, saw opportunity in the Mexican crisis: with the United States engulfed in a civil war of unprecedented proportions, France could use its neighboring republic's financial irresponsibility as an excuse for military intervention to establish a French foothold in the New World.

In Paris and in Rome, Mexican politicians and clerics in exile took advantage of their connections with the French imperial family and inside the papal court to win over key players to the idea of using European military strength to dislodge the Liberals from power.[10] They insisted that a long-suffering people, deprived of social peace by a corrosive demagogy, would welcome Europe's intervention as the nation's salvation. Spurred on by these voices, Napoleon III decided to sponsor a monarchical regime headed by a European prince. Hardened, well-trained French troops would pacify the country and place an Austrian archduke on the throne of Moctezuma. To disguise his expansionist intentions, Napoleon courted the other creditor nations—Spain, England, and even the United States, which turned him down—and negotiated a tripartite military intervention.

By early 1862, all the interventionist armies had landed in Veracruz. By early April the Spanish and British envoys reached an agreement with the Juárez government, but the French, whose objectives went beyond the settlement of debt payments, decided to go on to Mexico City. The expeditionary corps' advance proved more difficult than at first expected. Defeated at the outskirts of Puebla in May (*Cinco de Mayo*), they would not take Mexico City until a year later.

It was then, under the auspices of the French army, that the "Assembly of Notables" drafted the baroque resolution that called for the "restoration" of monarchy. As we have mentioned, their wild enthusiasm for a form of government "which modern science exalted and held up as perfect" struck a discordant note in Mexican nineteenth-century political discourse. At independence, Mexico, unlike the rest of Spanish America, had taken the path that Brazil, the South American giant, would follow. It established an imperial government within a framework of negotiated emancipation, headed by former counterinsurgent officer Agustín de Iturbide, who had led the last push towards putting an end to colonial rule. But after his fall in 1823, and despite the growing sensation that, with independence, Mexico had traded the fabled peace and prosperity of New Spain for political turmoil and economic stagnation, its politicians embraced the principles and mechanisms of a republican government, along with its inherent challenges, which Hilda Sabato so deftly describes in this volume.

For all the royalist fervor expressed by those who authored the 1863 *Resolution*, perhaps the most remarkable feature of Mexican monarchism during the first decades of the nineteenth century is its inconspicuousness, and the defensive, stilted quality of its rhetoric. Except for some exceptional moments, monarchy was, until the 1860s, an object of scorn and derision, the somewhat embarrassing cause of out-of-touch exiles, treacherous conspirators and a few Indian communities. It was not until 1840 that a serious politician, former Secretary of State José María Gutiérrez de Estrada, publicly discussed the possibility of re-establishing the system of government that had proven successful for almost three hundred years. Republicanism, he argued, was completely foreign to the Mexicans' character, their habits, and traditions. Unless the nation adopted a suitable system of government, it would be swallowed up by the United States.[11]

Gutiérrez de Estrada's monarchist manifesto effectively put an end to his political career. His pamphlet was confiscated a couple of days after being published, and he was indicted for speaking against the established form of government. He would leave the country for Europe, never to return. For years, he would try to entice the monarchs of the Old Continent with the possibility of establishing a European prince on a Mexican throne. Until the 1860s and the outbreak of the U.S. war, his proposals fell on deaf ears. In the court of Napoleon III, however, he found an emperor with grand American ambitions and an empress, Eugénie of Spain, with a zealous interest in his project for restoring the authority of the Catholic Church to what had been the crown jewel of the Spanish Empire.[12] In 1846, in the wake of a military coup against the government, the newspaper *El Tiempo*, which received financial support from the Spanish Legation, spoke of the virtues of constitutional monarchy. This newspaper's proposal of a European monarch for Mexico was fiercely condemned by the Mexico City press, and shut out from substantive public debate.[13] The din of a disastrous war with the United States completely drowned out the monarchist argument.

Again, in 1854, the Santa Anna dictatorship explored the possibility of setting up a monarchy headed by a Spanish prince—with Santa Anna holding the reins of power behind him. Little came of the secret negotiations, except their later being held up as further evidence of the regime's treasonous and tyrannical nature. Thus, during most of the nineteenth century, monarchy had represented a change so radical, a regime with such negative connotations, that it was barely even mentioned as a possible option. But, as the 1863 *Resolution* showed, the outbreak of civil war in the United States and French commitment to military involvement in the New World brought about dramatic change: the old, discredited project of reestablishing a Mexican empire, which had for years been the stuff of conspirators and vilified politicians, suddenly became viable.[14]

The Mexican crown was offered to a young Austrian who was perhaps more akin to the interests of Napoleonic diplomacy—which sought to ingratiate itself with Vienna after having defeated the Austrian armies during the wars for Italian unification—than to the sympathies of most Mexican Conservatives. Ferdinand Maximilian was said to have Liberal sympathies, and he had been the last imperial viceroy of the kingdom of Lombardy-Venetia

(1857–59), where his failure to quell Italian nationalism led to his destitution. He and his intelligent, driven wife Charlotte of Belgium seemed destined to the soporific life of princes who were not first in the line of succession. When offered the Mexican crown, he agreed to accept it if the "will of the nation" endorsed the assembly's decision. When his election was ratified by the certificates of allegiance of numerous municipal governments, Maximilian—who would henceforth use only the Mexicanized version of his name, Maximiliano—accepted to leave his castle on the Adriatic and arrived in Mexico City in June 1864. Again, two governments—the imperial government in Mexico City and the Republic's in Paso del Norte, on the U.S. border—fought to define the fate of the nation and the nature of its government.

FOR THE FIRST TIME since the fall of Iturbide, in a city occupied by French troops and with the republican press stunned and muzzled, monarchist discourse could flow freely. During the early years of the Second Empire, it even became an artificial *status quo* upheld by restrictive press legislation—which forbade the condemnation of the nation's "elected form of government"— and consequently, an empty shell that various factions filled with different contents. The defense of monarchy was expressed in the hyperbolic, baroque prose of the 1863 Assembly of Notables, and in the vengeful tone of Conservative newspaper *El Pájaro Verde*, the sentimental articles of Catholic *La Sociedad* and the well-reasoned, technical arguments of *La Razón*. It was clear from the get-go that monarchy meant very different things to different people.

Men of diverse political inclinations rallied to Maximiliano's regime. Most—but not all—Conservative military men, members of the church's hierarchy, and militant Catholics collaborated with the empire. Those officers who had a price put on their head by the republican government argued that they had no choice but to join the ranks of the empire. Those who were convinced that a "Catholic polity" had to be "Catholically governed" hoped the Hapsburg prince would restore the harmony between spiritual and temporal authority, and save the nation from the "social revolution" which threatened to engulf it.[15] Some Conservative politicians, who still believed that all could be solved if public administration was organized along rational, "scientific" lines—lawyers Aguilar y Marocho and Teodosio Lares, and engineer Joaquín Velásquez de León, for example—saw in the Empire an unexpected opportunity to further their project. They sought less to restore a golden age gone by than to find a way to structure politics in a world in which revolution had shattered certainties and made political legitimacy contingent and contentious.

In many ways, these Conservatives tried to sell monarchy as a system that could domesticate the alluring but dangerous values of the new order: "If liberty means deliberate choice, limited by the prescriptions of duty; if the dignity and decorum of the citizen are rooted in strict obedience to law and profound abeyance to authority; if social guarantees only exist where instead of rebels and conspirators, one finds a compact mass of true patriots . . . you, who have spent your life visiting the remote counties of the Old World, in order to make a philosophical study . . . tell us, where, but in the nations where thrones have withstood the test of time, are men freer, happier and more civilized?"[16]

Less articulate than the Conservative ideologues were some regional and local elites who also supported the empire. Among them stood out some important indigenous leaders such as Otomí general Tomás Mejía of Queré-taro, Manuel Lozada of Nayarit, and Opata chief Tanori of Sonora, who, as local military leaders, resented the centralizing policies of the national state and liberalism's encroachments on communal lands and local religious practices. Endowed with flexible ideological convictions, many had been displaced or felt threatened by the Liberals' triumph. Less predictable was the support of radical federalist governor Santiago Vidaurri, whose auda-cious political and commercial ventures are featured in Patrick Kelly's arti-cle, and of moderate Liberals who, despite their republican credentials, joined the ranks of the empire: noted political, scientific and literary figures like José Fernando Ramírez, José María Lacunza, and Manuel Orozco y Berra; jurists and provincial luminaries such as Manuel Siliceo, Jesús López Portillo, and Pedro Escudero y Echanove; and men who, until then, had shunned politics, like large land-owner and linguist Francisco Pimentel, or chemical engineer Vicente Ortigosa. They apparently saw the possibility of stabilizing Mexican politics through monarchical rule—and, even though they would have been a little ashamed to admit it, by France's military pres-ence, which liberated civilian government from the costly, precarious negotia-tions with undisciplined men of arms that had been the norm for decades.

After years of violent and inconclusive civil war, disappointed by the intransigence of both the constitution's defenders and its enemies, these men believed that only a strong government could guarantee peace and safe-guard the conquests of revolution. They were seduced by the checks-and-balances mechanisms they thought were built into modern monarchy. They thought it would defuse political wrangling by eliminating the "fighting arena" on which political factions had torn at each other and made government impossible. A system in which Mexicans could be "anything they wanted, except Emperor" would channel political ambition and provide government decisions with the finality required for effective rule of law, and the imperial family's permanence would offset the volatility of competitive politics.[17] Furthermore, politicians of all stripes hoped that a government of order, with firm dynastic connections to the major European powers, would be able to attract the investment necessary to develop the country through railroads and industrialization.[18]

This is perhaps the vision of empire that Maximilian found most congenial. In his speech accepting the Mexican throne, he had stressed his commitment to governing through "wisely liberal institutions."[19] But he was probably more attracted by the idea of liberalism than by its concrete practices. His regime never had a constitution; the Empire's "Provisional Statute" set up the administrative structure of the imperial government, but it did list a series of "individual guarantees."[20] The emperor, "representing National Sovereignty," held both executive and legislative powers, and, in practice, the army—much of it under foreign command—administered justice and did much of the policing.

The imperial couple prepared a draft constitution, which set up a council of state and a senate, two "intermediary bodies," that were popular among the *imperialistas* for their moderating influence. They were nevertheless made up mostly of men close to or designated by the emperor. Maximilian would name all the members of the council, while the three-hundred-member senate would include the empire's dignitaries—princes, bishops, university presidents, members of the High Court, etc.—100 members chosen by the emperor, and another 100 elected by the people. Although little suggested that the young Hapsburg was at the forefront of liberal and democratic thought in the 1860s, the liberal *imperialistas* believed that the regime would abandon its authoritarian features as soon as the country was pacified and constitutional government, elections, and political representation would be restored.

Despite the diversity of its personnel, the imperial government undertook ambitious legislative endeavors, some innovative, others building on projects that had long been caressed by Mexican statesmen but that had failed to crystallize. Thus, under the impulse of Lares and Ortigosa, the empire sought to consolidate the state's administrative machinery by systematizing legislation, organizing the ministries, centralizing political initiatives, and clarifying and strengthening the chain of command. It also tried to bolster the executive's autonomy by limiting the reach of the judiciary and creating an imperial prosecutor. The empire thus published the first national civil code, drafted by a group of lawyers who had been entrusted with the task by President Juárez in 1861. The text forms the core of the republican code of 1870.

In their efforts to strengthen the national government, the *imperialistas* went where other centralists had not dared to go. When in power, the latter had simply called the states departments, and local authorities had been appointed by the national government. Conversely, Maximilian's collaborators undertook the most audacious overhaul of the nation's territorial division: following Orozco y Berra's profound geographic, historical, and ethnographic research, they broke up the states' geographies of political and economic domination, and created fifty departments, along the French model. They hoped to make the hand of the state "present throughout" the nation's territory by decentralizing administration, but keeping local authority under the mandate of Mexico City. In order to prevent the domination of some by others, departments were designed to be of similar size, be able to maintain approximately the same population, and have access to comparable resources.

The imperial couples' enthusiasm for indigenous culture—both past and present, the latter seldom shared by their Mexican collaborators—generated laws and institutions that sought to solve one of independent Mexico's most intractable problems: how to integrate the majority Indian population into "modern," Spanish-speaking, Western-dressing, market-oriented Mexican society. The imperial couple founded the *Junta Protectora de Clases Menesterosas*, a consulting body that was to advise the underprivileged who felt abused and oppressed. Presided by Faustino Galicia Chimalpopoca, prominent Náhuatl connoisseur and former trustee of Mexico City's Indian communities, the *Junta* heard Indian pueblos report acts of injustice, misuse of legislation, and breaching of water rights, or express their opposition to the disentailment process or the meddling of priest or mayor in their rituals and celebrations.

The *Junta* did not defend what we would call today "indigenous rights." Its decisions—which were only rarely binding—consistently promoted the transformation of Mexico into a modern society, and condemned what they saw as the retrograde, wasteful, and distasteful habits of the Indians, such as, for example, the festive burials of small children.[21] It did seek to lend a sympathetic ear to the complaints and demands of marginalized groups within society, to give plaintiffs the legal information they needed to further their cause through the right channels, and to create a direct link between the emperor and his most disadvantaged subjects. It was also charged with writing legislation that would remedy some of the problems that affected Mexico's rural population. Fruit of its labors were the 1865 labor law, which sought to protect workers from extreme exploitation by forbidding corporal punishment and debt-peonage, establishing maximum working hours, and ordering land-owners and manufacturers to provide schooling for their workers' children; and the laws dealing with communal lands, which ordered that they be exempted from colonization ventures, and divided, as private property, only among the townspeople.[22]

Maximilian's empire would disappoint most of the disparate hopes it inspired. The war raged on, with the 30,000 strong French army and its Mexican allies controlling—with some exceptions—only the territory they occupied. Most of its hopeful, sophisticated legislative projects stayed on paper. The fact that the imperial government upheld liberal, reformist economic and religious principles—it ratified both the expropriation of church wealth and religious toleration—alienated the papal envoy, Francisco Meglia, who had been sent to Mexico to restore the church to its old prerogatives. Maximilian's vision of a church subordinate to the state and its interests—the emperor, for example, sought to transform priests into civil servants so that sacraments could be administered for free—estranged the ecclesiastical hierarchy and the most militant Catholics. By 1866, even the most intransigent of bishops, Michoacán's Clemente de Jesús Munguía, was convinced that the much maligned Benito Juárez suited the Mexican church better than this most Catholic—and meddlesome—prince.[23]

Maximilian also proved less pliant to French demands than expected. He refused, for instance, to turn over Sonora to his European sponsor in order to cover the nation's debts. In 1866, with Union victory in the United States and the increasingly disturbing advances of German unification, Napoleon III decided to cut his losses and put an end to his Mexican adventure. Without French military support and having disappointed its local adherents, the empire collapsed. In an act heavy with symbolism, the triumphant republicans executed Maximilian on a windswept hill outside Querétaro. They also swiftly eliminated the *imperialistas* they considered most troublesome: young general Miguel Miramón, who had led the fight against the 1857 constitution; the able military Indian leader Tomás Mejía, who had consistently opposed Liberal policies; the fiercely independent cacique of the north, Santiago Vidaurri. The republican triumph consecrated their version of the story as national history: the valiant, hardscrabble republic had defeated the imperialist ambitions of the despotic emperor of the French and his retrograde, traitorous, and fortunately very few Mexican allies. The 1857 constitution, banner of Mexico's "Second War of Independence," soaked with the blood of patriots, was enshrined as the only political possibility for the nation, its symbolic weight contributing to its clumsiness as an instrument of government.

IN THE LATE 1860S, the British Catholic historian, editor, politician, and renowned liberal Lord Acton cast a gloomy eye on recent events and on the profound changes brought about by their entangled histories. A great admirer of Maximilian, he deplored the death of "the fair haired stranger who devoted his life to the good of Mexico, and died for guilt which was not his own." The Austrian prince had fallen, "and carried with him in his fall the independence of the people he had come to save."[24] He also lamented the Confederacy's defeat; "the spurious liberty of the United States," he declared, was "twice cursed," for "by exhibiting the spectacle of a people claiming to be free, but whose love of freedom means hatred of inequality, jealousy of limitations of power, and reliance on the State as an instrument to mould as well as to control society, it calls on its admirers to hate aristocracy and teaches its adversaries to fear the people."[25]

Acton's despair is understandable; his staid liberalism, according to which liberty was made possible by curtailing the power of government and not through political empowerment, was turning into an anachronism. The demands made by the new guiding principles of democracy and nation were sweeping away with the often complex balancing acts between constitutional law, representative government, and local and regional self-government—which was especially dear to the British aristocrat's heart—that had characterized much of governance during the first half of the nineteenth century. In the Americas, these mechanisms had been largely compatible with established social hierarchies, traditional conceptions of authority, decentralized territorial arrangements and the government of the "reasonable," or the "most able," and not of "the many."

The crisis of the 1860s engendered different political responses that sought to deal with the transformations of markets and production, and discipline the powerful revolutionary currents of nationalism, republicanism, and socialism. To Acton's distress, these transformations unnerved systems of rule, and altered many of the key concepts—the sovereign people, freedom, citizenship, democracy—that had articulated public discourse, political legitimacy, and membership in the political community. The effervescence of the 1860s engendered powerful and diverse reactions, molded by local circumstances, shifts in global and continental geopolitics, and the transnational circulation of men and ideas, as well as the transformation of agriculture, trade and technology.

Thus, the state of Buenos Aires' efforts to maintain its independence, Meiji Japan's policies for economic modernization and political centralization, France's Second Empire and the French Communes, Spain's expansionist revival under Prime Minister Leopoldo O'Donnell's *Unión Liberal*, the Confederate States of America, the Canadian Confederation, and Mexico's Second Empire were political experiments that sought to find bearings in a convulsed world. In some ways, the Mexican *imperialistas* were in a more vulnerable position than others engaging in radical experimental politics. They were unlike the Southern secessionists, who sought to preserve a strained political and economic system that was riddled with tensions, but highly profitable to its beneficiaries. They were also unlike the Spanish *unionistas*—with whom they shared a longing for the political stability that had eluded most of the Catholic monarchy's heirs—that momentarily bolstered the Bourbon monarchy's declining prestige through economic growth and aggressive policies abroad, in that the Mexican Conservatives and moderate Liberals who rallied to the empire saw little in the past that was worth restoring, and failed to set up the empire's material underpinnings. However, like Maximilian's government, these alternative—if more solidly grounded—regimes also failed, as the territorially bounded sovereign state became the model, if not the norm.

In Mexico, as monarchy caved in, the construction of the modern nation-state would be undertaken using the standards of federalism and popular democracy. This was not, as we have seen, an inevitable outcome. Nevertheless, the 1867 Liberal triumph over the empire and foreign intervention effectively welded what had been a controversial, partisan proposal to the patriotic—and, unlike what had happened in 1848, successful—defense of national sovereignty. In retrospect, Conservative propositions became irrelevant; their architects were branded misguided traitors and were confined to the very edges of the political stage. As Charles Hale argued, an ideology of combat became one of Mexico's most enduring unifying political myths.[26] If the application of the 1857 Fundamental Law proved problematic, it nevertheless provided, at least until 1917, a stable legal framework for a country that had been searching, in vain, for a workable constitution. With the failure of the monarchical experiment, the secular, "democratic, representative, popular" republic became the only paradigm in Mexican politics.

Suggested Readings

Bazant, Jan. *Alienation of Church Wealth in Mexico: Social and Economic Aspects of the Liberal Revolution 1856–1875.* Cambridge: Cambridge University Press, 1971.

Corti, Egon Ceasar. *Maximilian and Charlotte of Mexico.* New York: Knopf, 1928.

Dabbs, Jack Autrey. *The French Army in Mexico, 1861–1867: A Study in Military Government.* The Hague: Mouton and Co., 1963.

Hamnett, Brian. *Juárez.* New York: Longman's, 1994.

Pani, Erika. "Dreaming of a Mexican Empire: The Political Project of the Imperialistas." *Hispanic American Historical Review* 82 (February 2002): 1–31.

Sinkin, Richard N. *The Mexican Reform, 1856–1876: A Study in Liberal Nation-Building.* Austin: University of Texas Press, 1979.

Thomson, Guy. *Politics, Patriotism and Popular Liberalism in Mexico: Juan Francisco Lucas and the Puebla Sierra, 1854–1917.* Wilmington, DE: SR Books, 1999.

Villegas, Silvestre, ed. *Antología de textos: La Reforma y el Segundo Imperio.* Coyoacán: UNAM, 2008.

Notes

1. "Dictamen acerca de la forma de gobierno," July 10, 1863, in Ignacio Aguilar y Marocho, *La familia enferma* (México City: Jus, 1969), 165–88.

2. Between 1821 and 1855, the young nation went from empire to republic and drafted three constitutions—of which one was not promulgated—two "constitutive laws," and three sets of "constitutional," "organic," or "administrative . . . bases" for the government of the Republic. See Felipe Tena Ramírez, *Leyes fundamentales de México, 1808–2002* (Mexico City: Porrúa, 2002).

3. For the decidedly unrevolutionary character of the Ayutla "Revolution," see Edmundo O'Gorman, "Precedentes y sentido del plan de Ayutla," in *Plan de Ayutla: Conmemoración de su primer aniversario* (Mexico: UNAM, 1954), 169–204.

4. Thomas Bender, "Freedom in an Age of Nation-Making," *A Nation among Nations: America's Place in World History* (New York: Hill and Wang, 2006), 116–81; Sven Beckert, "Emancipation and Empire: Reconstructing the Worldwide Web of Cotton Production in the Age of the American Civil War," *American Historical Review* 109 (2004): 1405–38.

5. Varios mexicanos, "Consideraciones sobre la situación política y social de la República Mexicana" (1847), in Mariano Otero, *Obras* (Mexico: Porrúa, 1967), 1:122–28.

6. "Proyecto de constitución. Dictamen de la comisión," Felipe Tena Ramírez, *Leyes fundamentales de México, 1808–2002* (Mexico: Porrúa, 2002), 525.

7. See his encyclical *Quanta Cura,* December 8, 1864, and the accompanying *Syllabus of Errors,* http://www.papalencyclicals.net/Pius09/p9quanta.htm.

8. *Opúsculo escrito por el Ilmo. Sr: Obispo de Michoacán Clemente de Jesús Munguía en defensa de la soberanía, derechos y libertades de la Iglesia atacadas en la Constitución*

civil de 1857 y en otros decretos expedidos por el actual gobierno de la nación (Morelia: I. Arango, 1857), 18.

9. "Dictamen," in Aguilar y Marocho, *La familia*, 165.

10. See Genaro García, ed., *Correspondencia secreta de los principales intervencionistas mexicanos*, 3rd ed. (Mexico: Porrua, 1992). For the key role played by Pelagio Antonio Labastida y Dávalos, who was soon to become Mexico's Archbishop, see Marta Eugenia García Ugarte, *Poder político y religioso: México, siglo XIX*, 2 vols. (Mexico: Miguel Ángel Porrúa, 2011) 1:851–74; 2:925–1060.

11. José María Gutiérrez Estrada, *Carta dirigida al Ecsmo Sr: Presidente de la República, sobre la necesidad de buscar en una Convención el posible remedio de los males que aquejan a la República; y opinions del autor acerca del mismo asunto* (Mexico: Ignacio Cumplido, 1840).

12. Gabriela Tío Vallejo, "La monarquía en México: Historia de desencuentros; El liberalismo monárquico de Gutiérrez Estrada," *Secuencia: Revista de historia y ciencias sociales* 30 (1994): 33–56.

13. Miguel Soto, *La conspiración monárquica en México, 1845–1846* (Mexico: EOSA, 1988).

14. Erika Pani, "La innombrable: Monarquismo y cultura política en el México decimonónico," in *Prácticas populares, cultura política y poder en México, siglo XIX*, ed. Brian Connaughton (Mexico: UAM-I, 2008), 369–94.

15. "Moralidad pública," *La Sociedad*, June 30, 1866.

16. "Dictamen," in Aguilar y Marocho, *La familia*, 183.

17. "Derechos del hombre bajo las monarquías" *La Razón*, November 17, 1864; "El Emperador y los partidos" *La Razón*, October 21, 1864; "Algo más sobre partidos," *La Razón*, October 22, 1864.

18. Barbara A. Tenenbaum, "Development and Sovereignty. Intellectuals and the Second Empire," in *Los intelectuales y el poder en México: Memorias de la VI Reunión de historiadores mexicanos y estadounidenses*, ed. Roderic A. Camp and Josefina Z. Vázquez (Mexico: El Colegio de México, Los Angeles: University of California Press, 1991).

19. "Contestación de Su Alteza Imperial y Real el Archiduque Fernando Maximiliano," April 10, 1864, in *Boletín de las leyes del Imperio mexicano, o sea código de la restauración* (1863–65), 1:547.

20. "Estatuto provisional del Imperio Mexicano," April 10, 1865, in Tena Ramírez, *Leyes*, 670–80.

21. "Informe del comandante militar de San Luis de la Paz al Mariscal Bazaine," September 1865, Archivo General de la Nación, Junta Protectora de Clases Menesterosas, vol. 2.

22. "Ley sobre trabajadores, November 1, 1865," in *Colección de leyes, decretos y reglamentos que interinamente forman el sistema politico administrative y judicial del imperio* (Mexico: Andrade y Escalante, 1865), 6:184–87; "Ley sobre terrenos de comunidad y de repartimiento, June 26, 1866," AGN, JPCM, vol. 4.

23. Pablo Mijangos, *The Lawyer of the Church: Bishop Clemente de Jesús Munguía and the ecclesiastical response to the liberal revolution in Mexico (1810–1868)*, PhD Thesis, UT-Austin, 2009.

24. "The Rise and Fall of the Mexican Empire" (1868) in John Emerich Edward Dalberg Acton, *Historical Essays and Studies*, 1907, e-book published by The Liberty Fund.

25. Lord Acton, "The Civil War in America and Its Place in History" (1866) in *Historical Essays and Studies* (London: McMillan, 1907), 142.

26. Charles A. Hale, "Los mitos políticos de la nación mexicana: El liberalismo y la revolución," *Historia Mexicana* 46 (1996): 821–37.

CHAPTER NINE

Arms and Republican Politics in Spanish America
The Critical 1860s

Hilda Sabato

By the 1860s America was basically a republican hemisphere. While European nineteenth-century experiments with republics had been short-lived, across the Atlantic the postcolonial polities in the making, with the sole exception of Brazil, had followed the initial example of the United States: in the 1810s and '20s, after severing their links with the Spanish empire, they had adopted republican forms of government. After four to five decades of sustained experimentation with self-government, internal and external pressures grew to challenge the results of these experiences. This move reached its peak with the "restoration" of monarchy in Mexico and the reintegration of the Dominican Republic as a colony of Spain, so forcefully described by Erica Pani and Anne Eller in the preceding essays in this volume.[1]

The monarchic drive did not reach the rest of Spanish America, but the new developments affected the course of the republics at a very particular time in their institutional history. During the first half of the nineteenth century, governments had usually been ephemeral, leaderships contested, territorial boundaries uncertain, and political regimes subject to successive changes. By the 1850s, this picture had started to change; most nations had settled their territorial claims, and they had adopted the basic institutions of constitutional liberalism, while in some of them, liberal political groups were able to reach and remain in power for several years. Soon, however, instability returned; this time not only due to internal conflicts, but also on account of the effects of events well beyond their borders. The antirepublican mood that prevailed in Europe, together with the attempts of some of its larger powers to interfere in the Americas, encouraged the most conservative groups in their confrontation with the liberals, and internal partisan conflicts escalated. At the same time, the devastating civil war in the United States, a country that had served as a model polity, shattered some of the certainties that had sustained the widespread republican convictions. Thus, the

1860s' wave of national and international conflicts, as well as their outcomes, had important effects in the ways of the republic in Spanish America both in the field of ideas as in the practical world of politics.

A crucial dimension of nineteenth century republicanism occupied center stage during the decade: the model of defense and the role of armed institutions in the polity. The "crisis of the '60s" had direct bearings upon this dimension of the political life of the republics, which was deeply embedded in the traditions and practices of Spanish-American self-government. To assess this impact is, therefore, a way to delve into the core republican dilemmas of this period. In fact, after independence, the history of arms and armies was closely tied to the shaping of the new polities. The institutional and political choices made in this regard by the postrevolutionary elites were directly connected to the values and institutions of self-government. The initial model, based upon the figure of the citizen in arms, was later modified and adjusted mainly on account of practical considerations and actual power disputes, but the basic pattern lasted for many decades. The ideological controversies and political confrontations of the 1860s brought about fresh perspectives and institutional novelties that contributed to question that pattern, yet it was only by the last decades of the nineteenth century that the post-independence model was finally replaced by a new understanding of national defense and military forces.

AFTER THE SEVERANCE of the colonial links with Spain and Portugal, the territories that had been under imperial rule entered a long and complex process of redefinition of sovereignties and formation of new polities. Attempts at nation building followed different directions, and many projects were tried and failed. But no linear or predetermined path led to the establishment of the sixteen individual nation states that eventually consolidated during the second half of the nineteenth century.[2] There was, however, a common denominator to that process: The polities in the making all adopted the principle of popular sovereignty for the foundation and legitimization of political power, thus shifting the grounds upon which collective life rested.[3] The political no longer referred to a transcendent-divine instance; it was considered a human construct.[4]

Nineteenth-century Latin America was, therefore, part of the larger and complex history of political transformation that involved the English, American, and French revolutions, the foundation of constitutional monarchies, and the invention of a federal republic in the United States. Within that framework, while Brazil opted for a constitutional monarchy, the Spanish Americans soon chose the republican way, and with few exceptions, they mostly stuck to it for good.[5] There was no single republican model, and the label applies to a wide variety of endeavors across the continent and throughout the century. This diversity notwithstanding, it is possible to find some shared patterns of change; the problems faced by the different nations-in-the-making were often similar, as were some of the directions they actually followed to solve them. For starters, in their initial drive towards nation building, the post-independence leaderships resorted to the available republican examples. The United States featured in a prominent place, but other historical cases appealed in various ways to the founding fathers and their successors: the classical republics, the Italian postclassical and early modern city-states, the United Provinces of the Netherlands (late sixteenth to late eighteenth century), and France, plus the highly prestigious English constitutional monarchy and the short liberal experiences in Spain (1812 and 1820–23)—which had a direct influence in the subcontinent. None of these examples amounted to a unique model to be imported, yet all of them provided a set of institutions and traditions that could be adapted and adopted by the locals. Besides these external models, exchanges and comparisons among the Hispanic-American experiences were widespread, as were references to the Brazilian case—a constitutional monarchy subject to both praises and critique.[6]

In this context of political creativity and experimentation, a topic dear to the republican tradition would have a prominent place in the public debates of the new polities: the problem of how to protect freedom in the face of both external and internal threats. The conviction that its defense should be in charge of those who belonged to the polity, the citizens, and that relying on professional soldiers—"mercenaries"—opened the door to corruption and tyranny goes way back in republican history, and was still invoked in the nineteenth century. In the past, however, that principle had been often overlooked in the face of the empirical demands of war, when—in the name of efficiency—professional armies had complemented or even replaced citizen militias.[7]

In matters of defense, the Spanish-Americans turned to these republican legacies and experiences, and early on they introduced the notion of the citizen in arms as a key piece in the construction of the new polities and in the design of their defense strategies. Yet the postrevolutionary elites did not start from scratch. Rather, they had to cope with the de facto militarization that outlived the wars of independence, as well as with the traces of colonial institutions and practices that were still in operation.

In America, for centuries, the Spanish Crown had kept regular forces of professional soldiers, as well as a rather irregular system of militias, manned by the *vecinos* (residents), for local defense purposes. At the beginning of the nineteenth century, this military landscape was put to the test of the widespread wars of independence, which entailed a wide-ranging mobilization of people and resources across the vast territories of the subcontinent. They resulted in a substantial and sustained increase in the numbers, assets, and political importance of the professional armies, while militias also expanded but in a rather unsystematic way. Other, "irregular" forces also made their appearance in the war scene, organized by local groups in order to take part in the conflicts.[8]

These developments had deep consequences for the ensuing conflict-ridden process of the formation of new polities, but despite widespread political instability, republican values soon prevailed, and in military matters, this meant a generalized preference for the militia. This formerly colonial institution was redefined in connection with the new concepts of the body politic and the sovereign people as it embodied the principle of the citizen in arms. At the same time, the republican governments sought to curtail the power that standing armies had amassed during the former wars and reduce their manpower. But in most places they survived and coexisted with militias in rather unstable patterns of military organization.

DURING THE FIRST DECADES after independence, the institution of the militia went through the ups and downs typical of a period of intense political experimentation. By the 1860s, however, it was firmly established as a key military institution in most countries of the subcontinent. The traditional generic term *milicias* was sometimes replaced by other names such as *guardias nacionales, guardias cívicas,* and *cuerpos cívicos,* which carried slightly different connotations and evoked distinctive legacies.[9] All of these shared not just the basic principle of armed citizenship, but also key aspects of their organization and operational structure.[10]

Thus, almost everywhere, the militia followed a highly inclusive pattern: all free adult male nationals had to enroll.[11] The prevailing regulations opened the way to the participation of large sectors of the male population, including workers and peasants, Indians and free blacks. Enrollment took place at the local level; men were nominally incorporated to the regiment in their place of residence, they had to take part in regular training exercises, and they had to eventually go into effective service—usually remunerated. Militia duty was supposed to remain limited in time and restricted geographically, except during emergencies (wars, for example), when troops could be taken far away from their places of origin and kept for longer periods on duty.

Even though enrollment was usually mandatory, not all men served. Exemptions and exceptions abounded, as did the hiring of replacements, and the great majority of the recruits came from the lower classes and the middling sectors, both urban and rural. Presumably, all members of the militia were equals, free citizens only temporarily subject to relations of subordination. In fact, however, these military bodies created and reproduced their own internal hierarchies, and were held together by vertical links of obedience and loyalty to chiefs and commanders, as well as by horizontal ties of comradeship.

Militias had their roots and main fields of action at the provincial and municipal levels, and were embedded in local partisan networks. They responded to regional leaders, governors, and *comandantes*[12] and were part of the decentralized webs of political power, which operated with a great degree of autonomy vis-à-vis the central government. This situation was not just the result of political practices; it was firmly grounded on ideas and principles related to the quest for a decentralized state pattern. Very much like in the United States during the disputes between Federalists and Anti-Federalists, and later on through the first half of the nineteenth century, the early civic model of the militia soon overlapped with the states' rights theory, whereby militias controlled by the states "would provide the ultimate check on federal power if such power ran amok."[13] In countries like Argentina and Mexico, for example, provinces or states claimed for their share of sovereignty and competed with the federal government in military matters. In Peru, Ecuador, and Colombia, political disputes pitted different regions against each other—with their respective armed forces—and also against attempts at centralization. The question of federal vs. local control of armed resources became, therefore, a key issue in the political struggles of the century.[14]

DESPITE THE INITIAL PREFERENCE for the militia as a force best suited to the republic, by the 1860s, for different reasons, most countries in Spanish America had settled for a combination of professional and citizens' armies in rather unstable patterns of shared and contested military arrangements.[15] Although the two institutions presumably had different functions and responsibilities, once in the field, they shared most of the burdens and obligations of military duty. Moreover, the existence of rules that prescribed the relationships between them did not suffice to guarantee a smooth partnership or a regulated subordination. In most places the militia was considered to be auxiliary to the army and only under special circumstances could the former be summoned beyond its allocated geographical area and assigned duties similar to those of the professionals. These restrictions, however, were seldom regarded, so that there is a long list of examples that show overlapping and frictions between them on the subject of powers and jurisdiction. Such ambiguous arrangements resulted in the fragmentation of military power, whereby sustained control of armed resources escaped any single authority.

The eruption of "irregular" forces complicated matters further. Many of these self-convened organizations, like the *guerrillas* in the Peruvian *sierra* or the *montoneras* in Argentina, considered themselves to embody the principle of armed citizenship, and acted in the name of their rights to defend freedom and combat despotism.[16] They often intervened in political struggles as allied forces to partisan groups of different sorts, not necessarily "irregular," and in different combinations with formal armies and militias.

This rather messy coexistence of armed forces fragmented military power in many parts, all of them with claims to a legitimate use of their coercive capacities. Although this situation was an outcome of the implementation of republican values and institutions, it became a topic of public and political debate. Disputes erupted between those who insisted on the role of the militia in the polity and on the benefits of a fragmented military power—on civic as well as federalist grounds—and those who strove to strengthen the standing army and ensure its supremacy. Even though the existing professional armies also showed signs of internal divisions, collusion with local interests, and some tendency to insubordination, their advocates considered it to be more adequate than the militia to secure the monopoly of violence in the hands of a national state. In that direction, they pushed forward for a systematic improvement of the army in terms of its discipline, hierarchical structure, and technical equipment. The controversy lasted for decades, and it overlapped with other issues regarding the shape and features of the state in the republics.[17] In the last decades of the century, the success of the centralizing model favored the standing army above the militia and the national guard, which were subordinated to the former or altogether eliminated as relevant military forces.

THE CENTRALIZED STATE WAS, therefore, not the starting point of our story but rather, an end result that was not necessarily in the minds and wills of all those who set up to create and organize new polities after the demise of the Spanish empire. The inclination towards republican forms of government did not include a precise recipe towards nation building, and beyond some shared principles and references to the same historical models, competition among different projects as well as conflicts of interests and political tendencies were the rule. By the 1860s, most of the republics had more or less established their national boundaries and defined their institutional organization according to the basic tenets of constitutional liberalism. The abolition of slavery, the end to Indian *tributo* (head tax), and a specific endorsement of civil liberties and the separation of powers prevailed. These common grounds did not preclude, however, the persistence of rivalries that were played out in different scenarios and animated a vibrant political life. Liberals had gained power in most places, but they were usually internally divided and also challenged by other political forces, particularly by conservatives of various kinds. Partisan competition and confrontations were the rule within the frameworks defined by the established republican principles and practices.

The early adoption of popular sovereignty to found and legitimize power had led to the development of institutions and procedures of self-government. By the 1860s, all countries considered elections as the legal road to public office; they were held regularly and constituted a matter of public debate and legislative consideration. Men from a wide social spectrum attended the polls and participated in a civic ritual that was quite different from our contemporary electoral days. A tightly knit organization of followers was the key to success so that partisan leaders had to actively recruit their potential voters beforehand, ensure their loyalty through personal links and exchanges, and build collective forces ready to take part in the partisan displays of the electoral game. Elections were, therefore, an occasion for the mobilization of men who mostly came from popular sectors and for the enactment of a ritual performance that often included different degrees of disorderly or turbulent behavior.[18]

In this context, claims and accusations of fraud and manipulation were frequent, and while the periodical exercise of the suffrage was a means of checking these and other eventual abuses of power, the regular control of those elected rested mainly in the hands of "public opinion" on the one side, and of the citizens in arms, on the other. The former was a key instance of political legitimation. Newspapers were the main actor in this regard, and while the partisan press prevailed, it shared the scene with more independent periodicals and other publications whose voice mattered. Associations originating in civil society, such as social clubs, learned societies, religious brotherhoods, Masonic lodges, literary circles, mutual aid societies, and artisan associations also played a growing role in the public sphere.[19] In this way, the strong personal ties so characteristic of the patrimonial-based politics of the first half of the century were now interwoven with other types of political links and interpersonal relationships.

Today we are familiar with the role of the public opinion in our democracies, but armed citizenship is no longer mentioned as a valid means of keeping government power in check. For most of the nineteenth century, however, it was a key dimension of republican regimes. As guardians of popular sovereignty, citizens had the right and the obligation to defend freedom and to bear arms in the face of any abuses of power. This principle was grounded on the theory of natural rights—which was widely accepted at the time and had precedence over positive law—and it opened the way to challenge the existing authorities on the charge of alleged despotism and to the deployment of armed resources to back this challenge. These actions were a regular feature of Spanish-American politics and were usually headed by political leaders who thus mobilized their following in the name of "the people" to question and eventually depose those in power.[20] This was not an exceptional move; rather, it was an accepted way of political intervention, and the fragmentation of military power facilitated this dynamics. While in the United States there were few such armed rebellions based upon similar arguments, and they were generally rapidly subdued, most countries to the south experienced frequent actions of this sort, both successful and unsuccessful.[21] In Mexico, for example, more than 1,500 *pronunciamientos* were staged between 1821, when the Plan de Iguala proclaimed independence, and 1876, when the Plan de Tuxtepec opened the road to power for Porfirio Díaz. These were manifestos put forward to question, formulate demands to, and put pressure upon the authorities, which very often culminated in a military action against them. In Argentina, at the other end of the subcontinent, a nineteenth-century observer counted 117 *levantamientos* (uprisings) between 1862 and 1868.[22]

None of these reached the scale—in terms of duration, geographical reach, and number of casualties—of the American Civil War, which may also be considered a case of internal insurrection in a country that had previously known only a handful of such events. In the United States, the highly coveted political stability reached after some initial fears was suddenly shattered by a conflict that evoked the volatile and strongly despised Spanish-American "anarchy" and exposed the fragility of the U.S. political order. In the southern republics, in turn, the northern war was seen with great concern by liberals, who were not only worried about the final outcome of the conflict, but also alarmed to see how far violence could go in confrontations between nationals who legitimized their claims in shared republican terms and responded to different allegedly legitimate political and military authorities. Also, the war served the critics of republicanism who had long blamed its ideals and practices for what they considered the recurrent political turbulence of their countries, and now could resort to the U.S. commotion to prove their point: There were no exceptions to the tumultuous nature of the republic.

These concerns did not suffice to curve the long-standing Spanish-American role of the use of force in regular politics, which was deeply enmeshed in a complex web of norms and practices whose contours responded to widely accepted, albeit variable, rules of the political game. In that context, armed confrontations took place as part of a competitive political life driven by struggles for power and disagreements over the territorial and institutional shaping of the republics. Political actors resorted to all recognized means available in order to dispute their claims and were ready to fight their opponents also through the use of force—a move that was not necessarily considered illegitimate. At the same time, if resorting to violence could count as legitimate, the outcome of an armed confrontation did not suffice to grant legality to the victors, and these had to validate their titles at the polls, as well as in the realm of public opinion. Thus, revolutions were embedded in republican politics and belonged to the usual repertoire of most political players.

THE POLITICAL DYNAMIC briefly portrayed above was not contrary to self-government; rather, it amounted to a particular way of understanding republican politics, which was strongly shaped by a civic rhetoric that favored *vita activa* and resulted in a relatively broad definition of citizenship. In practical terms, it relied strongly upon the organized mobilization of the people in vertically commanded groups—electoral clienteles, militia regiments, partisan networks, etc.—under the aegis of deeply divided leaderships. At a time when the centralization of state power was a highly contested proposition, political life was—with few exceptions—strongly decentralized. Local and regional leaderships struggled to keep political (and military) power in their hands, a modus operandi that conspired against any attempt at creating an overall hegemonic instance of domination. The fragmentation of military forces—the double tiered system of a standing army and militia with strong local roots—was at the heart of the system, and its persistence was strongly upheld by important sectors of the ruling elites as well as by wider sectors of the population. This institutional and political pattern resulted in recurrent instability, which was not the outcome of the failure to play the game of the republic, but on the contrary, a result of a specific way of abiding by its rules.[23]

This system had always raised some concerns among the contemporaries; on different occasions, regimes in power sought to discipline politics by concentrating all authority in the hands of a strong figure very much in the classical manner of republican "dictators" or by appealing to a conservative corporate order reminiscent of the Spanish colonial traditions.[24] These experiments succeeded in certain periods and places until around the middle of the century, when liberals managed to set up new rules that confirmed republican values and practices and at the same time introduced liberal institutions intended to establish limitations to the exercise of government power. Their initial success soon experienced the consequences of the new international scenario of the early 1860s, which came to alter the previous picture. On account of this change—as this book clearly shows—critics of republicanism found more room to put forward their positions, and in some cases, like Mexico and Santo Domingo, they were able to recruit enough support to espouse the colonialist moves of European powers and to depose the republic in favor of monarchical rule. These events, as well as the American Civil War, entered the public debate in the rest of the Spanish-American nations, and qualms regarding political turmoil, instability, and violence became widespread. These issues did not just remain as a banner for conservatives; increasingly, liberal-oriented groups were also discussing the prevailing system as new ideas regarding the republican order started to compete with the old.

In this context, the use of force in politics was revisited, not only as a result of the ideological and political novelties described above, but also on account of the concrete experience of war on a new scale. Such was the case of Mexico and the Dominican Republic, studied by Pani and Eller, as well as of several other Spanish-American countries that went through this type of international conflict. Thus, after Spain occupied the Peruvian Chincha Islands in 1864, Peru and Chile, later supported by Bolivia and Ecuador, fought the Spanish who were finally defeated in 1866. The bloodiest conflict of all took place from 1864–65 to 1871, and involved Paraguay on one side and Argentina, Brazil, and Uruguay on the other. In the following decade, the Pacific war (Chile against Peru and Bolivia) belonged to the same set of conflicts between nation states.

These confrontations were of a different magnitude than the usual internal struggles. The countries involved, therefore, soon had to face the fact of their military flaws, as well as the crude realities of large-scale violence. Fragmented forces, which lacked a central command and a coordinated leadership, could hardly meet the new challenges. In Mexico, Benito Juárez had dissolved the standing army in 1860, which was replaced by a combination of forces with strong local roots and a leading presence of the national guard. Yet this arrangement proved rather fragile during the French invasion, and the republican forces could only succeed once Napoleon III had retrieved his army home. So when the war ended, Juárez decided to reinstate a professional army under a national central command.[25] In the case of Chile, the conflict with Spain made clear that the country was in poor shape in military matters, and in the following years the authorities devoted their effort to improve the armed forces, particularly the navy, a move that would prove decisive in the following War of the Pacific.[26]

In the Southern Cone, the War of Triple Alliance lasted for almost six years, and had dramatic consequences for all involved—and most particularly for Paraguay. Argentina, Brazil, and Uruguay joined forces against that nation and entered into a spiral of violence that did not only affect the armies in the field but also was projected within each nation. This episode meant armed confrontation in an unforeseen scale and brought about important military changes as the following account on the case of Argentina will show.

THE ORIGINS OF the war speak about the fragility of the notion of national politics at the time. The spark that triggered the initial skirmishes had to do with a partisan controversy in Uruguay, which soon involved friendly groups in the neighboring countries. The Brazilian government intervened in favor of one of the parties (*Colorados*), while Paraguay supported the other (*Blancos*). In the case of Argentina, the *Liberales* in power had a long-standing relationship with the Colorado Party across the river, while their rival *Federales* were allies to the Blancos. Soon after the conflict began, however, this initial scenario of partisan struggles that cut across formal country borders developed into a formal war among nations, a typical geopolitical struggle for the consolidation of the nation-states—as Luc Capdevilla has perceptively indicated.[27]

In Argentina, the first steps towards the alliance against the Paraguayan regime were met with enthusiasm in the capital city of Buenos Aires, and the Liberal government was optimistic about the rapid resolution of the whole story. As the conflict escalated, however, resistance mounted. First, although the Federales were strongly divided on the issue, party leaders in the western and northwestern provinces were firmly against the war, and declared their friendship with Paraguay. Other political groups, initially pro-government, also shifted sides, albeit for different reasons. And so did some important members of the intellectual elite of the country. Secondly, the war effort required the recruitment of thousands of soldiers and national guards. The draft became widespread and triggered open resistance; groups of guards already on the way to the front mutinied and escaped, and others hid before being taken. A mounting popular antiwar mood spread all over the country. Thirdly, various leaders of the Federales joined forces and, by the end of 1866, they launched a wide-ranging rebellion not only to protest the war but also to try to topple the Liberales in power. The government brought back troops from the front, waged a strong repressive action against the rebels, and defeated them after long and bloody confrontations.

By 1868, most Argentine men were back from the front. President Bartolomé Mitre (1862–68), who had been commander in chief of the allied forces, left that post in order to resume his duties at home. The armies that were then occupying Paraguay consisted mainly of Brazilian troops; by 1870, they won the war, after the total annihilation of the Paraguayan forces, the physical destruction of the country's resources, and the extermination of a large number of its male population.

In Argentina, the military scenario changed considerably in those five years. When the war began, the standing army was poorly manned (6,000 soldiers in all), badly equipped, and scarcely disciplined. The officers were old favorites and partisans of Mitre, who found in these military comrades the loyal muscle needed to keep the country under control. But they were scarcely fit for the change of scale brought about by this war. During the conflict, the national government made huge efforts to modernize and regulate the forces, and the army that returned home was considerably improved in matters of equipment, training, and hierarchical structure.

At the same time, despite its problematic performance during those years, the national guard remained a key resource in the hands of the provincial authorities. Some of them had been reluctant to respond to the federal government's call for recruitment, and had protected their citizens from this extraordinary effort. Others were forced to comply and sometimes face the resistance of the draftees. The rebellion of the Federales, in turn, was launched in the name of the national guard, and it was also national guards disciplined to aid the standing army who manned the units that came from Paraguay to crush the rebels.

In the end, the war had become very unpopular, while it had paradoxically strengthened national unity. The political cost was mainly paid by the party in power, as well as by the defiant Federales, who were as good as eliminated from the political scene. President Mitre's chosen candidate for the 1868 succession was defeated by Domingo F. Sarmiento (1868–74), who came to office when the Argentine war effort was almost over. He was a champion of national state consolidation and was convinced of the need to modernize and at the same time discipline the professional army and the militia, under strict control of a strong executive. Abraham Lincoln was, in that respect, his role model, and he insisted on citing his example in the question of subduing the aspirations of military autonomy on the part of the states. His intentions as well as his policies were successful inasmuch as his administration empowered the standing army with measures geared towards the modernization and professionalization of the institution. The attempts at subordinating the national guard to the federal government and concentrating all military power at that level were, in turn, less successful, and military decentralization remained a much-proclaimed principle and a prevalent fact for at least another decade.[28]

LIKE IN ARGENTINA, in the rest of the countries involved in these larger wars, military organization was subject to practical changes, which in turn resulted in new challenges to the prevailing traditions. The previous relative consensus regarding the use of force in politics was weakened, standing armies were modernized and could operate with greater efficiency than before, and militia forces experienced increasing difficulties to sustain their autonomy. These changes did not amount to an overall eradication of the dual military system, but rather to recurrent debates and political disputes around these issues, as well as to discussions regarding the different alternatives. In fact, it was not until the following decades that in the context of wider changes in the relationships between politics and society, the dual system was dismantled. By then, the whole edifice of the former republican experiment was coming, once again, under heavy fire, both in the realm of ideas and in the empirical world of politics. Latin-American societies were experiencing important transformations: Most countries were going through a relatively sustained process of economic expansion as they developed closer links with the world markets, while the social structure became more diversified and complex. At this point, liberals themselves were strongly revising their former certitudes and embracing fresh perspectives. A rising creed put forward an entirely new concept of order, which favored stability and discipline rather than civic involvement and the active mobilization typical of elections and revolutions of old. To achieve that order, their advocates strove to centralize authority in a strong national state that would monopolize the use of force, discipline the elites, and reshape the citizenry. In that context, military matters became a focus of reform, designed to concentrate armed power in the hands of the state. In most countries, militias and national guards were either eliminated or put under the control of standing armies, and governments made sustained efforts to modernize, discipline, and subordinate the latter under a single, centralized command. Such was the case, for example, in Mexico after the ascent to power of Porfirio Díaz in 1876; in Argentina, starting during the presidencies of Avellaneda and Roca (1874–80 and 1880–86), and in Colombia, with the restriction of the role of militias after 1878.[29] These goals were not evenly reached, yet they were pursued throughout the entire region, and they succeeded in changing the ideological and political foundations of the Latin American republics for the years to come. And although no linear or gradual path led from the "crisis of the 1860s" to the new era, that momentous decade had anticipated some of the issues that would be at the heart of the decisive reforms of the fin-de-siècle.

Suggested Readings

Chust, Manuel and Juan Marchena eds. *Las armas de la nación: Independencia y ciudadanía en Hispanoamérica (1750–1850)*. Madrid: Iberoamericana, 2007.

Escamilla, Juan Ortiz, coord. *Fuerzas militares en Iberoamérica, siglos XVIII y xix*. México D.F./Zamora, Michoacán/Jalapa, Veracruz: El Colegio de México, El Colegio de Michoacán y Universidad Veracruzana, 2005.

Foote, Nicola and René Harder Horst eds. *Military Struggle and Identity in Latin America: Race, Nation, and Community during the Liberal Period*. Gainesville: University Press of Florida, 2010.

Garavaglia, Juan Carlos, Juan Pro Ruiz, and Eduardo Zimmermann, eds. *Las fuerzas de guerra en la construcción del Estado: América Latina, siglo XIX*. Rosario: Prohistoria, 2012.

Macías, Flavia, and Hilda Sabato. "La Guardia Nacional: Estado, política y uso de la fuerza en la Argentina de la segunda mitad del siglo XIX," *PolHis* 11 (2012).

Malamud, Carlos, and Carlos Dardé, eds. *Violencia y legitimidad: Política y revoluciones en España y América Latina, 1840–1910*. Santander: Universidad de Cantabria, 2004.

Palacios, Guillermo, and Erika Pani, coords. *El poder y la sangre: Guerra, Estado y Nación en la década de 1860*. México D.F.: El Colegio de México, 2014.

Rabinovich, Alejandro. *La société guerrière: Pratiques, discours et valeurs militaires dans le Rio de la Plata, 1806–1852*. Rennes: Presses Universitaires de Rennes, 2013.

Sabato, Hilda. "Soberania popular, cidadania, e nação na América Hispânica: A experiência republicana no século XIX." *Almanack Braziliense* 9 (2009).

Thomson, Guy. "Bulwarks of Patriotic Liberalism: The National Guard, Philharmonic Corps and Patriotic Juntas in Mexico, 1847–88." *Journal of Latin American Studies* 22 (1990).

Notes

1. I wrote most of this article during my stay as a Humboldt Foundation Forschungspreisträger at the Lateinamerika Institut of the Freie Universität Berlin (2013). My deep acknowledgement to those institutions, as well as to the University of Buenos Aires that financed part of the basic research for this piece.

2. Fifteen republics, plus one constitutional monarchy, Brazil, Argentina, Bolivia, Chile, Colombia, Ecuador, Paraguay, Peru, and Uruguay in South America, and Mexico, Costa Rica, El Salvador, Guatemala, Honduras and Nicaragua in North and Central America. I am considering here only continental Latin America, and therefore I have not included the countries of the Caribbean basin. Panama is not in this list because it only became definitively independent from Colombia in 1903.

3. Hilda Sabato, "Soberania popular, cidadania, e nação na América Hispânica: A experiência republicana no século XIX," *Almanack Braziliense* 9 (2009), and "La reacción de América: La construcción de las repúblicas en el siglo XIX," in *Europa, América y el mundo: Tiempos histórico*, ed. Roger Chartier and Antonio Feros (Madrid: Marcial Pons, 2006). See also Elías Palti, *El tiempo de la política: El siglo XIX reconsiderado* (Buenos Aires: Siglo XXI, 2007) and James E. Sanders, *The Vanguard of the Atlantic World: Creating Modernity, Nation and Democracy in Nineteenth-Century Latin America* (Durham, NC: Duke University Press, 2014).

4. I use "the political" in the sense defined by Pierre Rosanvallon in *Pour une histoire conceptuelle du politique* (Paris: Seuil, 2003).

5. The main exception was Mexico. Cf. Erica Pani's piece in this volume.

6. José Antonio Aguilar Rivera, *En pos de la quimera: Reflexiones sobre el experimento constitucional atlántico* (México, D.F.: Fondo de Cultura Económica/CIDE, 2000); José Antonio Aguilar Rivera and Rafael Rojas, coords., *El republicanismo en Hispanoamérica: Ensayos de historia intelectual y política* (México, D.F.: Fondo de Cultura Económica, 2002); Natalio Botana, *La tradición republicana: Alberdi, Sarmiento y las ideas políticas de su tiempo* (Buenos Aires: Sudamericana, 1984); J. Miller, "The Authority of a Foreign Talisman: A Study of the U.S. Constitutional Practice as Authority in Nineteenth Century Argentina and the Argentine's Elite Leap of Faith,"

American University Law Review 46 (1997); R. Piza Rocafort, "Influencia de la Constitución de los Estados Unidos en las constituciones de Europa y América," *Cuadernos del CAPEL* 23 (1987); Rafael Rojas, *Las repúblicas de aire: Utopía y desencanto en la revolución hispanoamericana* (Buenos Aires: Taurus, 2010); Julio Saguir, *¿Unión o secesión? Los procesos constituyentes en Estados Unidos (1776–1787) y Argentina (1810– 1862)* (Buenos Aires: Prometeo, 2007); Eduardo Zimmermann, "Historia global y cultura constitucional: Una nota sobre la traducción y ciruculación de doctrina jurídica en la Argentina del siglo diecinueve," *Nuevo Mundo/Mundos Nuevos*, May 30, 2014.

7. For the USA experiences and debates on this topic see, among others, Jerry Cooper, *The Rise of the National Guard: The Evolution of the American Militia, 1865–1920* (Lincoln: University of Nebraska Press, 1997); Saul Cornell, *A Well Regulated Militia: The Founding Fathers and the Origins of Gun Control in America* (New York: Oxford University Press, 2006); M. Muehlbauer and D. Ulbrich, *Ways of War: American Military History from the Colonial Era to the Twenty-First Century* (New York: Routledge, 2014); Lawrence Delbert Cress, "An Armed Community: The Origins and Meaning of the Right to Bear Arms," *Journal of American History* 71 (June 1984); E. Wayne Carp, "The Problem of National Defense in the Early American Republic," in *The American Revolution: Its Character and Limits*, ed. Jack P. Greene (New York: New York University Press, 1987). For a broader appraisal of the topic of the citizen in arms in the Anglo-Saxon world, see Edmund Morgan, *Inventing of the People: The Rise of Popular Sovereignty in England and America* (New York: Norton and Co., 1988). A very interesting perspective on the same subject for France in Pierre Rosanvallon, *Le sacré du citoyen: Histoire de la répresentation démocratique en France* (Paris: Gallimard, 1998). For a broad overview of the history of the militia, see Jan Metzger, *Die Milizarmee in klassischen Republikanismus: Die Odyssee eines militärpolitischen Konzeptes von Florenz über England und Schottland nach Nordamerika (15.–18. Jahrhundert)* (Bern, Stuttgart, Wien: P. Haupt, 1999).

8. See, among many others, Manuel Chust and Juan Marchena, eds., *Las armas de la nación: Independencia y ciudadanía en Hispanoamérica (1750–1850)* (Madrid and Frankfurt a. M.: Iberoamericana/Vervuert, 2007); Juan Marchena and Manuel Chust, eds., *Por la fuerza de las armas: Ejército e independencias en Iberoamérica* (Castelló de la Plana: Universitat Jaume I, 2008); Juan Ortiz Escamilla, coord., *Fuerzas militares en Iberoamérica siglos XVIII y XIX* (México, D.F.: El Colegio de México, El Colegio de Michoacán y Universidad Veracruzana, 2005); and Tulio Halperin Donghi, *Reforma y disolución de los imperios ibéricos, 1750–1850* (Madrid: Alianza, 1985).

9. "Guardia Nacional" prevailed in the second half of the nineteenth century and was used, for example, in Argentina, Mexico, Peru, and Colombia. It was meant to give "national" character to the traditionally local militia.

10. There is a vast bibliography on militia and armed citizenship in Latin America, which interested readers may consult online at American Civil Wars: A Bibliography, https://sites.google.com/site/americancivilwarsbibliography.

11. In the 1840s, in some places, like Venezuela and Peru, militia requirements included property qualifications, but these limitations were later eliminated, and like in the rest of the subcontinent, personal autonomy and local residence were the main conditions for enrollment, which was usually but not always mandatory.

12. The traditional figure of the "caudillo" or the "cacique" fits well into this picture. Yet these terms have lost much of their initial appeal for historians. Recent historiography has criticized the widespread use of those categories to subsume the complex picture of political relationships during the first half of the nineteenth century to the dual image of the caudillo and his retinue. These reservations are even more pertinent for the second half of the century. For a critique of the concept in the River Plate area, see José Carlos Chiaramonte, "Legalidad constitucional o caudillismo: El problema del orden social en el surgimiento de los estados autónomos del litoral argentino en la primera mitad del siglo XIX," *Desarrollo Económico* 26 (1986) and Noemí Goldman and Ricardo Salvatore, comps., *Caudillismos rioplatenses: Nuevas miradas a un viejo problema* (Buenos Aires: Eudeba, 1998).

13. Cornell, *A Well Regulated Militia*, 5.

14. The example of the United States, with its strongly federal institutional arrangement was always cited in Spanish-American public debate, particularly when discussing the role of the militia. See, among others, Hilda Sabato, *Buenos Aires en armas: La revolución de 1880* (Buenos Aires: Siglo XXI, 2008).

15. This coexistence was similar to what scholars call "the dual army tradition" for the United States, where the Constitution formalized the existence of both regular and militia forces, and "recognized that both the federal government and the individual states can raise and maintain military forces." Muehlbauer and Ulbrich, *Ways of War*, 113.

16. On "irregular" forces, see Ariel de la Fuente, *Los hijos de Facundo: Caudillos y montoneras en la Provincia de La Rioja durante el proceso de formación del Estado argentino, 1853–1970* (Buenos Aires: Prometeo, 2000); various articles in Garavaglia, Ruiz and Zimmermann, *Las fuerzas de guerra*; and Macías and Sabato, "La Guardia Nacional."

17. On different definitions of the state and the role of the armed forces, see D. H. Deudney, "The Philadelphian system: sovereignty, arms control, and balance of power in the American states-union, circa 1787–1861," *International Organization* 49 (1995).

18. During the last twenty years, elections and electoral practices in nineteenth-century Latin America have been widely studied, and we have now a bibliographical corpus that covers most of the countries of the region for the best part of that century.

19. There is a vast bibliography on these topics. For a more general coverage of the different aspects of institutions and practices in the public realm, see Carlos Forment, *Democracy in Latin America, 1760–1900, Volume I: Civic Selfhood and Public Life in Mexico and Peru* (Chicago: University of Chicago Press, 2003); François-Xavier Guerra, *Modernidad e independencies* (Madrid: Mapfre, 1992); François-Xavier Guerra and Annick Lempériere, eds., *Los espacios públicos en Iberoamérica: Ambigüedades y*

problemas; Siglos XVIII–XIX (México: Fondo de Cultura Económica, 1998); Nils Jacobsen and Cristóbal Aljovín, eds., *Political Culture in the Andes, 1750s–1950s* (Durham, NC: Duke University Press, 2005); Palti, *El tiempo de la política*; Pablo Piccato, "Public Sphere in Latin America: A Map of the Historiography," *Social History* 35 (May 2010); Hilda Sabato, "On Political Citizenship in Nineteenth-Century Latin America," *American Historical Review* 106 (October 2001); Sanders, *The Vanguard*; Víctor Uribe Urán, "The Birth of a Public Sphere in Latin America During the Age of Revolution," *Comparative Studies in Society and History* 42 (April 2000).

20. For recent interpretations of nineteenth-century Latin American revolutions, see the following collective volumes: Malamud and Dardé, *Violencia y legitimidad*; Rebecca Earle, ed., *Rumours of War: Civil Conflict in Nineteenth-Century Latin America* (London: Institute for Latin American Studies, 2000); Ricardo Forte and Guillermo Fajardo, coords., *Consenso y coacción: Estado e instrumentos de control politico y social en México y América Latina (siglos XIX y XX)* (Mexico, D.F.: El Colegio de Mexico y el Colegio Mexiquense, 2000); Chust and Marchena, *Las armas de la nación*. For the study of specific cases not included in those volumes, see, among others, Cristóbal Aljovín de Losada, *Caudillos y constituciones: Perú, 1821–1845* (Lima: Pontificia Universidad Católica del Perú y Fondo de Cultura Económica, 2000); Paula Alonso, *Between Revolution and the Ballot Box: The Origins of the Argentine Radical Party* (Cambridge: Cambridge University Press, 2000); Natalio Botana and Ezequiel Gallo, *De la república posible a la república verdadera (1880–1910)* (Buenos Aires: Ariel, 1997); Laura Cucchi and María José Navajas, "Garantizar el orden: debates sobre el derecho de la revolución y el federalismo en el Congreso Naconal durante la intervención a Corrientes en 1878," *PolHis* 11 (2013); Will Fowler, "El pronunciamiento mexicano del siglo XIX. Hacia una nueva tipología," *Estudios de historia moderna y contemporánea de México* 38 (2009); François-Xavier Guerra, "El pronunciamiento en México: Prácticas e imaginarios," *TRACE* 37 (2000); Leonardo Hirsch, "Entre la 'revolución' y la 'evolución': Las movilizaciones del Noventa," *PolHis* 9 (2012); Marta Irurozqui, *"A bala, piedra y palo": La construcción de la ciudadanía política en Bolivia, 1826–1952* (Sevilla: Diputación de Sevilla, 2000); Eduardo Míguez, *Mitre montonero: La Revolución de 1874 y las formas de la política en la organización nacional* (Buenos Aires: Sudamericana, 2011); Sabato, "El ciudadano en armas," *Buenos Aires en armas*, and "Resistir la imposición: Revolución, ciudadanía y república en la Argentina de 1880," *Revista de Indias* 246 (2009).

21. The best known examples for the United States are the Whiskey Rebellions of 1794, Fries' Rebellion of 1800, the Baltimore Riot in 1812, the Dorr Rebellion of 1842, and the post-Civil War insurgencies in the South. The Civil War itself may be considered a case of internal rebellion, where militias played a significant role, particularly in the formation of the Confederate army. See Cornell, *A Well Regulated Militia* and Muehlbauer and Ulbrich, *Ways of War*, among others.

22. The figures for Mexico in Fowler, "El pronunciamiento," 5, and for Argentina, in Carlos Malamud, "Elecciones, política y violencia: Las revoluciones argentinas de 1890 y 1893," in Forte and Guajardo, *Consenso y coacción*, 12.

23. A worthwhile comparison could be made with other nineteenth-century republican experiences, certainly in Europe and even in the United States before the Civil War. Most of them did not prove too stable, a problem that led in many cases—such as in Spain and France, among others—to their downfall and replacement for other political regimes. Spanish Americans, instead, insisted on the republic, warts and all, so that instability remained a long-lived feature of its political life.

24. These were ideal models that never entirely materialized, but figures such as Juan Manuel de Rosas in Buenos Aires and Gaspar de Francia in Paraguay may be associated with republican dictators, while conservatives who, at different times, reached power in Mexico and Colombia sought to re-establish a corporate order.

25. Hernández López, "Juárez y los militares" and "Las fuerzas armadas."

26. Rafael Sagredo Baeza, "Guerra y honor nacional: Chile y Perú contra España (1864–1866)," in Guillermo Palacios and Erika Pani, coords., *El poder y la sangre: Guerra, estado y nación en la década de 1860* (México, D.F.; El Colegio de México, 2014).

27. Luc Capdevila, *Una guerra total: Paraguay, 1874–1870: Ensayo de historia del tiempo presente* (Asunción and Buenos Aires: Centro de Estudios Antropológicos de la Universidad Católica y Editorial Sb, 2010). There is quite a vast bibliographical corpus on the War of the Triple Alliance. For a brief account of its consequences in Argentina, see Hilda Sabato, *Historia de la Argentina, 1852–1890* (Buenos Aires: Siglo XXI editores, 2012).

28. On the Argentine army during the War of the Triple Alliance, see Hilda Sabato, "La fuerza de las armas. Estado, guerra y revoluciones en la Argentina de la década de 1860, in Palacios and Pani, *El poder y la sangre*, and *Historia de la Argentina*; on Sarmiento and the U.S. example, see, among others, Botana, *La tradición republicana.*

29. On these changes, see for Mexico, Alicia Hernández Chávez, "Origen y ocaso del ejército porfiriano," *Historia Mexicana* 153 (1989) and Brian Connaughton, Carlos Illades, and Sonia Pérez Toledo, dirs., *La construcción de la legitimidad política en México* (Zamora, Michoacán/Mexico, D.F.: El Colegio de Michoacán, Universidad Autónoma Metropolitana, Universidad Nacional Autónoma de México y El Colegio de México, 1999). For Argentina, Beatriz Bragoni, "Cuyo después de Pavón: consenso, rebelión y orden político, 1861–1874" in Bragoni and Míguez, coords., *Un nuevo orden político*; Luciano de Privitellio, "El ejército ante el cambio de siglo y 1930: Burocratización y nuevos estilos políticos," in *AA.VV: La construcción de la Nación Argentina: El rol de las Fuerzas Armadas* (Buenos Aires: Ministerio de Defensa de la Nación, 2010); Macías and Sabato, "La Guardia Nacional"; Sabato, *Buenos Aires en armas*, "Resistir la imposición" and *Historia de la Argentina*. For Colombia, Ricardo Esquivel Triana, "La formación militar en Colombia, 1880–1884," in Torres del Río and Rodríguez Hernández, *De milicias reales a militares contrainsurgentes*; Sanders, *Contentious Republicans*; and for Peru, Mücke, *Political Culture.*

CHAPTER TEN

Cuba, the Atlantic Crisis of the 1860s, and the Road to Abolition

Matt D. Childs

By the time the U.S. Civil War erupted in 1861, emancipation of enslaved Africans had been taking place in the Western Hemisphere for nearly eighty years. Abolitionists throughout the Atlantic World hoped the Civil War would not only end slavery in the United States, but also catalyze emancipation processes elsewhere in places such as Brazil and Cuba. Past experiences in the Americas during the Age of Revolutions had demonstrated that military conflicts could ignite actions to weaken and destroy slavery. The intellectual, political, and economic changes that broke the chains of colonial rule could simultaneously corrode and reinforce the manacles of slavery. For example, during the American Revolution, antislavery measures gained traction in the northern United States through warfare and gradual emancipation laws even while slavery in the southern United States gained a stronger foothold. The intertwined process of emancipation and warfare abolished slavery in the French colony of Saint Domingue, which gave rise to the independent Republic of Haiti in 1804 and the first independent country in Latin-American history. Once independence armies marched through Latin America from Mexico in the north to Argentina in the south from 1810 to 1830, military conflicts decisively weakened slavery by turning one-time slaves into free soldiers when they joined revolutionary movements. In the ensuing decades from 1830 to the 1850s, the institution of slavery never recovered from the independence struggles, and the newly independent Latin-American nations gradually abolished slavery. Would the American Civil War initiate a second wave of emancipation struggles in the 1860s tied to military conflict and political changes?[1]

While the historical record of warfare followed by emancipation was a common occurrence in the slave societies of the Americas during the nineteenth century, the demographic and economic record told a far different story. By the 1860s the slave population in the Americas reached its highest point in its entire history dating back to the sixteenth century. By 1861 when the Civil War began, six million Africans and their descendants were enslaved in the United States, Brazil, Cuba, and Puerto Rico. The total enslaved population had dramatically increased—not decreased—during the nineteenth century—from roughly two million in 1800 to six million in 1860.[2] Economically, cotton in the United States, coffee in Brazil, and sugar in Cuba produced new slave regimes that breathed new life into the institution. Scholars of Atlantic slavery such as Dale Tomich, Anthony Kaye, Christopher Schmidt-Nowara, and Rafael Marquese have labeled these nineteenth-century slave regimes as a "Second Slavery" to contrast with the "First Slavery" of the colonial era.[3] From demographic and economic perspectives, the institution of slavery prior to the eruption of the Civil War appeared as dynamic, profitable, and more resilient than at any other time in its history, even if politically it appeared increasingly obsolete in a hemisphere of nations governed by varying degrees of republicanism and liberalism.

The U.S. Civil War, however, once again paired military warfare with emancipation, which made slavery seem less secure on the nearby island of Cuba. Similar to the "protective wall" metaphor used by Rafael Marquese in his chapter to explain how slavery in the United States provided security for Brazilian slavery, once the U.S. Civil War erupted, Cuban slavery no longer seemed so secure. The outbreak of the Civil War in the United States brought forth an anonymous plea to Isabella II of Spain in 1862 on the subject of Cuban slavery. British abolitionists (who most likely were its actual authors despite the claim that it was written by a Cuban), later published the letter as a *Memorial to the Queen of Spain*. The purpose of the *Memorial* derived from the "actual circumstances of the United States" where more than a year of warfare offered a cautionary tale on the future of slavery in Cuba. The author pessimistically noted that his message would simply be dismissed as the "gloomy philanthropic vertigo of some dreamer," but nonetheless insisted that the U.S. Civil War "surrounded and affected us to a contagious degree" and that a "comparison of the two analogous situations—that of Cuba and of the Southern section of the United States" was necessary. Drawing upon the experience of the United States, *The Memorial* explained that Cuba had two likely routes to emancipation: (1) bloody warfare as exemplified by the U.S. Civil War; or (2) controlled legislative action. The onset of the Civil War provided an urgent example for Cuba to avoid an apocalyptic outcome that could bring emancipation through slave rebellion. The 1862 *Memorial* urged Spain to save its colony of Cuba through legislative and gradual measures to peacefully and authoritatively end slavery without losing political control of the island. Despite the author's conclusion that his plea would likely be received by the Queen of Spain as a "beatific vision of hermit, resembling so many foragers of wise chimeras, inspired by a profound ecstasy of social love," his vision of Cuba's two paths toward abolition in 1862—insurrection or legislative—proved insightful for what transpired in the 1860s.[4]

Rather than a divided path where Cuba had to choose either insurrection or controlled legal steps, the Cuban road to abolition would wind through a combination of international pressure, legislative action, and insurrection by the slaves themselves. All of these actions would take place during the 1860s, yet final abolition would not occur until 1886. The American Civil War of the 1860s created a crisis for the Cuban plantation system that provided the context to place the abolition of slavery on the political horizon. Put another way, while the American Civil War should not be regarded as the single most important causal factor in bringing about the abolition of Cuba slavery, it most certainly created a crisis that catalyzed and accelerated the end of Cuban slavery.

Three events in the 1860s put Cuba decisively on the path toward ending slavery. First, the Lincoln administration demonstrated its commitment to preventing U.S. citizens from participating in the transatlantic slave trade from Africa to Cuba with the Lyons-Seward Treaty of 1862, which empowered the British to stop and seize slave ships operated by U.S. nationals. Second, a period of reform politics in metropolitan Spain witnessed the foundation in Madrid of the Spanish Abolitionist Society in 1865 and Spain's abolition of its transatlantic slave trade to Cuba in 1867. And third, when independence sentiments gripped Cuban patriots in 1868 with the start of the Ten Years' War, slaves could emancipate themselves by joining the rebel army. Collectively through international treaties and imperial policies the supply of African slaves to Cuba was shut down in the 1860s, and then through warfare on the battlefield slaves struck for their own freedom. As a result of actions in the 1860s, Cuban slavery would never recover its prior strength.

CUBA HAS THE DUBIOUS distinction of operating the longest running transatlantic slave trade in history. The first slaves arrived in the 1490s, and final abolition of the transatlantic slave trade only came in 1867. Unlike the United States that produced a slave population that grew by natural increase, Cuba remained dependent on the transatlantic slave trade to sustain its population, which made the actions in the 1860s all the more important for understanding the onset of abolition during the era of the U.S. Civil War. Despite its long history, however, it was only after the Haitian Revolution in the 1790s that Africans in large numbers were imported to the island. While no consensus has emerged over exact figures for total imports from 1790 to 1867, scholars have estimated that from 700,000 to as many as one million slaves entered Cuba. The massive importation of slaves and the radical transformations of Cuban society are all the more apparent given that in the previous 280 years only 100,000 slaves had been imported into the island. From a comparative perspective, this intense importation in a short period of time is all the more striking. For example, during the entire history of the slave trade to the United Sates roughly 400,000 slaves had been imported. The Cuban slave trade of the nineteenth century alone doubled the total volume of the United States slave trade for its entire history.[5]

Cuba's dependence on the transatlantic slave trade emerged during a precarious moment in the history of international slaving. The 1791 Haitian Revolution that destroyed the largest slave-based economy in the Caribbean and liberated roughly 400,000 Africans from bondage marked the beginning of the end for New World slavery. Yet it was precisely the destruction and liberation created by the Haitian Revolution that provided the structural opening for Cuba to enter the world sugar and coffee markets. In addition, the early nineteenth century witnessed a dramatic change in countries participating in the transatlantic slave trade with Britain abolishing the trade in 1807 and the United States abolishing the trade in 1808. Great Britain made a radical volte-face from being the largest transporter of slaves in the 18th century to championing the abolitionist cause in the nineteenth century. Animated by humanitarian and economic motives, the British exerted considerable pressure on Spain to abolish the trade. Consequently, although the transatlantic slave trade flourished in the nineteenth century and would last in Cuba until 1867, from the early 1800s Cuban slaveholders believed the trade could be abolished at any moment due to foreign pressure. The Spanish crown won the allegiance of many Cuban slaveholders by defending slavery even while they signed various treaties to limit the trade because they often turned a blind eye towards the new regulations.[6]

On the surface, Cuba's very profitable formula, dating to the 1790s, of sugar production fueled by enslaved Africans from the transatlantic slave trade looked essentially no different before the eruption of the U.S. Civil War in 1861. What had changed, however, was the world around Cuba. In 1790, when slavery rapidly expanded, Cuba was one among many colonies and nations where the institution existed. By 1860, however, slavery had been abolished in Haiti since 1794 and for nearly three decades on nearby British islands; the Revolution of 1848 brought an end to slavery in the remaining French colonies, and most Latin-American countries had abolished slavery.

The sectional politics of the 1850s made it clear to many Cuban slave owners that slavery did not have a secure future in the United States even though some continued to pursue a policy of annexation. For example, Cuban intellectual José Antonio Saco campaigned for annexation to the United States in the 1830s and 1840s. He and others believed the United States had shown that political liberty for whites could coexist with slavery for blacks. By the 1850s, however, with the rising tide of political divisions in the United States that could envelop Cuba, Saco and others now campaigned against annexation and for Cuban representation within the Spanish empire. Cuban masters could only find solace with their Brazilian counterparts where slavery would last until 1888. But even in Brazil the transatlantic slave trade was abolished in 1850.[7]

Cubans responded to the economic and political changes shaping Atlantic slavery beyond their control by turning to indentured and contract laborers. Beginning in the 1840s, Cuban plantation owners participated in the international Chinese coolie labor market that brought indentured laborers to the United States, Mexico, South America, and other destinations. From 1847 to 1874, Cuban planters imported roughly 125,000 Chinese contract laborers as they strategized how to survive in a world where slavery's demise seemed all the more probable with the Civil War raging in the United States. Chinese indentured servants primarily worked cutting cane alongside enslaved Africans on some of the largest sugar plantations in Cuba. In additional to agricultural tasks, many also found employment in domestic service and the artisanal trades in urban areas. Desperately seeking out other sources of bond labor, some plantation owners even went to the extreme of importing indigenous laborers from the Yucatan during its 1848 Caste War. The trade never flourished on a level similar to the importation of Chinese indentures. Mexican president of Indian ancestry Benito Juárez indignantly outlawed the inhumane practice in 1861 when the Civil War began. Exact figures for the Yucatan Indian trade remain elusive, but the most scholarly study estimates Cuba imported roughly 2,000 indigenous laborers during the 1850s. Experimenting with these different labor strategies taught Cuban masters they could extend slavery by finding a supplemental labor force while the supply of enslaved Africans diminished in the 1860s, but they could not find a permanent substitute for enslaved Africans.[8]

Changes in international and imperial politics in the 1860s resulted in unleashing the forces that would bring about the abolition of Cuban transatlantic slave trade. The U.S. Civil War dealt a devastating blow to Cuban slaveholders who depended on the slave trade to field laborers to work their plantations. Despite the abolition of the slave trade to the United States in 1808, many Americans continued to participate in the practice by serving as the major transporters of Africans to Cuba. In the period from 1808 to 1860 nearly one-third of all vessels that transported Africans across the Atlantic were either ships owned by U.S. merchants or ships built and serviced in U.S. ports. American citizens may have transported twice as many Africans to other countries such as Cuba and Brazil as they did to their own ports. Although the American government had declared the slave trade a crime of piracy as early as 1820, the United States Federal Navy did not routinely police the waters of the Caribbean and simply did not prosecute Americans who profited from the trade. The British protested the involvement of U.S. citizens in the slave trade to Cuba but did not patrol waters off the coast of Cuba in search of Americans involved in the trade. The British government reasoned that the risk of naval battles was too great to jeopardize relations between the two countries. Consequently, U.S. ships participating in the trade often unloaded their cargo in Havana or on hidden cays in the Bahamas for later transport to the island. In addition, the knowledge of the reluctance of the British Navy to pursue American ships resulted in many slavers flying an American flag as cover to avoid stop and seizure.[9]

The outbreak of the U.S. Civil War provided the opportunity for Lincoln to demonstrate to Great Britain its anti-slave trade policy that had important repercussions for Cuba. If Lincoln turned a blind eye to the slave trade, as previous American presidents had done before him, he might appear as encouraging the practice and therefore alienate the abolitionists in the British parliament and foreign office. Moreover, with the inability of the Federal Navy to police waters in search of the illegal slave traders as they were preoccupied with the naval blockade of the South, the North needed the aid of Britain to make sure a clandestine trade would not flourish under the direction, protection, and benefit of the Confederate states. As part of a strategy to win over Britain to the North's cause, the federal government began to prosecute Americans for participating in the slave trade for the first time in forty years. In 1862, as a sign of the seriousness of the Lincoln administration's effort to end U.S. citizens participating in the slave trade, Nathaniel Gordon became the first and only American to suffer capital punishment for participating in the slave trade. As somebody who had shipped slaves from West Africa to Cuba, his prosecution and execution sent a deadly warning to slave traders that American participation in the Cuban trade would no longer be tolerated.[10]

Following the execution of Gordon and the increased attention to suppressing the slave trade, a cooperative approach emerged between the United States and Britain in ending American participation in the slave trade to Cuba. American Secretary of State Seward and Lord Lyons, the British Ambassador in Washington, DC, quickly negotiated the Lyons-Seward Treaty of 1862 as discussed by Richard Huzzey in his chapter. The treaty allowed for a mutual right of search and the establishment of courts to try cases arising from captures. Not only had Lincoln acted against slave traders by prosecuting and punishing them, but he also authorized the British government to now pursue and stamp out the Atlantic slave trade even if that included American-owned and operated vessels. The impact on the Cuban trade was significant according to the Anglo-American mixed commission that operated in New York after the treaty had been signed. The commissioners believed that as many as 170 slaving voyages had been organized in New York prior to 1862, but by 1863 the city had virtually ceased operating as a center for organizing slaving voyages to Cuba after the Lyons-Seward treaty went into effect.[11]

Following the 1862 treaty and in the remaining years of the Civil War, Britain pursued a far more aggressive policy of patrolling slave trading ships in the Caribbean. Slave traders could no longer simply hoist an American flag to avoid arrest and prosecution by the British Antislavery squadron. Throughout the nineteenth century Cuba had long employed and depended on foreign participation in the transatlantic slave trade to the island to ensure a constant and ready supply of labor. While Spaniards and Cubans had participated in the slave trade, their efforts alone were not enough to meet demands on the island. As has been well remarked by contemporary observers such as Alexander Humboldt to historians, Cuba's slave population did not grow by natural increase because of unequal sex ratios between males and females; frequent outbreaks of diseases such as cholera, malaria, and yellow fever; overwork in the fields; and the high profitability of the sugar industry that often made it cheaper to buy imported laborers than grow a slave population by natural increase. Consequently, Cuba's slave population was sustained through imports, many of those carried by American slave trading merchants.[12] For example, recent evidence unearthed in Havana has shown the wide-scale participation of American slave traders in the Cuban trade. Even the enslaved Africans who would famously rise up and seize the *Amistad* ship are now believed to have been transported across the Atlantic to Cuba by an American merchant.[13] As a result of the American Civil War, American slave traders who had long served as one of the key suppliers for enslaved Africans to Cuba had been removed from Caribbean waters. For example, in the year before the Lyons-Seward Treaty went into effect, Cuba imported 23,964 slaves; in the year after the treaty Cuba only imported 7,507. Abolition in Cuba appeared all the more likely in the near future.[14]

Equally significant during the 1860s was the formation of the Spanish Abolitionist Society that included Spaniards, Cubans, and Puerto Ricans. Christopher Schmidt-Nowara's pioneering study, *Empire and Antislavery* (1999) and his chapter in this volume remain the most authoritative and insightful accounts on the emergence and actions of Spanish Abolitionist Society. Following a course of action similar to British abolitionists earlier in the century, the Spanish Abolitionist Society began by focusing on abolishing the transatlantic slave trade and then turning to the institution of slavery itself. Reform politics in Spain during the 1860s further contributed to an atmosphere of abolition. In 1865 Spain formed the *Junta de Información*, a council composed of Cuban, Puerto Rican, and Spanish representatives to discuss and formulate economic and social policies for the Caribbean colonies. Many abolitionists won seats on the *Junta*, including long-time Cuban opponent of the slave trade José Antonio Saco. According to Schmidt-Nowara, the new interest in abolition and the activities of the Spanish Abolitionist Society emerged out of the "United States' Civil War and renewed British and North American pressure on the slave trade to Cuba, [which] led the Spanish and Antillean slave owners to seek political and economic reforms in the colonies, abolition of the slave trade, and some form of gradual emancipation controlled by slave owners."[15]

The Spanish Abolitionist Society that emerged in Madrid in 1865 counted Spanish, Cuban, and Puerto Rican members. The society flourished as Madrid's public sphere became a place where Spaniards and Creoles representing both imperial and colonial interests could debate and attack slavery through the press. Creole critics of the colonial order forged alliances in Madrid with Spanish reformers and politicians to begin the process of dismantling Caribbean slavery. The politics of abolition ended up dividing Cubans and Puerto Ricans over what measures to take and how fast abolition would happen. Cuba had a population of 370,000 slaves in 1862 whereas Puerto Rico only had 40,000.[16] Cuban slave owners battled against the threat of immediate abolition proposed by some members of the Spanish Abolitionist Society. Speaking on behalf of Cuban slave owners Carlos Drake Nuñez del Castillo, the count of Vega-Mar conceded that abolition was inevitable, but he hoped to pursue a policy of indemnification and a long apprenticeship system. As the talk of ending slavery intensified, Cuban slave owners hoped to pacify abolitionists while buying time to reform slavery and foster the growth of an enslaved population on the island by natural increase. In 1867 Cuban slaveholders finally agreed to abolish the transatlantic slave trade.[17]

The reform politics that emerged in Spain in the 1860s did not end with the abolition of the Cuban slave trade in 1867. The inability for the *Junta de Información* to resolve colonial issues was indicative of larger political problems and divisions on the Iberian Peninsula. In September of 1868 naval officers revolted in Cádiz, and shortly thereafter revolutionaries took Madrid, proclaiming a liberal republic. Actions and reactions in Spain helped to catalyze political movements in the colonies. The unwillingness for the new liberal republican government to extend reforms enacted on the Iberian Peninsula to its Caribbean colonies resulted in many Cubans rallying around Creole planter Carlos Manuel de Céspedes from Bayamo and his call for independence, known to history as the *Grito de Yara*—named after the location where he issued his pronouncement. Capitalizing on the opportunity created by political divisions in Spain between monarchists and republicans, the movement for Cuban independence quickly gained momentum in the eastern portion of the island and was part of a larger drama of Spain's Caribbean possessions fighting for independence in the 1860s.[18]

Cuba was not alone in pursuing paths of open rebellion and reformist politics in the Spanish Empire. On the nearby island of Puerto Rico, a separatist insurrection broke out in October 1868 known to history as the Grito de Lares. The revolt called to arms slaves, laborers, and landowners who rebelled against the colonial state, slavery, and the economic power of Spanish merchants. The uprising only lasted three days and was easily suppressed. However, the movement gave impetus to colonial reforms and pushed Puerto Rico to end slavery, with final abolition coming five years later in 1873. As covered in the chapter by Anne Eller, Spanish imperial politics of the 1860s resulted in reconquering Santo Domingo and occupying the Dominican Republic from 1861 to 1865. As various chapters in this volume explore, the U.S. Civil War put the Monroe Doctrine temporarily on hold and provided new opportunities for Spain to reconceptualize its empire and extend dominion into the Caribbean. These hopes of returning to former imperial glory while the United States was on the sidelines were quickly crushed by a locally based insurgency that defeated the Spanish forces and had them withdraw from Santo Domingo in 1865.

The Cuban insurrection for independence would last longer than movements in Puerto Rico and the Dominican Republic and produce a far more contradictory record on slavery, abolition, and independence. In launching the Cuban rebellion on October 10, 1868, Carlos Manuel Céspedes began the movement symbolically and strategically by gathering slaves on his sugar mill, La Demajagua, and granting them their freedom. Addressing them as "citizens," he told them they were now "free" to join the fight to "conquer liberty and independence" for Cuba. Céspedes action ushered in Cuba's first war for independence, known to history as the Ten Years' War (1868–78), but he was insistent that the goal of the movement was ending colonial rule, not abolishing slavery. This wartime measure for military purposes favored male slaves who could earn their freedom on the battlefield. Some Cuban masters shared Céspedes' ideological convictions and individually emancipated their slaves in public ceremonies when they joined the cause. The early leaders of the independence movement, including Céspedes, came from regions in the East where in some districts the slave population numbered less than 10 percent of the total population, and thus, their own decision to individually free their slaves did not appear that radical or financially costly to them or to local society. In the western portion of island, however, where slave populations remained heavily concentrated, such actions would indeed threaten the planter class. Consequently, as a strategy to win over recruits to support Cuban independence from the powerful planter class in the west to their cause and not alienate the economic elite, Céspedes and others adopted a policy of gradual abolition after independence with indemnification for masters.[19]

The politics on the ground, however, confounded such attempts to neatly draw distinctions between a war to abolish colonialism and a war to postpone abolition of slavery. First, the independence army needed soldiers. As cane fields turned into battlefields, slaves did not hesitate to join the rebel cause, regardless of their master's position on slavery. The fielding and deploying into battle of slaves turned soldiers served to make abolition a priority of these political and military conflicts, even if leaders were reluctant to publicly endorse such motivations. Cuban slaves may have understood these dynamics far earlier and with greater prescience than Lincoln did for the U.S. Civil War. Even before Lincoln issued the Emancipation Proclamation and black regiments such as the First South Carolina Volunteers and the Fifty-Fourth Massachusetts were formed, slaves working in Cuban cane fields were heard singing: "Advance, Lincoln, advance / You are our deliverance."[20]

The enslaved and freed population of African descent in Cuba eagerly joined the independence movement if it meant both personal and political freedom. Detailed statistics on the Cuban rebel army remain elusive, but the actions required in addressing the number of slaves and freed people who joined the cause, and the people of African descent that climbed up leadership ranks during the course of the war, illustrate that the rebel army was far from simply a white-led and white-directed movement. Yet, despite the constituency of the rebel army, the leadership constantly stated that the war was not about abolition, and the discussion of slavery would have to wait until independence had been achieved. These assertions, however simply fell on deaf ears. Those who wanted to discredit the movement by portraying it as a race war to destroy slavery, attack the white population, and overturn existing social and political relations emphasized slave participation. Moreover, slaves themselves insisted that freedom was precisely what the war meant to them as they fled the plantations and flocked to the army encampments.

In attempting to clear up the confusion, Céspedes outlined how slaves could be emancipated and freed in an official decree issued on December 27, 1868. First, all slaves belonging to pro-Spanish enemies of the independent cause would be considered free and their owners would not receive compensation, echoing provisions stated in Lincoln's Emancipation Proclamation. Second, slaves could join the rebel cause with the consent of their pro-independence masters, and their owners would be compensated for their financial loss. Third, masters could "lend" their slaves to the rebel cause and then would have them returned after fighting had ended. In addition, individual runaway slaves who fled pro-independence Cuban masters and sought security in the rebel army would be returned to their owners. In contrast to returning runaways, firmly established maroon communities that recognized rebel leadership and assisted the war effort would be considered free. Ironically for slaves, the best opportunity to control their own destiny and join the rebel cause out of their own volition was to have a pro-Spanish master. And conversely, the least possibility for slaves being empowered to decide their own freedom during the Ten Years' War was if their master happened to be proslavery, and pro-independent Cuba. Céspedes' attempt to clarify the issue through an official proclamation only revealed how clearly the Cuban rebels could not decide what to do about slavery. The rebel army offered several other decrees during the course of the war that granted freedom on a conditional basis but did not question the institution of slavery as a system.[21]

By 1870 regional differences in Cuba paralyzed the war to spread out of the east, which resulted in a standstill that would last until 1878. In the east central town of Puerto Príncipe, desertions and surrenders occurred between 1870 and 1872, most prominently among white members and leaders of the rebel army. This resulted in shifting the perceived racial identity of the movement from one that was multiracial to one that was black. By 1873, surrenders and desertions had become so numerous that Spain had firmly regained control of the area. In other areas, however, an opposite scenario played itself out. In Santiago and Guantanamo where the white population made up only 25 percent of the total population, opportunities abounded for slaves and free people of color to join the movement. The highest-ranking officers of color came from these regions, most notably the mulatto Antonio Maceo, who proved to be the decisive military leader in engineering the campaigns that won the rebel army a stronghold in the region. In response to Maceo's achievements, however, rumors spread that he conspired to take over the movement and turn Cuba into another Haiti. Whether as a result of white desertion and surrender, or the inability to acknowledge the achievements of people of color on the battlefield, the rebel army remained divided by race and slavery.

Finally recognizing the military and political stalemate that had befallen the independence movement, in February of 1878 the rebel leadership and Spain worked out a peace agreement known as the Pact of Zanjón. The peace treaty provided a political pardon for insurgents and recognized the legal freedom for slaves in the insurrection. Over 16,000 slaves received their freedom by the treaty, which presented a glaring contradiction for Cuban slavery. Slaves engaged in rebellious acts attempting to overthrow Spanish colonialism received their freedom while those who demonstrated loyalty by not joining the insurgency remained enslaved. Antonio Maceo and others did not recognize the treaty and famously issued his "Protest of Baragua," vowing to continue the fight for independence and abolition, the initial goals of the Grito de Yara as expressed by Céspedes when the movement began. After several months, however, Maceo and others were forced into exile. The inability to adopt a clear and unified position on abolition, and more broadly, race relations, proved the ultimate downfall of the Ten Years' War.[22]

Cuban slavery survived the Ten Years' War, but it most certainly would never be the same. Demographics alone reveal a dramatic decline in the slave population. At the closing of the slave trade and the onset of the independence war the enslaved population numbered 363,288. Ten years later the slave population enumerated in the 1877 census listed 199,094. When the 16,000 slaves emancipated by the terms of the Pact of Zanjón were subtracted from the 1877 census totals, roughly 184,000 slaves labored on the island at the end of the war. The decade that spanned the Ten Years' War fundamentally restructured the slave population in Cuba.[23]

Few historians have studied the transition from slave labor to free labor with the care of historian Rebecca Scott. In accounting for this gradual transition she has singled out several economic, political, and social factors produced in the context of the Ten Years' War and its aftermath that played a decisive role in ending slavery. In 1870 Spanish delegate to the Cortes and abolitionist Segismundo Moret introduce a bill into parliament for the "gradual abolition of slavery." The law most certainly was a response to counter the moral high ground the rebel army had claimed in recruiting slaves to their cause. The Moret Law—as the bill became known—freed all children born to slave mothers since September 1868 when the liberal republic began and all slaves upon reaching the age of sixty. The abolition of the transatlantic slave trade in 1867 had deprived Cubans of a slave labor force through imports, and now the passage of the Moret Law in 1870 shut down any possibility for the slave population to grow and reproduce itself by natural increase as occurred in the United States. Cuban slavery would slowly become extinct when the currently enslaved population reached its death.

Although the Moret Law did not directly impact the vast majority of enslaved laborers already working on the island, and children born to slave mothers would still be the legal charges of masters until they reached majority age, it did usher in important changes. The actions of slaves reveal they understood that the legal foundations for slavery as a system were crumbling. Scott has shown that in the wake of the Moret Law, slaves called upon the state more frequently to exercise certain rights that they had been granted since the early colonial period. For example, Cuban authorities recorded an increase in complaints against abusive masters, an increase in *coartacíon* agreements whereby slaves could purchase their own freedom by paying their assessed value to their masters in installments over time, and day-to-day acts of resistance increased as well. If Cuban masters attempted to minimize the impact of the Moret Law through subterfuge such as changing the birth dates and ages of their labor force, slaves fought valiantly for its implementation.[24]

The second legal change in slavery that made gradual abolition possible was the passage of the *Patronato* Law in 1880. The law left in place the fundamental labor relations between masters and slaves but changed them legally to something akin to an apprenticeship system that had marked the final years of slavery in the British Caribbean. The law redefined master-slave relationships and renamed owners *patronos* and slaves *patrocinados*. Its most important provision was that one-quarter of the slaves held by each master in 1884 were to be freed at the end of the year. This emancipation of one-fourth would then be followed over the next three years so that by 1888 all slaves on the island would be emancipated and slavery abolished. The passage of the law also empowered a series of local and regional boards to oversee the process, referred to as *juntas*. These local committees had powers to oversee and regulate self-purchase, and if slaves could document abuse they could be given their freedom under Article 4 of the *Patronato* Law. The intent of the *Patronato* Law was to guide Cuba peacefully from slave labor to free labor without disrupting the plantation system and while maintaining a disciplined and subordinated labor force.

The *Patronato* Law specified slavery's expiration date, but many slaves did not wait around for eight years for it to go into effect. Similar to Brazil in its last years of slavery, the enslaved fled from the plantations. With only limited years of labor before final abolition, many masters simply calculated it was not worth it to hunt their slaves down and have them returned. *Coartación* agreements became easier to achieve with the local *juntas* now charged to oversee the process. Masters had no choice but to work out relationships for post-emancipation labor while they still had some coercive sway over their laborers. Many relinquished their legal control over laborers in exchange for a commitment to continue working for them once emancipated. Scott found that emancipation by "mutual accord" between masters and slaves outnumbered all other avenues for freedom under the *Patronato* Law. As with the Moret Law, now that there was an intervening legal force between masters and slaves, slave complaints for abusive masters increased dramatically, especially since documented abuse could result in freedom according to Article 4 of the *Patronato* Law. Collectively, these changes empowered slaves to simply make the disciplined relations masters held over slaves obsolete and the system unworkable. Two years before the system was scheduled to come to an end, Cuban masters conceded that the *Patronato* Law was impractical and agreed to end slavery by royal decree on October 7, 1886. In effect, slaves' actions most decisively sped up the emancipation process.[25]

CUBA'S LONG ROAD to abolition finally came to an end in 1886, leaving only Brazil as the last slave society in the Americas. But here as well, as Rafael Marquese's chapter shows, abolition was just around the corner in 1888. In explaining the emancipation process in Cuba, the catalyst and part of the cause can be attributed to the U.S. Civil War broadly, and more specifically three events in the 1860s that emerged during and after the bloody conflict between the North and the South. With the Lyons-Seward treaty of 1862, British and U.S. forces could join to put an end to American participation in the slave trade to Cuba. The abolitionist impulse extended to Spain in 1865 with the formation of the Spanish Abolitionist Society that worked to abolish the transatlantic slave trade in 1867. The following year in 1868, the Ten Years' War erupted, resulting in thousands of slaves entering the military conflict and emancipating themselves on the battlefield. Cuban slavery would survive the crisis of the 1860s that was initiated in no small part by the U.S. Civil War. When the final abolition of Cuban slavery arrived in 1886, the crisis of the 1860s born out of the U.S. Civil War most certainly began the process that resulted in the destruction of Cuban slavery.

Suggested Readings

Barcia, María del Carmen. *Burguesía esclavista y abolición*. Havana: Editorial de Ciencias Sociales, 1987.

Berbel, Marcia, Rafael Marquese, and Tâmis Parron. *Escravidao e politica: Brasil e Cuba, 1790–1850*. São Paulo: Editor Hucitec, 2010.

Bergad, Laird W. *The Comparative Histories of Slavery in Brazil, Cuba, and the United States*. New York: Cambridge University Press, 2007.

Blackburn, Robin. *The American Crucible: Slavery, Emancipation and Human Rights*. London: Verso, 2011.

Ferrer, Ada. *Insurgent Cuba: Race, Nation, and Revolution, 1868–1898*. Chapel Hill: University of North Carolina Press, 1999.

Graden, Dale T. *Disease, Resistance, and Lies: The Demise of the Transatlantic Slave Trade to Brazil and Cuba*. Baton Rouge: Louisiana State University Press, 2014.

Manuel, Moreno Fraginals. *El Ingenio: Complejo económico social Cubano del azúcar*, 3 vols. Havana: Editorial de Ciencias Sociales, 1978.

Murray, David. *Odious Commerce: Britain, Spain and the Abolition of the Cuban Slave Trade*. Cambridge: Cambridge University Press, 1980.

Schmidt-Nowara, Christopher. *Empire and Antislavery: Spain, Cuba, and Puerto Rico, 1833–1874*. Pittsburgh: University of Pittsburgh Press, 1999.

Scott, Rebecca J. *Degrees of Freedom; Louisiana and Cuba after Slavery*. Cambridge, MA: Harvard University Press, 2005.

———. *Slave Emancipation in Cuba: The Transition to Free Labor, 1860–1899*. Princeton, NJ: Princeton University Press, 1985.

Notes

1. For recent interpretations of the process of abolition from hemispheric perspectives, see Laird W. Bergad, *The Comparative Histories of Slavery in Brazil, Cuba, and the United States* (New York: Cambridge University Press, 2007); Christopher Schmidt-

Nowara, *Slavery, Freedom, and Abolition in Latin America and the Atlantic World* (Albuquerque: University of New Mexico Press, 2011); and Robin Blackburn, *The American Crucible: Slavery, Emancipation and Human Rights* (London: Verso, 2011).

2. Blackburn, *American Crucible*, 6; Bergard, *Comparative Histories*, ch. 2; Schmidt-Nowara, *Slavery, Freedom, and Abolition*, 93, 133.

3. Dale Tomich, *Through the Prism of Slavery: Labor, Capital, and World Economy* (Lanham MD: Rowan and Littlefield, 2004); Dale Tomich and Michael Zeuske, "Introduction, The Second Slavery: Mass Slavery, World-Economy, and Comparative Histories," *Review: Fernand Baraudel Center* 31 (2008): 91–100; Kaye, Anthony E., "The Second Slavery: Modernity in the Nineteenth-Century South and the Atlantic World," *Journal of Southern History* 75 (August 2009): 627–50; Christopher Schmidt-Nowara, "Empires against Emancipation: Spain, Brazil, and the Abolition of Slavery," *Review: Fernand Baraudel Center* 31 (2008): 101–20; and Márcia Berbel, Rafel Marquese, and Tâmis Parron, *Escravidao e politica: Brasil e Cuba, 1790–1850* (São Paulo: Editor Hucitec, 2010).

4. *Memorial to the Queen of Spain for the Abolition of Slavery in the Islands of Cuba and Puerto Rico* (New York: Dick and Fitzgerald, 1862).

5. A reliable series of annual import figures remains to be constructed for the Cuban transatlantic slave trade, but estimates of imports for different periods of the nineteenth century can be found in: Gloria García, "Importación de esclavos de ambos sexos por varios puertos de Cuba, 1763–1820," in *Historia de Cuba: La colonia, evolución socioeconómica y formación nacional e los origines hasta 1867*, ed. María del Carmen Barcia, Gloria García and Eduardo Torres-Cuevas (Havana: Editorial Política, 1994), 471–73, table 11; Juan Pérez de la Riva, *El Monto de la Inmigración Forzada en el siglo xix* (Havana: Editorial de Ciencias Sociales, 1979), table 3; David Eltis, *Economic Growth and the Ending of the Transatlantic Slave Trade* (Oxford: Oxford University Press, 1987), 245; Laird W. Bergad, Fe Iglesias García, and María del Carmen Barcia, *The Cuban Slave Market, 1790–1880* (Cambridge: Cambridge University Press, 1995), 27; the extremely valuable transatlantic slave trade database by David Eltis et al. continues to be updated, and with each update Cuban import figures increase. The open-access database is available on the web at http://www.slavevoyages.org/.

6. For the international politics of the Cuban slave trade see David Murray, *Odious Commerce: Britain, Spain and the Abolition of the Cuban Slave Trade* (Cambridge: Cambridge University Press, 1980); Rodolfo Sarracino, *Inglaterra: sus dos caras en la lucha cubana por la abolición* (Havana: Editorial Letras Cubanas, 1989); Christopher Schmidt-Nowara, *Empire and Antislavery: Spain, Cuba, and Puerto Rico, 1833–1874* (Pittsburgh: University of Pittsburgh Press, 1999).

7. Schmidt-Nowara, *Empire and Antislavery*, 25–36.

8. For the use of Chinese laborers see, Kathleen López, *Chinese Cubans: A Transnational History* (Chapel Hill: University of North Carolina Press, 2013); Lisa Yun, *The Coolie Speaks: Chinese Indentured Laborers and African Slaves in Cuba* (Philadelphia: Temple University Press, 2008); Juan Pérez de la Riva, "Demografía de los culíes chinos en Cuba (1853–1874)," in *El barracón y otros ensayos* (Havana: Editorial

de Ciencias Sociales, 1975): 469–507; for the importation of Yucatecan laborers, see Paul Estrade, "Los colonos yucatecos como sustitutos de los esclavos negros," in *Cuba la perla de las Antillas: Actas de las I Jornadas sobre "Cuba y su historia,"* ed. Consuelo Naranjo Orovio and Tomás Mallo Gutiérrez (Madrid: Ediciones Doce Calles, 1994), 93–107.

9. Dale T. Graden, *Disease, Resistance, and Lies: The Demise of the Transatlantic Slave Trade to Brazil and Cuba* (Baton Rouge: Louisiana State University Press, 2014), 12–26; Arthur F. Corwin, *Spain and the Abolition of Slavery in Cuba, 1817–1886* (Austin: University of Texas Press, 1967), 142–45; and David R. Murray, *Odious Commerce: Britain, Spain, and the Abolition of the Cuban Slave Trade* (Cambridge: Cambridge University Press, 1980), 304.

10. Amanda Foreman, *A World on Fire: Great Britain's Crucial Role in the American Civil War* (New York: Radom House, 2011), 237; Murray, *Odious Commerce*, 305.

11. Murray, *Odious Commerce*, 306.

12. For Humboldt's classic comments on the slave population see, Alexander Humboldt, *Ensayo político sobre la isla de Cuba* (1826; reprint, with an introduction by Fernando Ortiz, Habana: Fundación Fernando Ortiz, 1998), ch. 3, 109–10 in particular. For historians' discussion of the demographics of Cuban slavery, see Laird W. Bergad, Fe Iglesias García, and María del Carmen Barcia, *The Cuban Slave Market, 1790–1880* (Cambridge: Cambridge University Press, 1995), 35–36; and Graden, *Disease, Resistance, and Lies*, 51–58.

13. Michael Zeuske, "Rethinking the Case of the Schooner Amistad: Contraband and Complicity after 1808/1820," *Slavery & Abolition* 35 (2014): 155–64.

14. Peres de la Riva, *El monto*, 43–44; Murray, *Odious Commerce*, 308; Corwin, *Spain and the Abolition of Slavery in Cuba*, 147.

15. Christopher Schmidt-Nowara, *Empire and Antislavery: Spain, Cuba, and Puerto Rico, 1833–1874* (Pittsburgh: University of Pittsburgh Press, 1999), 100–101.

16. Bergad, *Comparative Histories*,128–29; Luis A. Figueroa, *Sugar, Slavery, and Freedom in Ninetenth-Century Puerto Rico* (Chapel Hill: University of North Carolina Press, 2005), 48.

17. Schmidt-Nowara, *Empire and Antislavery*, 102–3.

18. For a succinct treatment on the politics in Spain in the 1860s and its repercussion for Cuban slavery see, Schmidt-Nowara, *Empire and Antislavery*, 126–35.

19. For an excellent and concise overview of slavery during the Ten Years' War, see Ada Ferrer, "Armed Slaves and Anticolonial Insurgency in Late Nineteenth-Century Cuba," in *Arming Slaves: From Classical Times to the Modern Age*, ed. Christopher Leslie Brown and Philip P. Morgan (New Haven, CT: Yale University Press, 2006), 304–29. More extensive and in-depth treatments can be found in Ada Ferrer, *Insurgent Cuba: Race, Nation, and Revolution, 1868–1898.* (Chapel Hill: University of North Carolina Press, 1999), esp. chapters 1–2; Rebecca J. Scott, *Slave Emancipation in Cuba: The Transition to Free Labor, 1860–1899* (Princeton, NJ: Princeton University Press, 1985), 45–62; and María del Carmen Barcia, *Burguesía esclavista y abolición* (Havana: Editorial de Ciencias Sociales, 1987), 138–48.

20. Nicola Miller, "'The Great and Gentle Soul': Images of Lincoln in Latin America," in *The Global Lincoln*, ed. Richard Carwardine and Jay Sexton (Oxford: Oxford University Press, 2011), 212.

21. Carlos Manuel de Céspedes, "Decreto de 27 de Diciembre de 1868 sobre la esclavitud," in *Documentos para la historia de Cuba*, ed. Hortensia Pichardo (Havana: Editorial de Ciencias Sociales, 1971), 1:370–73. For an English translation of the decree, see Carlos Manuel de Céspedes, "Freedom and Slavery," in *The Cuba Reader: History, Culture, and Politics*, ed. Aviva Chmosky, Barry Carr, and Pamela Maria Smorkaloff (Durham, NC: Duke University Press, 2003), 115–17.

22. Ferrer, *Insurgent Cuba*, 40–69.

23. For the Ten Years War impact on slave population figures, see Kiple, *Blacks in Colonial Cuba*, 7–8, 65–71; Fe Iglesias García, "El censo cubano de 1877 y sus diferentes versiones," *Santiago* 34 (June 1979): 167–214; Ferrer, *Insurgent Cuba*, 29–36; and in particular the careful interpretation of these figures in Scott, *Slave Emancipation*, 72–87.

24. Scott, *Slave Emancipation*, 63–83.

25. Ibid.

CHAPTER ELEVEN

The Civil War in the United States and the Crisis of Slavery in Brazil

Rafael Marquese

Despite all their economic, social, political, and cultural differences, the U.S. republic and the Brazilian Empire shared a few characteristics. Both emerged from the crisis of European colonialism and, consequently, represented the rise of new independent political units in the global arena. The two countries also had continental dimensions, resisting indigenous populations, and agricultural economies based on slave labor. Moreover, there was an increasing political and economic convergence between their slave systems starting in the 1830s. On the one hand, the dramatic growth of coffee production in Brazil was accompanied by the emergence of the United States as the main importer of the Brazilian product. On the other hand, in the context of growing tensions between Brazil and Britain over slavery, the North American republic played a fundamental role for the South American empire. By providing boats, capitals, and its flag for illegal transatlantic slave trading operations, and adopting external policies that openly supported slavery, the United States became a sort of protective wall for the defense of Brazilian slavery in the world-system until the early 1850s.[1]

The destinies of slavery in the two countries diverged only in the second half of the nineteenth century. The United States abolished the institution in the early 1860s with an extremely violent civil war that emancipated more than four million slaves without compensation for slaveholders. Brazil continued to depend on slave labor until the late 1880s, but after the passing of a free-womb law on September 28, 1871, it was clear that the system—which had around one and a half million captives when the law was passed (almost 16 percent of the Brazilian population)—was coming to an end. After the closing of the transatlantic slave trade in 1850, in a society lacking positive rates of slave reproduction, the prospects of slavery's expansion in Brazil vanished. Abolition in 1888 also came without compensation to former slaveholders, but the process was not marked by the large-scale bloodshed that characterized emancipation in the United States.

Thus we are dealing with two distinct solutions to the problem of slavery. The key question is whether these processes were interconnected, considering the links the two slave systems had in the antebellum period. This chapter will explore this issue by identifying and analyzing the straight connection between the abolition of slavery in the United States and its subsequent counterpart in Brazil. This approach is not new, since some historians have explored the impact of the U.S. Civil War on the Brazilian Empire. On the specific issue of slavery, scholars have suggested how the origins of the free-womb law can be traced back to the widespread perception among imperial political agents that Brazil had become internationally isolated after the defeat of the Confederate States of America (CSA).[2] None of these studies, however, have systematically explored the many relations between, on the one hand, the U.S. Civil War, the abolition of slavery in 1865, Reconstruction, and the U.S. economy after the war, and, on the other, the destinies of Brazilian slavery between 1861 and 1889.

Such a task cannot be fully explored here. The aim of this essay is to provide a broader framework to understand how the U.S. Civil War triggered the crisis of slavery in Brazil. There were two aspects of this process: first, the political impact of the Civil War, abolition in 1865, and Reconstruction on the political debates and parliamentary decisions regarding slavery in Brazil, especially in the period between 1861 and 1871; second, the impact of U.S. economic growth in the postbellum era on the social relations of slavery in the Brazilian empire after the passing of the free-womb law. This will allow us to track the broader global impact that the U.S. Civil War had on the crisis of Brazilian slavery.

AFTER A FOUR-MONTH deliberation in the Chamber of Deputies, the bill freeing the children of slave mothers born after 1871—offered by the Visconde do Rio Branco (José Maria da Silva Paranhos)—reached the Senate on September 4, 1871. Senator Zacarias de Góis e Vasconcelos, a powerful and highly esteemed politician from Bahia, presented an interpretation about the origins of the proposal at the beginning of the debates. After Emperor D. Pedro II mentioned in his *Fala do Trono* of 1867 (which opened the parliamentary debates) that the empire could not postpone a solution to the problem of slavery anymore, Senator Zacarias said:

> The government, gentlemen, should not remain silent on the issue for a powerful reason, . . . and that is the fact that slavery had not only come to an end in the United States, but that the Spanish government is also

ready to end it in Cuba. While the great American Republic had slaves, Mr. President, the issue could be ignored. . . .

Mr. [Francisco do Rego] Barros Barreto [PE]:—We were shielded.

Mr. Zacarias: For the monarchy, alone in America, to maintain this institution; but as soon as the events that, as we all heard, led the North to fight a war against the South and beat it until slavery was extinguished, passing an amendment on December 18, 1865 to the article of the Constitution that legitimized the institution, after that day we had no more excuses. Thus, gentlemen, with Brazil alone as the only slave country in America, it was impossible to keep such an institution alive among us (Supported). There was no need for a war against us to push us toward emancipation; the world laughing at us was enough; becoming the scorn of all nations, which described Brazil as a friend of slavery willing to maintain the institution for an indefinite period of time, was enough. The government that decided to ignore the general will and resist the pressure could not make it because the individual initiative of senators and deputies, who somehow had remained silent while believing that the government was studying the question, would bring insurmountable obstacles for the government.[3]

Spoken in the first session of the Senate debates on the issue, after bitter arguments in the Chamber of Deputies and in newspapers between May and August of 1871, these words revealed the existence of a consensus among the political agents of the empire about the origins of this discussion. Both for defenders and opponents of the project proposed by the Rio Branco cabinet, the defeat of the CSA in the U.S. Civil War and the abolition of slavery after the passing of the thirteenth amendment to the Constitution isolated Brazil from the concert of civilized nations, especially after the Spanish Empire (also influenced by the results of the U.S. Civil War) took the first step to abolish slavery in its Caribbean possessions with the passing of a free-womb law in 1870.[4]

Perhaps the most significant moment of the quoted passage, however, was the brief comment of Francisco do Rego Barros Barreto: "We were shielded." The great historical shift experienced by Brazil in the 1860s clearly appeared in the words of the senator of Pernambuco. Indeed, before 1861, the slave power in the U.S. republic provided one of the most powerful pro-slavery arguments to Brazilian intellectuals and politicians. Between the proclamation of Brazilian independence in 1822 and the attack to Fort Sumter, Brazilian slavery was criticized both internally and externally. Besides the threat to national sovereignty presented by the British pressure against the transatlantic slave trade, there was within Brazil a continuous opposition to slavery that appeared in newspapers, in the Parliament, and in the actions of slaves themselves. This opposition, however, was defeated by the proslavery forces that ruled the country after 1837. In the first two decades of D. Pedro II's reign (1841–89), the *saquaremas* (the powerful Conservative group that was connected to coffee production in the Paraíba do Sul River basin, which included parts of the provinces of Rio de Janeiro, São Paulo, and Minas Gerais) managed to impose their proslavery platform on the national political agenda. If, on the one hand, Great Britain pushed Brazil to abolish the transatlantic slave trade in 1850, on the other, the *saquaremas* in the following years saw the U.S. South as the most perfect example of a successful slave society in the modern world, considering it the bulwark of slavery in the West. Brazil was protected by the strength of Southern slavery in the world arena.[5]

This interpretation influenced the initial reactions to the Civil War, which was immediately described in the Brazilian press as a conflict over slavery. Along with Britain and France, the Brazilian Empire recognized the state of belligerence of the CSA already in 1861, or, in other words, acknowledged their right to eventually become independent. Despite the official position of neutrality, the Brazilian government could not hide its sympathies for the South.[6]

Until late 1862 Brazil expected—as did the rest of Europe—that sooner or later the Union would be confronted with intervention by European Great Powers and forced to accept CSA independence. The battle of Antietam; the preliminary Emancipation Proclamation on September 22, 1862, confirmed on January 1, 1863; and the Union victories in the Mississippi Valley and in Gettysburg in July 1863 completely changed those predictions.[7] Brazil became aware of a possible Southern defeat and of the consequences of emancipation in 1863. One of the first signs of the shifting conditions of Brazilian slavery came from D. Pedro II himself, who had been well informed of the Civil War events because of the diplomatic correspondence coming from the United States. In his recommendations of January 14, 1864 to Zacarias de Góis e Vasconcelos (who had just been nominated chief of the new ministerial cabinet), the emperor wrote:

> The successes of the American Union force us to think about the future of slavery in Brazil so that we can avoid a repetition of what happened with the trade in Africans. The most useful measure, it seems to me, is granting freedom to the children of slaves who are born in a certain

number of years from now. I have been thinking about how to enact the measure; this is one of those that need strength to remedy the evils that it will necessarily generate, as far as circumstances permit. I recommend the reading of the dispatches of our minister in Washington, which contain many considerations about this subject.[8]

The shield seemed to be breaking apart. After the serious diplomatic crisis that marked the end of the transatlantic slave trade and almost led to a war against Great Britain, Brazil lived a relatively calm period regarding slavery. But the development of the North American conflict risked isolating the country once again, leading the Brazilian government to consider alternative solutions to the problem of slavery. Inspired by experiences in the northern United States and in many Spanish-American Republics, proposals for a free-womb law had already circulated in Brazil during the crisis with Great Britain.[9] Now, in 1863, the law seemed to be the only alternative to the radicalization of tensions and an eventual civil war, as had been the case in the United States.

The chronological coincidence between the end of the U.S. Civil War and the Paraguayan War, however, postponed antislavery politics at the center of imperial power. The immediate cause of this huge conflict—the most serious one in South America during the nineteenth century—was the dispute between the Empire of Brazil and the Republics of Argentina, Uruguay and Paraguay over the hegemony at the River Plate zone.[10] After 1865 the Brazilian priority was the quick ending of the Platine conflict, which contrary to all expectations lasted for five long years (1865–70). But the Paraguayan War did not stop studies and debates about the problem of slavery. At the request of D. Pedro II, José Antonio Pimenta Bueno, the Marquis of São Vicente, senator and member of the Council of State (Conselho de Estado), prepared between late 1865 and early 1866—concluding it on January 23—a number of projects for the emancipation of the children of slave mothers born after the passing of the law and ultimately the emancipation of all other slaves, with compensation to their former owners, on December 31, 1899. The attempt to submit the proposal to the Council of State in early 1866 failed because of the opposition of the cabinet chief at the time, Pedro de Araújo Lima, the Marquis of Olinda, to any measure against slavery in the context of the Paraguayan War. Zacarias de Góis, who was more receptive to the idea of emancipation, replaced Olinda on August 3.[11]

Already in its first month (on August 22) the new cabinet replied to a letter from the *Comité Français d'Émancipation* to D. Pedro II in which the signers (key figures of internationalist abolitionism such as Agustin Cochin and Henri Wallon) called for unequivocal actions against Brazilian slavery by the emperor, for the sake of his reputation in Europe.[12] According to the French abolitions, the Civil War had completely changed the prospects of slavery in the Americas, opening the breach that led to its abolition in Cuba and Brazil. Under the imperial constitution of 1824, D. Pedro II could not take control of the legislative process, as the Frenchmen living under the regime of Napoleon III believed. The reply from Minister of Foreign Affairs Martim Francisco Ribeiro de Andrade, however, was attuned to the trans-formations that were taking place in 1865 at the center of imperial power: "The emancipation of slaves, a necessary consequence of the abolition of the traffic," he wrote back, "is nothing but a matter of form and chance."[13]

In 1871 the proslavery opposition considered the reply to the French eman-cipation committee—which reverberated in the Brazilian press—the begin-ning of the parliamentary process leading to the passing of the free-womb law and a clear indication of the so-called "imperialism" of D. Pedro II, i.e., of his active and unconstitutional position in political affairs that, according to them, had no relation to the Moderating Power (Poder Moderador).[14] The efforts of the monarch to convince imperial politicians to debate the womb issue in the Parliament, which increasingly appeared in newspapers, would have to wait for the end of the Paraguayan conflict. In one sphere that was within the power of the emperor, however, the issue was debated earlier. The cabinet of Zacarias de Góis managed to do what the cabinet of Marquis of Olinda could not do: submit the project of Pimenta Bueno to the Coun-cil of State. During the sessions of April 2 and 9, 1867, councillors had long debates about the free-womb project that had been available since January 1866. Since the subject has been well explored by another historian,[15] I will merely outline how the United States appeared in these discussions.

The most important speech about this was by José Maria da Silva Paran-hos, a brilliant Conservative diplomat and statesman without direct con-nections with the world of slave production, who three years later would receive the title of Viscount of Rio Branco. He started by describing the emancipation process in the British and French empires, where slavery—a colonial (rather than national) issue involving significantly smaller slave populations than in Brazil—was the object of long deliberations and where these public debates frequently stimulated slave uprisings. By March 1867 Spain had still not solved the problem of slavery in Cuba and Puerto Rico.[16] While European colonial powers had to deal with great abolitionist pressures from within the metropolis, which ultimately led them to abolish slavery, such a threat did not exist in Brazil. What about the United States, "the only country where the issue was as significant as in Brazil"? It is well known that "rivers of blood and a tremendous civil war with consequences that still cannot be foreseen were necessary there." "The example of the United States," according to Silva Paranhos, should not stimulate Brazil to jump to conclusions about the future of slavery: at that moment (April 1867) it was still "an incomplete event, a solution imposed by one half of the nation against the other, a solution marked by political antagonisms and not the humanitarian question. For now this example seems to be more favorable to the status quo than to the innovation that Brazil wants. There is not a single party among us that completely embraced the abolition of slavery." Moreover, he finished, the experiment in mass emancipation of North American slaves was being observed with certain reservations around the world.[17]

What did Paranhos understand by "an incomplete event"? Despite the ratification of the thirteenth amendment in December 1865, the presidential Reconstruction of Andrew Johnson left the status of freedmen in a state of uncertainty during 1866. The meanings of freedom, the civil statute and the political rights of former slaves, their access to land, the work arrangements, the place of freedmen in the Southern economy and society, and the prospects of the economic recovery of cotton remained open one year after the end of the Civil War. Moreover, there was the possibility that former masters would quickly regain their political power in Southern states as a consequence of the pardons granted to Confederates by Johnson, which threatened to restart military conflicts. Only the beginning of Radical Reconstruction by Congress, the impeachment of Johnson in February 1868, and the election of Ulysses Grant at the end of that year led to more conclusive answers to these questions.[18] Notwithstanding this opposition to the free-womb law idea, the dominant view in the sessions of April 2 and 9, 1867, of the Council of State was that the potential international isolation forced Brazil to seek a solution to the problem of abolition. Thereafter the developments of Reconstruction would be carefully followed in Brazil and eventually politicized by competing parties.

The critical conjuncture of the Paraguayan War in 1868 turned it into a top priority for the emperor. The Zacarias cabinet, whose sympathies for a free-womb law were evident, was replaced in July 1868 by the Conservative Viscount of Itaboraí, a historical proslavery *saquarema* who opposed any measure related to emancipation but was considered more capable of conducting military affairs in the Plata. The weaknesses of the empire during the conflict were a consequence of the difficulties in assembling a national army in a slave society such as Brazil, difficulties that contributed to deepening the crisis of slavery.[19] After defeating the Paraguayan army, however, the Itaboraí cabinet paralyzed all attempts to pass the emancipationist project between 1869 and 1870.

In the context of increasing tensions between the *saquarema* ministry and D. Pedro II, a commission of the Chamber of Deputies started to work on the free-womb project of Pimenta Bueno on May 24, 1870. Despite a large number of obstacles, the commission presented its final report on August 16. According to the three congressmen of the commission who voted in favor of the report (the two votes against it came from congressmen connected to the *saquaremas*), emancipation would be much simpler in Brazil than in the United States because of the absence of sectional divisions over slavery. Brazil had neither abolitionist nor proslavery parties. The congressmen indicated the urgency of the issue given that courts in Spain had recently issued decisions about slavery in Cuba and Puerto Rico. Reform was risky but doing nothing in those circumstances would be riskier, since it would increase the disruptive potential of the global crisis of slavery in Brazil. With a hopeful tone, the signers of the report noted that the trajectory of Radical Reconstruction contradicted the negative predictions that had been predominant in Brazil: "The reports presented by the states of the South of the American Union about the labor of freedmen have exceeded the expectations of even the most optimistic observers. After the violent crisis experienced by those states, and the almost complete interruption of agricultural labor, came the favorable reaction and the freedmen have been working so hard that cotton production is approaching the levels of the years before the War of Secession."[20]

AFTER THAT MOMENT the success of Reconstruction became an important part of the antislavery platform. When taken to vote in the Plenary, however, the report of the commission was defeated by the strong proslavery position of the Itaboraí cabinet. The free-womb law could only be approved by a new cabinet. This was the main reason behind the renouncement of Itaboraí in September 1870 and, after a short period under the command of Pimenta Bueno (who lacked the political skills to gain the support of the Parliament), the ascension in February 1871 of the cabinet of Paranhos, now the Viscount of Rio Branco.[21]

The decision of Paranhos, who in 1867 was against the project of Pimenta Bueno, surprised many of his old fellows in the Conservative Party and became the object of harsh critiques during the emancipation debates of 1871.

The split in the hitherto united Conservative group over the free-womb issue was one of the main signs of the crisis of slavery and, as a matter of fact, of the monarchy itself after the 1860s. D. Pedro II, whose institutional apparatus in the Segundo Reinado had been largely built by proslavery forces, now openly opposed them. Paranhos/Rio Branco was perhaps the perfect embodiment of this rupture. How can we understand it? The direct experience of Paranhos with the impressment and command of former slaves in a multinational military alliance (in which Brazil was the only slave nation, with obvious implications for the affirmation of the empire in the regional concert) during the Paraguayan War, more specifically between the years of 1869 and 1870, certainly contributed to his change of mind. But the global transformations brought by the U.S. Civil War had a more decisive role. One of its consequences was the passing of the Moret Law in Spain on July 4, 1870.[22] The connection between one event and the other, as well as its implications for the Brazilian Empire, were at the center of the opening speech by Rio Branco on July 14, 1871, for the first round of debates on the free-womb law in the Chamber of Deputies:

> The example of an American and democratic people such as the United States was a very strong example on which the routine, the prejudice, and all the concerns of individual interests could rely, as they in fact did. Well, gentlemen, the idea of emancipation persisted and the American Union, the last example, after a civil war that generated rivers of blood, suddenly abolished all its slavery! Spain could not resist that influence, which came from such a close place, and the abolition of the servile condition almost became a universal fact.[23]

The event of a Civil War and the emancipation by force of arms of over 4,000,000 slaves, now turned into citizens, had been completed.

IN OCTOBER 1870 Brazilians got a new source of information. Published in New York, the monthly periodical *O Novo Mundo* aimed at providing to Brazilian readers the latest political, economic, and artistic news of the powerful republic of the United States, which had been experiencing dramatic growth and modernization in the aftermath of its sectional conflict. Its owner, José Carlos Rodrigues, had a long career as journalist and editor. *O Novo Mundo* was published without interruption between 1870 and 1879, a relatively long period under nineteenth-century conditions. After shutting down the journal and leaving the United States, Rodrigues became the main London correspondent of the prestigious *Jornal do Comércio*, which he bought after the proclamation of the republic in 1889.[24]

More important here is the fact that he became the main source of information about Reconstruction in the South for the Brazilian abolitionist movement during the 1870s and 1880s. Already in its first issue *O Novo Mundo* had two interconnected articles that clarified the editorial direction of the journal. The first reported the recovery of cotton production in the United States despite the problems in assembling a labor force composed of freedmen. The positive context was to a large extent a product of the Grant administration that had followed the chaotic period of Andrew Johnson: "In eighteen months the Union has been reorganized: prosperity in the South was stronger than in the period before the War: the negro, despite the antipathy of a large minority, the negro is a citizen in the full sense of the word—the law has been rigorously observed." On the same page an article described how North American and Spanish events made abolition a pressing matter for the Brazilian Empire: "Four years ago, when Mr. D. Pedro II declared that he would take measures to abolish the servile element of the Empire as soon as possible, the international press cheered Brazil for believing that the country had quickly accepted the moral of the war of the United States. 'And Spain,' it was said back then, 'will be the last country with slaves.' Fortunately, Spain has already declared that those born within its dominions are free; but unfortunately Brazil left to Spain the applause for abolishing slavery first." Given the refusal of the ministry to deal with the issue (the journalist referred to the Itaboraí cabinet, taken down one month earlier), the sacrifice would be great, perhaps comparable to what had happened in the United States. The risk, however, was worth it.[25]

At the turn of 1871 José Carlos Rodrigues continued to publish articles with a similar tone. *O Novo Mundo* published critiques of Spanish slave imperialism in South America during the U.S. Civil War, soon destroyed by the victory of the Union; praised the economic, social, and political success of abolition in the United States; and called for measures toward emancipation by the Brazilian Parliament, a process that would demand some patience from planters in the short run but that would later compensate them with the introduction of an order based on free labor.[26] There is a remarkable contrast between, on the one hand, the positive assessment of the reorganization of labor and the reconstitution of Southern cotton exports in these writings and, on the other, the negative perception of emancipation in the British and French Caribbean that had been predominant in Brazil during the 1840s and 1850s. In the earlier period external events were an important part of the defense of national slavery;[27] now, in 1870, the antislavery field was able to stress that emancipation in the largest slaveholding country of the Americas had been an economic success.

This shift in the perceptions of emancipation processes in American societies framed the parliamentary debates of 1871. During the legislative year started in May, the crucial (almost exclusive) theme was deliberating on the free-womb bill. As the most important members of the cabinet, senators Viscount of Rio Branco (minister of finance and president of the Council of Ministers) and Francisco de Paula Negreiros de Saião Lobato (minister of justice) became the greatest defenders of the project in the Chamber and Senate. In an intervention at the Senate on May 22, an argument that was reproduced in the Chamber of Deputies eleven days later, Saião Lobato stated that if slave owners and their parliamentary representatives opposed the free-womb law, abolition could soon come without compensation through revolutionary means. This was precisely the example provided by the United States, where the constant rejection of reformism in the South led to the revolution of 1861–65.[28] Rio Branco in turn stressed once again the international isolation of Brazil—according to him, a perception shared by everybody, including those who opposed the project—as the main reason for a free-womb law: "The war came in the United States and during this colossal fight all thinking men in Brazil asked themselves many times: 'There goes the last example that could provide us moral support in the civilized world against the aversion that slavery generates. After the end of slavery in the United States it is necessary to think that it should not exist in Brazil.' Was not this the general thought?"[29]

The proslavery field acknowledged that, indeed, the North American event had profoundly transformed the political conditions of slavery within the national space. The *saquarema* congressman João de Almeida Pereira Filho made one of the most relevant speeches about this on August 2. "Who would think 10 years ago," he asked, "that we were so close to a social revolution such as the one that will necessarily be brought by the government's project as it is now formulated? I was minister 10 years ago and I confess that I have had never seen the issue be seriously discussed." From a stable situation Brazilian slavery moved into a position of permanent instability after the French emancipation committee sent a letter, inspired by abolition in the United States, to D. Pedro II in July 1866. Even worse was the official answer from the Brazilian government, which set a terrible precedent; after that moment, Brazil became vulnerable to external pressures despite the fact that the idea of emancipation was not widely supported by national public opinion. Slavery was the basis of the material wealth of Brazil and the previous emancipation experiences in the Atlantic world indicated that this would be lost after the passing of the free-womb law. Every slave society in the Americas that was forced to abolish slave labor experienced economic setbacks, including the South: "The same United States that exported approximately five million cotton bales one year before the War, today produces less than three million bales, despite all the attention given to this cultivation, which they consider easy and advantageous, noting that this is now, already many years after the War. . . . If there in the United States, where they have canals, vast railways, a developed navigation system, a manufacturing industry that rivals those of Europe, professional instruction, this happens; what is going to happen to this unfortunate country?"[30]

THE CONGRESSMAN DID NOT provide the source of his numbers of cotton production, and nobody in the Plenary questioned their veracity. His intervention nonetheless suggests that Brazilian slaveholders explored the economic setbacks of the U.S. South as a strategy to curb initiatives against slavery in Brazil. Thus it became important for antislavery activists to demonstrate the success of Reconstruction. Few in the proslavery field, however, accepted the challenge to prove that the North American post-emancipation period had been an economic failure, perhaps because they recognized their own ignorance about the subject.

This became clear in a representation sent by property holders from Vassouras, one of many produced against the free-womb law by slave owners of the Vale do Paraíba. In the 1830s these same planters (or their parents) had petitioned the Brazilian Parliament against the anti-slave trade law of 1831, calling for the reopening of the transatlantic slave trade. In this they were successful because the Brazilian state never questioned the illegal property of the more than 700,000 Africans disembarked in Brazil between 1831 and 1850. In 1871, however, the correlation of forces was distinct: despite the widespread frustration among the great coffee planters of the region (in fact, the largest coffee producers in the world) with the bill, the Rio Branco cabinet took forward the process in Parliament. Thus it is not surprising that a few historians consider the episode of 1871 the beginning of the separation between the Brazilian monarchy and its social bases.[31]

Of the more than two dozen representations taken to the Parliament, fourteen were published on the pages of the *Diário do Rio de Janeiro*, the newspaper that more strongly opposed the free-womb project. Only two of them briefly mentioned the United States. The reference in the petition from Bananal stated that Brazil had no proslavery party as in the North American republic. The one from Vassouras not only reproduced the consensual argument (present in all petitions coming from the Vale do Paraíba) that the project represented an attack on domestic sovereignty and property rights but also criticized the government for not debating the issue with planters. It was necessary to learn about the post-emancipation period in other societies so that Brazilian property owners could know what they were dealing with: "Capable commissions should be established, as in the South of the United States, to study the evils that survived abolition, of how they were planned, to note how much is of interest in this revolution, which has just abolished slavery and suddenly released four million slaves in the middle of an extremely free society."[32]

Despite the request from Vassouras for more precise data on the Reconstruction process, the strategy of proslavery defenders in 1871 was emphasizing the local aspect of the problem in order to shift the terms of the debate imposed by the Rio Branco cabinet, which highlighted the international isolation of Brazil. In this sense, the intervention by Domingos Andrade Figueira is extremely significant because he was perhaps the main representative of the aspirations of the Vale do Paraíba coffee planters in the Chamber of Deputies. Disdaining the idea that Brazil would become isolated in the world as a slave society, Andrade Figureira argued in the session of August 9 that "not only there is no external pressure but this is also impossible to exist. The main nations engaged in this anti-emancipatory crusade in this century are England and the United States, precisely those with whom we maintain vast commercial relations." The English had a large volume of capital invested in Brazil, in the national debt, and in other enterprises (railroads, navigation companies, banks, etc.). "About the United States the Chamber knows that that great Republic, with its prospects of a great future, has currently been reducing, until it is utterly extinguished, the import rights over our production. Well, is this a country that can complain about slavery? Is this a country that can force upon us the abolition of slavery?" Andrade Figueira concluded that "the issue is completely domestic and we should solve it without worrying not only about external governments but also about foreign emancipation societies; we must deal with it exclusively inspired by the great national interests, with prudence, listening to these interests and avoiding shocks and disturbances."[33]

The attempt to "nationalize" the debate and push the cabinet to ignore the question failed: the Rio Branco ministry passed the free-womb bill in both houses and had it sanctioned by the imperial power on September 28, 1871.

ACCUSATIONS THAT THE GOVERNMENT'S victory in 1871 was based on practices of co-optation and patronage were true, but by themselves they do not explain the regional split that allowed the passing of the law. In the Chamber, where the decisive battle took place, most northern representatives (Piauí, Ceará, Rio Grande do Norte, Paraíba, Pernambuco, Alagoas, Sergipe, and Bahia) voted in favor of the law, unlike their southern counterparts (Espírito Santo, Minas Gerais, Rio de Janeiro, and São Paulo), who generally voted against it. Moreover, while northern provinces had a voting ratio of six to one, one in every four representatives from southern provinces voted in favor of the law.[34] In other words, the success of the Rio Branco cabinet depended on the almost unanimous support of the north and a few outliers in the south. It is not an overstatement to say that the macroregion of the Paraíba do Sul River basin stood in opposition to the rest of Brazil.

This political experience clearly embodied the risks of a regional split over Brazilian slavery, reminding masters in southern provinces of the previous history of the United States. The fading commitment of northern provinces to slavery was a product of the internal slave trade that replaced the transatlantic slave trade after its end in 1850.[35] The high prices of coffee in the 1850s drained slaves from small farms and cattle-raising enterprises, as well as from northern and southern cities, to plantations in Rio de Janeiro, São Paulo, and Minas Gerais; sugar mill owners managed to keep their slaves because of the high prices of the product. This pattern changed in the following decade with the drop in the volume of the domestic slave trade caused by, on the one hand, a crop failure in the early 1860s and, on the other, by the global "cotton famine." Northern Brazil indeed benefited the most from the North American conflict, with the expansion of cotton plantations in the north, from Pernambuco to Maranhão.[36]

Despite the relative decline of the domestic slave trade in the 1860s, it was clear to political and economic actors in 1871 that slaves were increasingly concentrated in the coffee-producing provinces of southern Brazil, a pattern that increased in the 1870s when the traffic reached its peak. The arrival of railroads on the coffee frontier, new tariff duties exemptions for coffee imports in the United States in 1872 (during the Civil War the product had been taxed as part of efforts to reorganize the treasury of the Union), and, especially, the high prices generated by the growth of North American demand significantly increased slave sales to coffee producers in the internal market.[37] After the 1870s, relations between Brazilian coffee producers and North American consumers—which had started in the 1830s—became increasingly closer, notwithstanding the fact that North American demand also stimulated other Latin-American countries to enter the market.[38]

U.S. economic growth in the aftermath of the Civil War had an impact on the stability of the Brazilian slave system, which had already been shaken by the passing of the free-womb law. This is clear whether we look at the coffee-, sugar-, or cotton-producing sectors. In 1861, the United States was the largest importer of coffee in the world, with an unmatched level of consumption per capita. In the following three decades consumption of the drink spread, geographically and socially, as a consequence of demographic growth, the expansion of commercial agriculture throughout the country (North, South, Midwest), and the rise of manufacturing production in the North. There were crucial innovations in the commercialization and distribution of the product in the aftermath of the Civil War, such as the use of paper bags in retail sales of roasted coffee (previously the final consumer had to purchase the green beans from retailers and roast them at home) and the creation of registered trademarks, with multiple firms operating in the importation and wholesale distribution on a national scale. Moreover, with the reduction in transportation costs on a global scale and population and income growth in the United States (a consequence of the accelerated industrialization and the growing commercialization of family agriculture), these practices helped expand the North American consumer market: coffee imports dramatically increased in the last thirty years of the nineteenth century, going from 231,170,000 to 748,810,000 pounds, and consumption per capita growing twofold (from six to thirteen pounds a year).[39]

In the 1870s Brazilian coffee producers could only fulfill that demand by expanding cultivation into frontier zones and purchasing slaves in the domestic slave trade. Here the other two impacts that the postbellum North American economy had on Brazilian slavery become clear. The same basic factors (population growth, industrialization, urbanization, and commodification of social relations in the country and the city) that stimulated the growth of North American demand for coffee had similar consequences for sugar production. The defeat of the CSA disrupted sugar production in Louisiana and left the North American market completely dependent on imports. North American consumption jumped from 440,000 tons of sugar in 1866 to 1,500,000 tons twenty years later. During this period Cuba was the United States' main supplier. Brazil, after losing access to the British market in the 1870s to beat sugar, also lost its competitiveness in the U.S. market in face of the higher productivity of the Cuban sugar industry.[40]

Finally, it is important to note the effects of the recovery of cotton production in the U.S. South. Cotton production for 1860 was 4,861 million bales; it dropped by the end of the Civil War to less than half of that figure. It was not long before production grew based on restrictions on the access to land for former slaves, the creation of a labor system based on sharecropping, and the hardening of race relations. In 1870 production reached almost pre-war levels (4,025 million bales); in 1878 it surpassed those levels, and ten years later—when slavery was abolished in Brazil—it reached around 7,000 million bales.[41]

The economic trajectory of the U.S. South in the 1870s was described on the pages of the *O Novo Mundo* as an example of the political success of Reconstruction. José Carlos Rodrigues frequently noted the growing racial violence promoted by the KKK and the conflicts over the political activities of freedmen and carpetbaggers; he didn't criticize the growing racism at the end of the Ulysses Grant administration; and he considered the election of Rutherford B. Hayes not only a corrective to these problems, but the end of sectional conflicts in the United States, thus reproducing the growing Northern view that opposed the radical abolitionism of old republicans and ultimately inspired the Compromise of 1877 that ended Reconstruction. Still, his assessment in 1879 was that the experience had been extremely positive and instructive to Brazil. Lacking the racism of North America, the Empire could go through a peaceful abolition process that would not destroy the agro-exporting sector.[42]

Leaving aside the optimism of José Carlos Rodrigues about how Brazilian slaveholders could learn from the recovery of cotton production in the U.S. South, the growth of U.S. cotton production was an important part of the crisis of slavery in Brazil. The flow of slaves into the coffee-producing South had significantly decreased in the 1860s, in part because Northern slaveholders were able to keep their captives in the context of rising cotton prices. This, however, was short-lived. By the mid-1870s cotton from northern Brazil had been displaced by the recovery of the U.S. cotton production in the world market. A harsh drought in the region, starting in 1877, worsened the crisis. Small slaveholders involved in the production of cotton and foodstuffs were forced to sell their captives to the coffee-producing South.[43]

In sum, by stimulating the growth of Brazilian coffee production while displacing Brazilian sugar and cotton in the world market, the economic performance of the United States in the last third of the nineteenth century contributed to widening the regional gap within the South American empire. In the 1870s the efficiency of coffee production led to an increasing concentration of slaves in the coffee plantations of Rio de Janeiro, Minas Gerais, and São Paulo and their decreasing presence in the cotton and sugar plantations and farms in the north of Brazil—thus leading to the gradual erosion of the national commitment to the institution, already evident in the behavior of imperial congressmen when voting on the free-womb law.

It is also possible to identify another consequence of the U.S. Civil War for the crisis of Brazilian slavery. A few years after the passing of the free-womb law, its political implications significantly transformed the conflicts between masters and slaves. The institution lost a lot of its legitimacy after 1871. Slaveholders themselves were to a large extent responsible for this, since they made very clear that the state was taking away their authority and that slave insubordination would grow as a result. Moreover, the concentration of slaves in coffee plantations was not only quantitative, but also qualitative: when purchasing captives in the internal market coffee producers preferred young men born in Brazil lacking strong family ties. They had to adapt to a more intense work routine than in the region from where they were coming.[44] Thus it is not surprising that the strongest center of slave resistance was the coffee frontier in the São Paulo province. In this region the actions of enslaved subjects combined, for the first time in the history of Brazil, with a systemic political movement against the institution.[45]

The Brazilian abolitionist movement emerged in the empire's public sphere around 1879–80 as a result of frustrations with the free-womb law. The first abolitionist victory came in early 1881 when the Assemblies of Minas Gerais, Rio de Janeiro, and São Paulo passed prohibitive taxes on the domestic slave trade, practically extinguishing the interprovincial traffic in Brazil. The initiative, in fact, did not come from abolitionists: its goal was mainly keeping the national commitment to slavery alive (thus stopping the advances of the abolitionist movement). The example of Ceará, one of the provinces that lost the largest number of slaves to coffee plantations in the 1870s and the first to witness the emergence of mass abolitionist movement in 1879, prefigured the experience of an abolitionist North and a Slave South that had marked the history of the United States. This was, in fact, one of the arguments for the prohibition of the interprovincial slave trade in the Assembly of São Paulo.[46]

As part of a strategy to articulate the abolitionist movement on a national scale, the newspaper *O Abolicionista* was founded in the capital of the Empire in 1880, precisely when agitations in Ceará were growing. The tra-

ditional *Gazeta da Tarde*, also published in the *Corte*, embraced the abolitionist cause. The propaganda strategy used in the free-womb law debates
became one of the strongest aspects of the campaign against slavery by
those abolitionist newspapers: the successful conclusion of the Civil War,
abolition, and Reconstruction in the United States was the perfect example for Brazil. During the 1880s it is also possible to track the links between
the editorial activities of José Carlos Rodrigues and his journal *O Novo
Mundo* (when he became the main informant of U.S. events, especially
the Reconstruction, for a Brazilian audience) and the abolitionist press,
which considered him the main expert on North American affairs.[47] The
heroes of the Civil War became heroes of Brazilian abolitionism: week after
week newspapers mentioned Lincoln, Sumner, Seward, Grant, Stowe,
Douglass, and others.[48] Proslavery defenders, on the other hand, remained
silent about the United States, a silence that had already marked the
free-womb law debates. The Brazilian abolitionist movement tried to build
international links to fight the institution in the country; after 1865 the international isolation of the empire favored the strategy. For slaveholders such
an option was impossible, unlike in the 1840s and 1850s, when the Southern
example was fundamental for the Brazilian defense of slavery in the world
system.

As a final remark, I would like to note two specific aspects of the impact
that the U.S. Civil War had on Brazilian slavery, each of them marked by
distinct temporal structures. First, there was the direct impact, witnessed by
contemporaries and with clear political implications. This impact led to the
creation and passing of the free-womb law and the framing of experiences
that ultimately guided the actions of political and social actors in the Brazilian Empire after 1871. In every debate where the global past and present
were discussed, the U.S. experience influenced the range of actions available
to Brazilian actors. Although it was used almost exclusively by abolitionists, the U.S. experience was open to multiple readings, both as a concrete
example and as a rhetorical weapon. Second, there was the impact of the
reorganization of the world economy in the aftermath of the Civil War.
Poorly understood by contemporaries, this may have been the most decisive force defining the range of actions available to Brazilians at the time.
The crisis of Brazilian slavery, with regional splits influencing it at every
step, must be understood as an economic crisis of global dimensions that
established the limits of the possible in local transformations.

The abolition of slavery in 1888 was the result of actions and decisions
taken within the limits of the Brazilian national state by multiple social

actors. But without the U.S. Civil War, the end of slavery in Brazil would not have happened the way it did. It seems likely that the institution would have continued into the twentieth century—and perhaps beyond.

Suggested Readings

Blackburn, Robin. *The American Crucible: Slavery, Emancipation and Human Rights*. London: Verso, 2011.

Conrad, Robert. *The Destruction of Brazilian Slavery, 1850–1888*. Berkeley: University of California Press, 1972.

de Azevedo, Célia Maria Marinho. *Abolionismo: Estados Unidos e Brasil, uma história comparada (século XIX)*. São Paulo: Annablume, 2003.

Horne, Gerald. *The Deepest South: The United States, Brazil, and the African Slave Trade*. New York: New York University Press, 2007.

Marquese, Rafael. "Capitalism, Slavery, and the Brazilian Coffee Economy." In *The Legacy of Eric Williams: Caribbean Scholar and Statesman*, edited by Colin A. Palmer (Mona, Jamaica: The University of the West Indies Press, 2015), 190–223.

Needell, Jeffrey D. *The Party of Order: The Conservatives, the State, and Slavery in the Brazilian Monarchy, 1831–1871*. Stanford, CA: Stanford University Press, 2006.

Parron, Tâmis. *A política da escravidão no Império do Brasil, 1826–1865*. Rio de Janeiro: Civilização Brasileira, 2011.

Toplin, Robert Brent. *The Abolition of Slavery in Brazil*. New York: Atheneum, 1975.

Notes

1. On the links between the U.S. and Brazilian coffee markets, see Rafael Marquese and Dale Tomich, "O Vale do Paraíba escravista e a formação do mercado mundial do café no século XIX," in *O Brasil Imperial, Volume 2—1831–1870*, ed. Keila Grinberg and Ricardo Salles (Rio de Janeiro: Civilização Brasileira, 2009), 339–83; Steven Topik and Michelle Craig McDonald, "Why Americans Drink Coffee: the Boston Tea Party or Brazilian Slavery?" in *Coffee: A Comprehensive Guide to the Bean, the Beverage, and the Industry*, ed. Robert W. Thurston, Jonathan Morris, and Shawn Steiman (Boulder: Rowman and Littlefied, 2013), 234–47; Rafael Marquese, "Estados Unidos, Segunda Escravidão e a Economia Cafeeira do Império do Brasil," *Almanack* 5 (2013): 51–60. On the political connections between Brazilian and U.S. slavery before the U.S. Civil War see Rafael Marquese and Tâmis Parron, "International Proslavery: the Politics of the Second Slavery," in *The Politics of the Second Slavery: Conflict and Crisis on the Nineteenth Century Atlantic Slave Frontier*, ed. Dale Tomich (Binghamton: SUNY Press/Fernand Braudel Series, in press); Gerald Horne, *The Deepest South: The United States, Brazil, and the African Slave Trade* (New York: New York University Press, 2007); Matthew Karp, *This Vast Southern Empire: Slaveholders at the Helm of American Foreign Policy* (Cambridge, MA: Harvard University Press, 2016); Leonardo Marques, *The United States and the Transatlantic Slave Trade to the Americas, 1776–1867* (New Haven, CT: Yale University Press, 2016).

2. Luiz A. Moniz Bandeira, *Presença dos Estados Unidos no Brasil* (Rio de Janeiro: Civilização Brasileira, 2007), 155–61; Robert Conrad, *The Destruction of Brazilian Slavery, 1850–1888* (Berkeley: University of California Press, 1972), 88–100; Robert Brent Toplin, *The Abolition of Slavery in Brazil* (New York: Atheneum, 1975), 41–43; Ricardo Salles, *Nostalgia Imperial: A formação da identidade nacional no Brasil do Segundo Reinado* (Rio de Janeiro: Topbooks, 1996), 158–67; Ricardo Salles, *E o Vale era o escravo: Vassouras, século XIX; Senhores e escravos no coração do Império* (Rio de Janeiro: Civilização Brasileira, 2008), 79–110; Roderick Barman, *Citizen Emperor: Pedro II and the Making of Brazil, 1825–1891* (Stanford, CA: Stanford University Press, 1999), 282–84; Célia Maria Marinho de Azevedo, *Abolicionismo: Estados Unidos e Brasil, uma história comparada (século XIX)* (São Paulo: Annablume, 2003); Maria Helena Pereira Toledo Machado, "Os abolicionistas brasileiros e a Guerra de Secessão" in *Caminhos da Liberdade: Histórias da Abolição e do Pós-Abolição no Brasil,* ed. Martha Abreu and Mateus Serva Pereira (Niterói: PPGHistória-Ed.UFF, 2011), 9–28.

3. *Annaes do Senado do Império do Brasil. 3ª Sessão em 1871 da 14ª Legislatura de 1 a 30 de Setembro* (henceforth cited as AS) (Rio de Janeiro: Typographia do Diário do Rio de Janeiro, 1871), 5:30.

4. Ramiro Guerra y Sánchez, *Manual de Historia de Cuba* (Havana: Editorial de Ciencias Sociales, 1971), 589–90; Rebecca J. Scott, *Slave Emancipation in Cuba: The Transition to Free Labor, 1860–1899* (Princeton, NJ: Princeton University Press, 1985), 65–66; Christopher Schmidt-Nowara, *Empire and Antislavery: Spain, Cuba, and Puerto Rico, 1833–1874* (Pittsburgh: University of Pittsburgh Press, 1999). See, also, Christopher Schmidt-Nowara and Matt Childs' chapters in this volume.

5. Tâmis Parron, *A política da escravidão no Império do Brasil, 1826–1865* (Rio de Janeiro: Civilização Brasileira, 2011); Marquese and Parron, "International Proslavery."

6. Silvana Mota Barbosa, "A Imprensa e o Ministério: escravidão e Guerra de Secessão nos jornais do Rio de Janeiro (1862–1863)," in *Perspectivas da Cidadania no Brasil Império,* ed. José Murilo de Carvalho and Adriana Pereira Campos (Rio de Janeiro: Civilização Brasileira, 2011), 123–47; Antonia F. de Almeida Wright, "Brasil-Estados Unidos, 1831/1889," in *História Geral da Civilização Brasileira,* Tomo II, *O Brasil Monárquico,* vol. 6, *Declínio e Queda do Império,* ed. Sérgio Buarque de Holanda (Rio de Janeiro: Bertrand, 1972), 232–35; Sérgio Buarque de Holanda, *História Geral da Civilização Brasileira,* Tomo II, *O Brasil Monárquico,* vol. 7, *Do Império à República* (Rio de Janeiro: Rio de Janeiro: Bertrand, 1972), 53–54.

7. See Howard Jones' chapter in this volume.

8. Hélio Vianna, *D. Pedro I e D. Pedro II: Acréscimos às suas biografias* (São Paulo: Companhia Editora Nacional, 1966), 176–77. See also Barman, *Citizen Emperor,* 284. For the diplomatic correspondence mentioned by D. Pedro II, see Moniz Bandeira, *Presença dos Estados Unidos,* 98–99.

9. On March 22, 1850, the deputy Silva Guimarães presented to the Chamber a bill for a free-womb law. The project was not discussed. For a discussion of its content see Agostinho Marques Perdigão Malheiro, *A Escravidão no Brasil: Ensaio Histórico, Jurídico, Social* (1866–67) (Petrópolis: Vozes, 1976), 2:286.

10. See, among others, Hendrik Kraay and Thomas Whigham, eds., *I Die with My Country: Perspectives on the Paraguayan War, 1864–1870* (Lincoln: University of Nebraska Press, 2005).

11. Joaquim Nabuco, *Um Estadista do Império: Nabuco de Araújo—Sua Vida, Suas Opiniões, Sua Época* (Rio de Janeiro: Garnier, 1897), 2:388–95; 3:27–42; Barman, *Citizen Emperor*, 300–303.

12. Perdigão Malheiro, *A Escravidão no Brasil*, 2:298.

13. Perdigão Malheiro, *A Escravidão no Brasil*, 2:300.

14. Jeffrey D. Needell, *The Party of Order: The Conservatives, the State, and Slavery in the Brazilian Monarchy, 1831–1871* (Stanford, CA: Stanford University Press, 2006), 272–314. According to the Brazilian Parliamentary Regime under the 1824 Imperial Constitution, the emperor of Brazil was the head of the Executive and the Moderating Power, but he could not as such initiate processes of law making—this would fit only to the Chamber of Deputies and to the Imperial Senate.

15. Salles, *E o Vale era o escravo*, 79–115.

16. See more on that in Schmidt-Nowara and Childs's chapters.

17. *Atas do Conselho de Estado*, ed. José Honório Rodrigues (Brasília: Senado Federal, 1973–78), 6:195.

18. Eric Foner, *Reconstruction: America's Unfinished Revolution, 1863–1877* (New York: Harper and Row, 1988), 77–345.

19. See Ricardo Salles, *Guerra do Paraguai: Escravidão e cidadania na formação do Exército* (Rio de Janeiro: Paz and Terra, 1990) and Wilma Peres Costa, *A Espada de Dâmocles: O Exército, a Guerra do Paraguai e a crise do Império* (São Paulo: Hucitec-Ed. Unicamp, 1996).

20. "Relatório final da Comissão especial da Câmara dos Deputados, encarregada de dar parecer sobre o elemento servil, 16 de agosto de 1870" in *A abolição no Parlamento: 65 anos de luta (1823–1888)* (Brasilia: Senado Federal, 2012), 1:387.

21. Needell, *The Party of Order*, 254–66.

22. On this free-womb law, see again Schmidt-Nowara and Childs's chapters.

23. *Discussão da Reforma do Estado Servil na Câmara dos Deputados e no Senado* (Rio de Janeiro: Typographia Nacional, 1871), 1:167–68.

24. On the trajectory of José Carlos Rodrigues and his journal *O Novo Mundo*, see Charles Anderson Gauld, "José Carlos Rodrigues. O Patriarca da Imprensa Carioca," *Revista de História* 16 (1953): 427–38; Gabriela Vieira de Campos, "O literário e o não-literário nos textos e imagens do periódico ilustrado *Novo Mundo* (Nova Iorque, 1870–1879)" (MA Thesis, Unicamp, 2001); Mônica Maria Rinaldi Asciutti, "Um lugar para o periódico *O Novo Mundo* (Nova Iorque, 1870–1879)" (MA Thesis, Universidade de São Paulo, 2010).

25. "Um administrador modelo," "A emancipação dos escravos," *O Novo Mundo* 1 (1870): 2.

26. See, respectively, "A Hespanha e o Chili, o Peru, a Bolivia e o Equador," *O Novo Mundo* 2 (1870): 19; "O Ano de 1870" *O Novo Mundo* 3 (1870): 34, which says that "*the Reconstruction has been concluded: the negro is not only a freedmen, but also a citizen;*

and the material wealth of the country is being recovered by the prudent and peaceful administration of the same person who smashed the terrible hydra of slavery"; "Agora é o Tempo Aprazado" *O Novo Mundo* 6 (1871): 82.

27. Parron, *A política da escravidão*. For the broader context see Seymour Drescher, *The Mighty Experiment: Free Labor versus Slavery in British Emancipation* (New York: Oxford University Press, 2002).

28. *Diário do Rio de Janeiro*, June 1, 1871, 1–2.

29. *Diário do Rio de Janeiro*, June 1, 1871, 2.

30. *Diário do Rio de Janeiro*, August 6, 1871, 1–2. Another example of how defenders of slavery in Brazil considered the Civil War a turning point can be found in the speech of the Baron of Três Barras at the Senate on September 15, 1871. The speech was reproduced in *Anexos aos Annaes do Senado—1871* (Rio de Janeiro: Typographia Nacional, 1871).

31. José Murilo de Carvalho, *A Construção da Ordem/Teatro de Sombras* (Rio de Janeiro: Civilização Brasileira, 2006), 322; Ricardo Salles, *E o Vale era o escravo*, 79–115. On the reaction of Vale planters against the free-womb law see also Laura Janargin Pang, "The State and Agricultural Clubs of Imperial Brazil, 1860–1889" (PhD dissertation, Vanderbilt, 1981), 84–184.

32. The petition from Bananal was published in the *Diário do Rio de Janeiro* on June 22, 1871; the one from Vassouras on July 25, preceded by another one from the same city on July 22. All others were published during 1871 on the same newspaper: May 24 (Paraíba do Sul), June 15 (Piraí), June 23 (Conservatória), June 29 (Corpo do Comércio do Rio de Janeiro), July 14 (Valença), July 18 (Campinas), July 24 (Clube da Lavoura e do Comércio), July 26 and 28 (both from Cantagalo), August 9 (Juiz de Fora), and August 17 (São Luís do Paraitinga).

33. *Diário do Rio de Janeiro*, August 10, 1871, 2.

34. Conrad, *Destruction of Brazilian Slavery*, Appendix, Table 25.

35. As historian Evaldo Cabral de Mello has emphasized in *O Norte Agrário e o Império, 1871–1889* (Rio de Janeiro: Nova Fronteira, 1984), 33, *"the support given by northern congressmen to its passing* [the Rio Branco law] *generated the first suspicions about the* [internal] *traffic among representatives of the coffee producing provinces, the earliest fears that it could work against slave interests."*

36. Jacob Gorender, *O Escravismo Colonial* (São Paulo: Fundação Perseu Abramo, 2011), 354–55; Robert W. Slenes, "The Brazilian Internal Slave Trade, 1850–1888: Regional Economies, Slave Experience, and the Politics of a Peculiar Market," in *The Chattel Principle: Internal Slave Trades in the Americas*, ed. Walter Johnson (New Haven, CT: Yale University Press, 2004), 325–70; José Flávio Motta, *Escravos daqui, dali e de mais além: O tráfico interno de cativos na expansão cafeeira paulista* (São Paulo: Alameda, 2012), 73–81.

37. On the arrival of railroads in the coffee-producing zones, see Pierre Monbeig, *Pioneiros e fazendeiros de São Paulo* (São Paulo: Hucitec, 1984), 174–76; Odilon Nogueira de Mattos, *Café e ferrovias: A evolução ferroviária de São Paulo e o desenvolvimento da cultura cafeeira* (São Paulo: Pontes, 1990), 78–90. José Carlos Rodrigues

noted the exemption of taxes over the coffee imported by the United States and celebrated it in *O Novo Mundo* 18 (1872): 94. On coffee prices in the U.S. market see Mauro Rodrigues da Cunha, "Apêndice Estatístico," in *150 anos de café*, ed. Edmar Bacha and Robert Greenhill (Rio de Janeiro: Marcelino Martins and E. Johnston, 1992), 334; on the sales of slaves see Slenes, "The Brazilian Internal Slave Trade," 331.

38. On this last point see Robert G. Williams, *States and Social Evolution: Coffee and the Rise of National Governments in Central America* (Chapel Hill: University of North Carolina Press, 1994), 28–40; Marco Palacios, *El Café en Colombia, 1850–1870: Una historia económica, social y política* (Bogotá: Editoral Planeta, 2002), 71; William Roseberry, *Coffee and Capitalism in the Venezuelan Andes* (Austin: University of Texas Press, 1983), 70–77.

39. Michael F. Jiménez, "'From Plantation to Cup': Coffee and Capitalism in the United States, 1830–1930," in *Coffee, Society and Power in Latin America*, ed. W. Roseberry, L. Gudmundson, and M. Samper Kutschbach (Baltimore: Johns Hopkins University Press, 1995), 39–42. See also Antônio Delfim Netto, *O problema do café no Brasil* (São Paulo: Unesp-Facamp, 2009), 20–21.

40. On these movements see "A History of Sugar Marketing," *U.S. Department of Agriculture*, Agricultural Economic Report n.197, February 1971, 10–11; Manuel Moreno Fraginals, *O Engenho: Complexo sócio-econômico açucareiro cubano* (São Paulo: Hucitec, 1989), 2:390–91; Peter L. Eisenberg, *Modernização sem Mudança: A indústria açucareira em Pernambuco, 1840–1910* (Rio de Janeiro: Paz and Terra, 1977), 48–49.

41. Department of Commerce/Bureau of the Census, *Historical Statistics of the United States, 1789–1945: A Supplement to the Statistical Abstract of the United States* (Washington, DC: U.S. Government Printing, 1949), 108; Foner, *Reconstruction*, 392–411; Gene Dattel, *Cotton and Race in the Making of America: The Human Costs of Economic Power* (New York: Ivan R. Dee, 2009), 293–347.

42. "Da Condição Econômica do Sul dos Estados Unidos," *O Novo Mundo* 13 (1871): 3; "Progresso dos Negros," *O Novo Mundo* 17 (1872): 75; "O aspecto político," *O Novo Mundo* 19 (1872): 114; "O trabalho dos emancipados," *O Novo Mundo* 25 (1872): 2; "Revista americana," *O Novo Mundo* 45 (1874): 161; "Os Estados do Sul e os Libertos," *O Novo Mundo* 46 (1874): 178; "Os Emancipados como Políticos," *O Novo Mundo* 49 (1874): 4; "O Trabalho dos Libertos," *O Novo Mundo* 98 (1879): 23; "Os Benefícios da Emancipação," *O Novo Mundo* 107 (1879): 250.

43. Slenes, "The Brazilian Internal Slave Trade," 338.

44. Richard Graham, "Another Middle Passage? The Internal Slave Trade in Brazil," in *The Chattel Principle: Internal Slave Trades in the Americas*, ed. Walter Johnson (New Haven, CT: Yale University Press, 2004), 311; Warren Dean, *Rio Claro: Um sistema brasileiro de grande lavoura, 1820–1920* (Rio de Janeiro: Paz and Terra, 1977), 135.

45. Toplin, *The Abolition of Slavery in Brazil*; Emilia Viotti da Costa, *Da Senzala à Colônia* (São Paulo: Brasiliense, 1989); Maria Helena P. T. Machado, *O Plano e o Pânico: Os movimentos sociais na década da abolição* (São Paulo: Edusp-Ed.UFRJ, 1994); Elciene Azevedo, *O direito dos escravos: Lutas jurídicas e abolicionismo na província de São Paulo* (Campinas: Ed. Unicamp, 2010).

46. Célia Maria Marinho Azevedo, *Onda Negra, Medo Branco: O negro no imaginário das elites, século XIX* (Rio de Janeiro: Paz and Terra, 1987), 114–58.

47. See the contributions by Rodrigues to the first issue of the *O Abolicionista* (November 1880—February 1881) and the frequent references to his work in the *Gazeta da Tarde*, starting in 1880. When giving a speech in the Chamber during the Projeto Dantas debates, which aimed at freeing slaves older than 60 years, Rui Barbosa discussed in detail the problem of economic decline in post-emancipation societies, comparing the British and French Caribbean to the U.S. South. One of his sources was José Carlos Rodrigues. The other was the work of George W. Williams, *History of the Negro Race in America from 1619 to 1880* (New York: G. P. Putnam's Sons, 1891), the first history of slavery and post-emancipation written by an African American in the United States, a direct participant both in the Civil War and in the politics of Reconstruction. "Parecer do Deputado Rui Barbosa ao Projeto Dantas, apresentado na sessão de 4 de agosto de 1884," in *A abolição no Parlamento: 65 anos de luta (1823–1888)* (Brasília: Senado Federal, 2012), 2:120–38.

48. One example: the obituary of Ulysses Grant in the *Revista Ilustrada* 416 (1885): 1–3, which had a nice picture of the general occupying the entire first page of the journal.

Contributors

MATT D. CHILDS, associate professor at the University of South Carolina, is author and editor of *The 1812 Aponte Rebellion in Cuba and the Struggle against Atlantic Slavery*; *The Yoruba Diaspora in the Atlantic World*; *The Changing Worlds of Atlantic Africa: Essay in Honor of Robin Law*, and *The Urban Black Atlantic during the Era of the Slave Trade*.

DON H. DOYLE, McCausland Professor of History at the University of South Carolina, is author and editor of several books, among them *The Cause of All Nations: An International History of the American Civil War*; *Secession as an International Phenomenon*; *Nations Divided: The Southern Question in America and Italy*; and *Nationalism in the New World* (with Marco Pamplona).

ANNE ELLER is an assistant professor of Latin American and Caribbean history at Yale University. Her book, *We Dream Together: Dominican Independence, Haiti, and the Fight for Caribbean Freedom*, will be published in 2016 by Duke University Press.

RICHARD HUZZEY is a senior lecturer in modern British history at the University of Durham. He is the author of *Freedom Burning: Anti-Slavery and Empire in Victorian Britain* and co-editor of *British Suppression of the Transatlantic Slave Trade*. He was previously co-director of the Centre for the Study of International Slavery at the University of Liverpool.

HOWARD JONES, university research professor of history emeritus at the University of Alabama, is author and editor of more than a dozen books, including *Blue and Gray Diplomacy: A History of Union and Confederate Foreign Relations*; *Union in Peril: The Crisis over British Intervention in the Civil War*; *Abraham Lincoln and a New Birth of Freedom: The Union and Slavery in the Diplomacy of the Civil War*; and a book on My Lai for the Pivotal Moments in American History series for Oxford University Press (forthcoming).

PATRICK J. KELLY teaches history at the University of Texas at San Antonio. He is the author of *Creating a National Home: Building the Veterans Welfare State 1865–1900* and co-editor, with Rhonda Minten, of *Living on the Edge: Texas during the Civil War and Reconstruction*. His articles on the transnational dimensions of the U.S. Civil War include "The North American Crisis of the 1860s," *Journal of the Civil War Era*, (2012), and "The European Revolutions of 1848 and the Transnational Turn in Civil War History," *Journal of the Civil War Era*, (2014).

RAFAEL MARQUESE, professor of history of the Americas at the Universidade de São Paulo (Brazil), is the author of *Feitores do Corpo, Missionários da Mente: Senhores, letrados e o controle dos escravos nas Américas, 1660–1860* (2004); *Administração & Escravidão: Ideias sobre a gestão da agricultura escravista brasileira* (1999); *Slavery and Politics: Brazil and Cuba, 1790–1850* (co-authored with Tâmis Parron and Márcia Berbel, 2016); *Escravidão e Capitalismo Histórico no Século XIX: Brasil, Cuba, Estados Unidos* (co-edited with Ricardo Salles, 2016).

ERIKA PANI, research professor at El Colegio de México, is author of "Dreaming of a Mexican Empire: The Political Projects of the 'Imperialistas,'" *Hispanic American Historical Review* (2002); *Para mexicanizar el Segundo Imperio; El imaginario político de los imperialistas;* and *Para pertenecer a la gran familia mexicana: Procesos de naturalización en el siglo XIX.*

HILDA SABATO, head researcher at the Consejo Nacional de Investigaciones Científicas y Técnicas (CONICET-Argentina), is the author of several books on the political history of nineteenth-century Argentina. Her recent books include *Historia de la Argentina, 1852–1890* (2012); *Buenos Aires en armas: La revolución de 1880* (Buenos Aires, 2008); *Pueblo y política: La construcción de la república* (Buenos Aires, 2005, reprinted in 2010; in Portuguese: 2012); *The Many and the Few: Political Participation in Republican Buenos Aires* (Stanford, 2001; in Spanish: 1998 and 2004).

STÈVE SAINLAUDE teaches history at L'Université Paris-Sorbonne and is the author of two books: *Le gouvernement impérial et la guerre de Sécession* and *La France et la Confédération sudiste,* along with several essays, among them "Alfred Paul, un consul dans la guerre de Sécession." He is about to publish an English edition of his work on French foreign policy and the American Civil War.

CHRISTOPHER SCHMIDT-NOWARA, Prince of Asturias Professor of Spanish Culture, Tufts University, was author of *Empire and Antislavery: Spain, Cuba, and Puerto Rico, 1833–1872; The Conquest of History: Spanish Colonialism and National Histories in the Nineteenth Century;* and *Slavery, Freedom, and Abolition in Latin America and the Atlantic World.* His sudden death in Paris in the summer of 2015 deprived our profession of a brilliant historian.

JAY SEXTON, Kinder Chair at the University of Missouri and distinguished fellow at the Rothermere American Institute at the University of Oxford, is the author and editor of several books and essays, including *Debtor Diplomacy: Finance and American Foreign Relations in the Civil War Era, 1837–1873; The Monroe Doctrine: Nation and Empire in Nineteenth-Century America;* and *The Global Lincoln* (with Richard Carwardine).

Index